MEDIEVAL EUROPE

A SHORT SOURCEBOOK

SECOND EDITION

C. Warren Hollister
University of California, Santa Barbara

Joe W. Leedom
Hollins College

Marc A. Meyer
Berry College

David S. Spear
Furman University

McGRAW-HILL, INC.

New York   St. Louis   San Francisco   Auckland   Bogotá
Caracas   Lisbon   London   Madrid   Mexico   Milan   Montreal
New Delhi   Paris   San Juan   Singapore   Sydney   Tokyo   Toronto

This book was set in Times Roman by Carlisle Publishers Services.
The editor was David C. Follmer;
   the production supervisor was Richard A. Ausburn.
The cover was designed by Carol Couch.
Project supervision was done by Carlisle Publishers Services.
R. R. Donnelley & Sons Company was printer and binder.

Cover photo: The Metropolitan Museum of Art, Robert Lehman Collection, 1975.
(1975. 1. 1912)

MEDIEVAL EUROPE

A Short Sourcebook

Acknowledgments appear on pages 273–280, and on this page by reference.

1 2 3 4 5 6 7 8 9 0 DOC DOC 9 0 9 8 7 6 5 4 3 2

ISBN   0-07-029617-0

Library of Congress Cataloging-in-Publication Data

Medieval Europe: a short sourcebook / [edited by] C. Warren Hollister
   ... [et al.].— 2nd ed.
      p.   cm.
   ISBN 0-07-029617-0
   1. Europe—History—476-1492—Sources.   2. Middle Ages—History—
   Sources.   I. Hollister, C. Warren (Charles Warren), (date).
   D113.M4   1992
   940. 1—dc20   91-43803

ABOUT
THE EDITORS

C. WARREN HOLLISTER is professor and Chair of Medieval Studies at the University of California, Santa Barbara, and president of the Medieval Association of the Pacific. He has published a number of books and articles. JOE W. LEEDOM is professor of history at Hollins College in Virginia and has published articles in such journal as *History* and the *American Journal of Legal History*. MARC A. MEYER is professor of history at Berry College in Rome, Georgia. He has published in the Revue Bénédictine and elsewhere and is editor of a forthcoming memorial volume for the great British historian, Denis Bethell. DAVID S. SPEAR is professor of history at Furman University in Greenville, South Carolina. He has published in a number of journals including the *Journal of British Studies* and *Annales de Normandie* and is editor of the Haskins Society *Newsletter*.

CONTENTS

PREFACE

This book of readings in medieval history is a thoroughly revised version of the first edition, published in 1982. The first edition was itself based on a longer, two-volume work, photocopied and bound at the University of California, Santa Barbara, and used there by students in Warren Hollister's course in medieval Europe. With the help of this work, and of his doctoral students and TAs at the time—Joe Leedom, Marc Meyer, and David Spear, all of whom have since gone on to successful academic careers of their own—Warren Hollister was awarded the campus-wide Academic Senate Teacher of the Year Prize for 1982. At about the same time, Joe Leedom, also using this sourcebook, won an identical prize as a visiting professor at the University of Maryland. Professors Spear and Meyer have received similar teaching accolades. We therefore have considerable confidence in the sourcebook's effectiveness. On the basis of student response, at UCSB and throughout the country, the collection has been reshaped into its present form.

The photocopied prototype and first edition have normally been assigned in conjunction with Professor Hollister's *Medieval Europe: A Short History* (currently in its 6th edition, 1990). Because literary passages abound in the Hollister text, they have not been stressed in the present sourcebook. Among other improvements, two Islamic jokes included in the first edition have been deleted here because nobody found them funny. And an early-medieval Irish treatise on geography has been omitted because nobody, including Professor Hollister, could understand it.

We believe that the Hollister textbook and our new sourcebook together provide an appropriate balance between the various subdisciplines of medieval European history. Owing to limitations of length, and to our decision to stress certain major themes, many well-known medieval sources are absent. But we are confident that the sources we have chosen constitute an effective instructional tool, proven in classrooms throughout the United States and polished by revision.

We are grateful to Professor Ralph V. Turner of Florida State University, vice-president of the Charles Homer Haskins Society, and to Marcia L. Colish of Oberlin College, president of the Medieval Academy of America, for their valuable comments. We are grateful, too, to hundreds of undergraduate students from around the country for their encouraging and candid evaluations. For the flaws that remain, we assume full responsibility.

C. Warren Hollister

Joe W. Leedom

Marc A. Meyer

David S. Spear

INTRODUCTION

Many students dislike reading historical sources, yet many professors assign them nonetheless. In our own view, a history course that does not require the reading of original documents is a contradiction in terms. Contemporary sources are the foundations on which historical scholarship is built—the raw materials with which all historians work. Source materials are often difficult to absorb because they lack the tidiness and clarity that one finds in a good work of historical interpretation, or in a good textbook. But one cannot hope to understand the historical edifice without examining its foundations.

This collection of translated documents has been designed for use in connection with Warren Hollister's *Medieval Europe: A Short History* but it can be used with other textbooks as well. Some of the translations are our own; some are the work of others. When translations were already available that were accurate, readable, and not prohibitively expensive, we used them—and we thank the translators and publishers who gave us permission to do so. The editorial headnote preceding each document provides essential information on its historical context but does not summarize its contents. We prefer to let the sources speak for themselves.

They will not always speak clearly; the human past was more complex and ambiguous than most textbooks make it out to be. But it is our hope that many readers will appreciate the challenge of being led beyond the generalizations of textbooks and lectures into the underlying human reality. In this book, as in others like it, the reader is led very gently. The documents that follow are a minute sampling of the historical records of the Middle Ages, carefully chosen and edited to illustrate historical trends and events that we regard as significant. In place of the documentary jungle through which the historical scholar must grope, we have provided a small, well-tended garden. In this respect, our book of readings offers only a foretaste of the historian's craft.

Reading an historical source is rather like reading a newspaper: both should be approached with a healthy touch of skepticism. When an event is reported, the careful reader will ask a series of questions about the accuracy and objectivity of the report: did the reporter witness the event? If not, how reliable were the sources used? Is the reporter caught up in some personal hostility or enthusiasm that might affect the tone of the report, or the selection of certain facts to the exclusion of others? Is the reporter reputable or reckless, shrewd or gullible?

Reports of past events are known to historians as *narrative sources,* and they must always be evaluated by the criteria suggested above. Whenever possible, relevant information about the narrators quoted in this sourcebook will be provided in an editorial headnote, just as a good newspaper provides the names and affiliations of the writers of its major articles and columns. If your own newspaper does not provide such information, beware of it. Likewise, in reading a work of nonfiction or in viewing a documentary film, you should always ask who produced it and for what purpose.

Many of our documents are not narrative accounts but official edicts, laws, charters, creeds, and letters. Known generally as *record sources,* these documents bring us face to face with the past, without the distorting lens of the biased, careless, or misinformed reporter. They are like the verbatim accounts that newspapers sometimes provide of speeches, diplomatic agreements, and court decisions. But here again, they must be read with discrimination and with certain questions in mind. First and most obviously, is the document absolutely authentic, or has it been forged or tampered with? (The speeches of members of Congress often appear in the *Congressional Record* in much improved form, and some were never delivered at all.) If authentic, does the source tell us what was occurring or what its framer(s) hoped might occur? Does a religious creed reflect general belief or is it a response to a growing number of people who believed otherwise? Does a law providing severe penalties for arson suggest that arson was being reduced or that it was increasing to dangerous proportions? Was a particular law, edict, or creed strictly enforced or largely ignored? Is a particular charter typical or atypical? Does a particular law code create new legal conditions or simply perpetuate old ones? What portions of the document are merely conventional formulas (like "Sincerely yours," or "I believe in a new beginning for this great country of ours, where Americans, regardless of creed or race, can live together in peace and prosperity," etc.), and what parts contain the meat of the message? Above all, what were the cultural attitudes and historical circumstances underlying the creation of the record source, and how does the source reflect them? Again, our editorial headnotes will provide some guidance in answering these questions.

In short, we hope that students who use this book will not simply read the sources but think critically about them as well. The development of a discriminating, sophisticated approach to historical documents can sharpen one's ability to evaluate evidence of all sorts—from campaign oratory, sales pitches, college catalogues, and books about biorhythms and UFOs to the evening television news and the morning paper.

PART ONE

THE EARLY MIDDLE AGES

During the turbulent centuries between about A.D. 300 and 1050, Western Europe underwent wave after wave of invasions. As a result of the first wave, Roman imperial government disintegrated in the West, giving way by A.D. 500 to a group of loosely organized Germanic kingdoms. Most of these kingdoms were themselves destroyed or transformed by subsequent invasions. East Roman armies reconquered Italy in the mid-sixth century but quickly lost much of it to the assaults of the Germanic Lombards. In the early eighth century, Muslim armies overwhelmed the Visigothic kingdom of Spain and struck deep into France. Between these major invasions Europe was afflicted by warfare between and within its kingdoms. The population declined, cities shriveled into villages, and commerce ebbed. Europe became a land of isolated agricultural settlements surrounded by forests and wastelands.

In the course of this troubled era, the cultural traditions of the Classical, Christian, and Germanic past gradually fused into a new, Western European civilization. Its great unifying force was the Christian Church, which had spread through the Roman Empire and eventually converted it. When Rome collapsed in the West, the Church remained to preserve its memory and perpetuate its culture. Christian missionaries labored to convert and civilize pagan tribes. Benedictine monasteries, planted in Germanic forests, became centers of devotion, learning, and agrarian enterprise, while in Rome, where emperors had once ruled the West, popes now claimed the allegiance of all Christians and directed the efforts of far-flung missionaries.

In the decades around A.D. 800, the emerging culture of Western Christendom experienced a period of political unification and expansion under a Frankish dynasty known as the Carolingians. The most celebrated of the Carolingian kings, Charlemagne, worked closely with the Roman popes and Benedictine monks to conquer and convert pagan tribes, to reform the Church, and to encourage learning.

In the years following Charlemagne's death in 814, his empire broke into pieces as a result of internal instability and attacks from without. Europe was struck by new waves of non-Christian invaders—Hungarian horsemen from the East, Muslim pirate bands from the South, and Viking seafarers from the North. These were to be the last invasions that Europe would suffer. Out of the chaos that they brought, strong Christian monarchies emerged in England and Germany. The kingdom of France—the western part of Charlemagne's former empire—remained decentralized, with a weak monarchy and increasingly strong regional principalities: Anjou, Poitou, Champagne, Normandy, and others. Italy survived the invasions to become a land of increasingly vigorous commercial cities.

By A.D. 1050 Europe was once again expanding. Hungary, Scandinavia, and Poland had been Christianized and brought under the loose jurisdiction of the Roman popes. Commerce was reviving, towns were growing along Europe's river valleys, and the population was increasing once again. The old civilization of Rome had evolved, through centuries of turmoil and struggle, into the civilization of Western Europe.

CHAPTER 1

THE TRANSFORMATION OF THE ROMAN WORLD

The documents in this chapter illustrate two major themes: (1) the Christianization of the Roman Empire, and (2) the administrative and military problems leading to the Empire's collapse in the West.

The process of Christianization progressed during the fourth century A.D. from the abolition of imperial persecutions of Christians to the establishment of imperial persecutions of non-Christians. The conversion of Constantine (document 1) and the edict granting Christians the same toleration that other religions enjoyed (document 2) were followed by imperial efforts to resolve theological disputes within the Christian community (document 3). Such involvement forced the emperors to take sides in the debate between two contending Christian groups: the Trinitarians (who believed that God was a Trinity of three equal Persons: Father, Son, and Holy Spirit) and the Arians (who believed that the Son was subordinate to the Father). By the end of the fourth century it had become imperial policy to tolerate only the Trinitarian Christians and to ban the religious activities of Arians and all non-Christian sects (document 4). Meanwhile the Visigothic sack of Rome proved deeply demoralizing to Christians and Pagans alike (document 5). Perhaps the keenest Christian theologian of the age, St. Augustine, interpreted Christianity in the intellectual context of Classical Antiquity and shaped Christian thought across the Middle Ages and beyond (document 6).

During the fourth and fifth centuries, the Roman Empire suffered from internal stresses and barbarian invasions. Imperial taxes were becoming increasingly severe and inequitable. Civic officials, who had abandoned their cities to avoid financial ruin, were ordered to resume their municipal duties (document 7). Others responded to the tax burden by fleeing the Empire to live among the barbarians (document 8). Germanic peoples overwhelmed most of the Western Empire, including remote Britain (document 9), and the final result of this Germanic inundation of Europe was the removal of the last Western Roman Emperor, Romulus Augustulus, in A.D. 476 (document 10). The Roman Empire endured in the East for another thousand years, centered on its great capital of Constantinople; the western provinces passed into the hand of Germanic kings but, as is illustrated by the example of Clovis, king of the Franks, these kings and their people themselves adopted Christianity and thus drew closer in culture and faith to the citizens of the late Empire (document 11).

READING 1

Lactantius on Constantine's Victory and Conversion, 312

The conversion of Constantine, the first Christian emperor, was of decisive importance to Roman and Christian history. Lactantius (c. 240-320), a Christian rhetorician and historian who was alive at the time of Constantine's victory at the Milvian Bridge, A.D. 312, provides a first-hand account of his rise to the western imperial office. Another contemporary, Eusebius of Caesarea, reports, perhaps with some credulity, that Constantine's motivation to provide his troops with Christian insignia was a dream in which he saw a fiery cross in the sky and the words, "In this, conquer!" Constantine clearly saw in the Christian God a bringer of victory, and he was not disappointed.

And now a civil war broke out between Constantine and Maxentius. Although Maxentius kept himself within Rome, because the soothsayers had foretold that if he went out of it he should perish, yet he conducted the military operations through able generals. In forces he exceeded his adversary; for he had not only his father's army, but also his own, which he had lately drawn together out of Mauritania and Italy. They fought, and the troops of Maxentius prevailed. At length Constantine, with steady courage and a mind prepared for every event, led his whole force to the neighborhood of Rome, and encamped them opposite to the Milvian Bridge.

Constantine was directed in a dream to cause the heavenly sign to be delineated on the shields of his soldiers, and so to proceed to battle. He did as he had been commanded, and he marked on their shields the letter X, with a perpendicular line drawn through it and turned round thus at the top, being the cipher of Christ. Having this sign, his troops stood to arms. The enemies advanced, but without their emperor, and they crossed the bridge. The armies met, and fought with the utmost exertions of valor, and firmly maintained their ground. In the meantime a sedition arose at Rome, and Maxentius was reviled as one who had abandoned all concern for the safety of the commonweal; and suddenly the people cried with one voice, "Constantine cannot be overcome!" Dismayed at this, Maxentius burst from the assembly, and having called some senators together, ordered the Sibylline books to be searched. In them it was found that

"On the same day the enemy of the Romans should perish."

From *Of the Manner in which the Persecutors Died*, tr. A. Roberts and J. Donaldson, *The Ante-Nicene Fathers of the Christian Church*, v. VII (New York, 1886), 301-303.

Led by this response to the hopes of victory, he went to the field. The bridge in his rear was broken down. At sight of that the battle grew hotter. The hand of the Lord prevailed, and the forces of Maxentius were routed. He fled towards the broken bridge; but the multitude pressing on him, he was driven headlong into the Tiber.

This destructive war being ended, Constantine was acknowledged as emperor, with great rejoicing, by the senate and people of Rome. The senate, in reward of the valor of Constantine, decreed to him the title of Maximus.

READING 2

The Edict of Milan, 313

The first imperial edict to prohibit the persecution of Christians was issued in 311 by the pagan emperor Galerius, as a deathbed response to the clear failure of the last imperial persecution. Galerius permitted Christians to practice their religion so long as they did so without offending public order. In 313 a much more sweeping edict of toleration was issued by Constantine and his co-emperor, Licinius. Although not actually issued from Milan, the edict promulgates an agreement that the two emperors had previously concluded there.

When we, Constantine Augustus and Licinius Augustus, had happily met at Milan, and were conferring about all things which concern the advantage and security of the state, we thought that amongst other things which seemed likely to profit men generally, the reverence paid to the Divinity merited our first and chief attention. Our purpose is to grant both to the Christians and to all others full authority to follow whatever worship each man has desired; whereby whatsoever Divinity dwells in heaven may be benevolent and propitious to us, and to all who are placed under our authority. Therefore we thought it salutary and most proper to establish our purpose that no man whatever should be refused complete tolera-tion, who has given up his mind either to the cult of the Christians, or to the religion which he personally feels best suited to himself; to the end that the supreme Divinity, to whose worship we devote ourselves under no compulsion, may continue in all things to grant us his wonted favour and beneficence. Wherefore

From *A New Eusebius: Documents Illustrative of the History of the Church to A.D. 337*, ed. J. Stevenson; London, 1957, pp. 300-302. By permission of the Society for Promoting Christian Knowledge.

your Dignity should know that it is our pleasure to abolish all conditions whatever which were embodied in former orders directed to your office about the Christians, that what appeared utterly inauspicious and foreign to our Clemency should be done away and that every one of those who have a common wish to follow the religion of the Christians may from this moment freely and unconditionally proceed to observe the same without any annoyance or disquiet. These things we thought good to signify in the fullest manner to your Carefulness, that you might know that we have given freely and unreservedly to the said Christians toleration to practice their cult. And when you perceive that we have granted this favour to the said Christians, your Devotion understands that to others also freedom for their own worship and cult is likewise left open and freely granted, as befits the quiet of our times, that every man may have complete toleration in the practice of whatever worship he has chosen. This has been done by us that no diminution be made from the honour of any religion. Moreover in regard to the legal position of the Christians we have thought fit to ordain this also, that if any appear to have bought, whether from our exchequer or from any others, the places at which they were used formerly to assemble, concerning which definite orders have been given before now, and that by a letter issued to your office—that the same be restored to the Christians, setting aside all delay and doubtfulness, without any payment or demand of price.

All these things must be delivered over at once and without delay by your intervention to the corporation of the Christians. And since the said Christians are known to have possessed, not those places only whereto they were used to assemble, but others also belonging to their corporation, namely to their churches, and not to individuals, we comprise them all under the above law, so that you will order them to be restored without any doubtfulness or dispute to the said Christians, that is to their corporation and assemblies; provided always as aforesaid, that those who restore them without price, as we said, shall expect a compensation from our benevolence. In all these things you must give the aforesaid Christians your most effective intervention, that our command may be fulfilled as soon as may be, and that in this matter, as well as others, order may be taken by our Clemency for the public quiet. So far we will ensure that, as has been already stated, the Divine favour toward us which we have already experienced in so many affairs shall continue for all time to give us prosperity and successes, together with happiness for the State. But that the tenor of our gracious ordinance may be brought to the knowledge of all men, it will be your duty by a proclamation of your own to publish everywhere and bring to the notice of all men this present document, that the command of this our benevolence may not be hidden.

READING 3

The Nicene Creed, 325

The Nicene Creed is a product of the Trinitarians' victory over the Arians at the Council of Nicaea, summoned by Constantine in 325. The outcome of this first universal council of the Church was strongly influenced by Constantine, who had himself been persuaded by important churchmen to support the Trinitarian position. The Nicene Creed expresses what would become the orthodox Christian position of the Trinity and the incarnation of Christ. It rejects explicitly the doctrine of the Alexandrian churchman Arius, who taught that only God the Father was eternal and that God the Son was His creation.

We believe in one God, the Father Almightly, maker of all things visible and invisible; and in one Lord Jesus Christ, the Son of God, the only-begotten of his Father, of the substance of the Father, God of God, Light of Light, true God of true God, begotten not made, being of one substance with the Father; by whom all things were made, both in heaven and in earth. Who for us men and for our salvation came down from heaven and was incarnate and was made man. He suffered and the third day he rose again, and ascended into heaven. And he shall come again to judge both the living and the dead. And we believe in the Holy Spirit. And whosoever shall say that there was a time when the Son of God was not, or that before he was begotten he was not, or that he was made of things that were not, or that he is of a different substance or essence from the Father, or that he is a creature, or subject to change or conversion—all that say so, the Catholic and Apostolic Church anathematizes[1] them.

From *The Seven Ecumenical Councils*, tr. A.C. McGiffert and E.C. Richardson; *Library of Nicene and Post-Nicene Fathers*, V, XIV, 2nd Series; New York, Charles Scribner's, 1900, p.3.

[1]"Anathema" is a curse, carrying the full authority of the Church, that banishes the recipient from the Christian community.

READING 4

Selections from the Code of Theodosius II

Around the year 438 the Emperor Theodosius II (408-450) published a law code intended as a convenient reference to all
imperial edicts since the time of Constantine that still remained
valid. The excerpts reproduced below are edicts of Emperor
Theodosius I (378-395), issued in his name and in those of his
several co-emperors. Notice the marked shift in imperial religious
policy since the Edict of Milan.

Emperors Gratian, Valentinian, and Theodosius Augustuses: An Edict to
Eutropius, Praetorian Prefect [A.D. 380]:

Crowds shall be kept away from the unlawful congregations of all the heretics.
The name of the One and Supreme God shall be celebrated everywhere; the
observance, destined to remain forever, of the Nicene faith, as transmitted long ago
by Our ancestors and confirmed by the declaration and testimony of divine
religion, shall be maintained.

On the other hand, that man shall be accepted as a defender of the Nicene faith
and as a true adherent of the Catholic religion who confesses that Almighty God
and Christ the son of God are One in name, God of God, Light of Light; who does
not violate by denial the Holy Spirit which we hope for and receive from the
Supreme Author of things; that man who esteems, with the perception of inviolate
faith, the undivided substance of the incorrupt Trinity. The latter beliefs are surely
more acceptable to Us and must be venerated.

Those persons, however, who are not devoted to the aforesaid doctrines shall
cease to assume, with studied deceit, the alien name of "true religion," and they
shall be branded upon the disclosure of their crimes. They shall be removed and
completely barred from the threshold of all churches, since We forbid all heretics
to hold unlawful assemblies within the towns. If factions should attempt to do
anything, We order that their madness shall be banished and that they shall be
driven away from the very walls of the cities, in order that Catholic churches
throughout the whole world may be restored to all orthodox bishops who hold the
Nicene faith.

Emperors Theodosius, Arcadius, and Honorius, to Rufinus, Praetorian Prefect
[A.D. 391]:

If any man should dare to immolate a victim for the purposes of sacrifice, or to
consult the quivering entrails, he shall be reported by an accusation that anyone

From *The Theodosian Code and Novels and the Sirmondian Constitutions*, tr. C. Pharr,
Princeton, 1952, pp. 450-51, 473.

may levy, and according to the example of a person guilty of high treason he shall receive the appropriate sentence, even though he has inquired nothing contrary to, or with reference to, the welfare of the Emperors. For it is sufficient to constitute an enormous crime that any person should wish to break down the very laws of nature, to investigate forbidden matters, to disclose hidden secrets, to attempt interdicted practices, to seek to know the end of another's life, to promise the hope of another person's death.

If any person should venerate, by placing incense before them, images made by the work of mortals, or should bind a tree with fillets, or should erect an altar of turf he has dug up, or should attempt to honor vain images with the offering of a gift, such a person, as one guilty of the violation of religion, shall be punished by the forfeiture of that house in which it is proved that he served a pagan superstition. For we decree that all places shall be annexed to Our fisc, if it is proved that they have reeked with the vapor of incense, provided, however, that such places are proved to have belonged to such incense burners.

If any person should attempt to perform any such kind of sacrifice in public temples or shrines, or in the buildings or fields of others, and if it is proved that such places were usurped without the knowledge of the owner, the offender shall be compelled to pay twenty-five pounds of gold as a fine. If any person should connive at such a crime, he shall be held subject to the same penalty as that of the person who performed the sacrifice.

It is Our will that this regulation shall be so enforced by the judges, as well as by the defenders and decurions of the several cities, that the information learned by the defenders and decurions shall be immediately reported to the courts, and the crimes so reported shall be punished by the judges. Moreover, if the defenders and the decurions should suppose that any such crime should be concealed through favoritism or overlooked through carelessness, they shall be subjected to judicial indignation. If the judges should be advised of such crimes and should defer punishment through connivance, they shall be fined.

READING 5

St. Jerome on the
Visigothic Sack of Rome, 410

St. Jerome (s. 340-420), who shares the title "Doctor of the Latin
Church" with two other major intellects of his generation—St.
Ambrose and St. Augustine (next document)—expresses here the
profound affection that he and his Christian contemporaries had
toward the Christian Roman Empire and their despair at its declining fortunes.

While these things were happening in Jerusalem, from the west a terrible rumor
came to us, that Rome is besieged, that the safety of the citizens is redeemed by
gold; despoiled and again surrounded, they lost their wealth and now are losing
their lives. The voice cannot continue, sobs interrupt its words. Captured is the city
that captured the world; it perished by famine before it died; and few were found to
be captured. The rage of the hungry sought nefarious food: men tore one another's
limbs; while the mother did not spare her infant at the breast—she ingested into
herself what before she had pushed out. "By night was Moab captured, by night her
walls fell." (Isaiah 15.1) "O God, the heathen have come into thy inheritance; they
have defiled thy holy temple; they have laid Jerusalem in ruins. They have given
the bodies of thy servants to the birds of the air for food, the flesh of thy saints to
the beasts of the earth. They have poured out their blood like water round about
Jerusalem, and there was none to bury them." (Psalm 79:1-3)

> Who can describe the horror of that night, and
> Who can shed enough tears for those deaths?
> Ruined is that ancient city that ruled so many years.
> Bodies in the streets! Countless images of death![1]

From St. Jerome, *Letter CXXVII* [A.D., 412], tr. J. W. Leedom.
[1]Virgil, Aeneid, II. 361-65

READING 6

Selections from St. Augustine's *City of God*

St. Augustine (354-430), as the opening paragraph makes clear, is
also responding to the trauma of the sack of Rome by the
Visigothic leader, Alaric. But his response is vastly more elaborate
than St. Jerome's; the result, *The City of God*, of which only a few
bare excerpts are provided here, is one of the great intellectual
endeavors of Western Civilization. Rather than simply lament the
decline of Rome, as Jerome had done, Augustine set about to
redefine the relationship between Christianity—the City of God—
and earthly states—the City of Man. This relationship between
believers and unbelievers underlies all of human history.

Rome had been invaded by the Goths under King Alaric and was staggered by
the impact of this great disaster; and the worshippers of false gods, whom we
customarily call pagans, working to turn this invasion into an accusation against
the Christian religion, began to curse the true God more sharply and more bitterly
than ever. Upon which I, burning with the zeal of the house of God, decided to
confute their blasphemies and errors in these books on the city of God.

The first five books of *The City of God* rebut those who think that the safety of
mankind depends on the cult of the gods whom the pagans worshipped, and who
contend that these disasters happened, and were as bad as they were, because of the
prohibition of that worship. The next five books answer those who, while saying
that mortals never have and never will be spared evils—some greater, some lesser,
varying with time and place and person—still argue that the cult of many gods, in
which sacrifices are made to them, is useful because of the life to be after death. In
these ten books, then, are refuted those two false notions that are contrary to the
Christian religion.

Of the twelve books following, the first four contain the beginning of the two
cities, of which the one is of God, the other of man; the second four, their course or
progress; the third, which is the last four, their ends. And all twenty-two books,
whether they are about one city or the other, took their title from the better of the
two, with the result that they were called by preference *The City of God*.

I place humanity into two groups, one that lives following man, the other that
lives according to God, and about which I might call two cities, that is, two
societies, of which one is predestined to reign eternally with God and the other to
undergo eternal punishment with the devil. But this is their end, which is to be
spoken of later. Now I must detail the paths of the two cities from the time when

From St. Augustine, *The City of God*, tr. J.W. Leedom.

two people first reproduced to the time when reproduction will come to an end. For the history of the two cities consists of the whole era or age in which the dying give way to the born.

Cain was born first among these two parents of mankind [Adam and Eve], a member of the city of men; Abel afterwards, of the city of God. It is known by experience that in every individual, as the Apostle has said, "it is not the spiritual which is first but the physical, and then the spiritual" (I Corinthians 15.46)—and this is true in the whole of humanity as well. When the two cities began their history through birth and death, first was born the citizen of this world, and after him the alien in this world who belongs to the city of God, predestined by grace, made elect by grace, a pilgrim below by grace, a citizen above by grace. So in himself a person first is reprobate, which by necessity is the beginning—but where we must not remain—and later becomes virtuous, to which we come as we progress and in which we may remain when we arrive. Consequently, not each bad person will be good, but no one will be good who was not first bad.

So it is written that Cain established a city, but Abel, being a foreigner, did not establish one. For in heaven is the city of the saints, although it produces its citizens here, in whom it waits until its kingdom shall come.

The earthly city has its good here, and its society delights in it with such delight as it can. But this kind of good is not the sort that causes no difficulties for those who admire it, so the earthly city is generally divided against itself by lawsuits; or by fights and battles; or by victories that are deadly or temporary. And when one part has risen up in war against the other, it seeks to be victorious over other peoples while itself a captive of vices. And it cannot dominate forever those it may overcome by conquest.

But it is not correct to say that the good things that this earthly city desires are not good, for it is made better, in a human fashion, by these. It desires an earthly peace for these lowest of things, a peace it hopes to come by through war; and if it wins and no one may resist it, there will be peace. This is a peace that requires hard fighting, this is a peace that "glorious" war can win. But if, neglecting the better things that pertain to the supernatural city (where there will be eternal victory and secure perpetual peace), while other things are desired because they are either believed the only good things or are loved more than better ones, it follows by necessity that new misery will augment the old.

Now the household of a person who does not live by faith seeks an earthly peace through the things of this earth; while a household of people who live by faith expects those blessings that are promised in eternity, and they use earthly and temporal things like a wanderer, not being captured by them, or diverted by them from those things that tend towards God. On that account, the things necessary for mortal life are used by both types of people and households; but the purpose of using such differs with each. So the earthly city, which does not live by faith, desires only an earthly peace, securing civil obedience and authority so that there may be a consensus about things useful in this mortal life. But the heavenly city, or that bit of it that sojourns in this mortal life and lives by faith, needs to use such peace only until this weak necessity shall pass. And so, while in the earthly city it leads its life as if in captivity, it does not balk at complying with the laws of the earthly city in the administration of those things that sustain and accommodate this mortal life, since life is common to both.

While this heavenly city is traveling on earth it finds citizens among all peoples and collects a pilgrim society of all tongues and in all tongues, not caring anything about differing customs, laws, institutions, not rescinding or destroying them, but serving and following them (because it allows diversity in different peoples) to the same earthly peace as they tend—as long as the religion which advises the following of the most true high God is not impeded. So the heavenly city uses the earthly peace for itself during its pilgrimage; it makes this earthly peace work for that peace of heaven which alone is truly peace, namely the most orderly and harmonious society in the enjoyment of God and of one another in God. And when we come there, there will be life, certainly, but not mortal life; no animal body corrupting the soul; but a spiritual one, one without wants and one subject in all parts to the will. While on earth the heavenly city has this peace through faith; and by this faith it lives justly, and makes the winning of this peace the goal of every good action, in which it is done for the sake of God and neighbors; for the life of every city is certainly a social life.

READING 7
More Selections from the Theodosian Code

These passages, dating from the early to the mid-fifth century A.D., serve as a chronicle of the declining military fortunes and increasingly desperate attempts to defend the Western Roman Empire.

Emperors Arcadius, Honorius, and Theodosius II Augustuses to the Provincials [A.D. 406]:

In the matter of defence against hostile attacks, We order that consideration be given not only to the legal status of soldiers, but also to their physical strength. Although We believe the freeborn persons are aroused by love of country, We exhort slaves also, by the authority of this edict, that as soon as possible they shall offer themselves for the labors of war, and if they receive their arms as men fit for military service, they shall obtain the reward of freedom, and they shall also

From *The Theodosian Code and Novels and the Sirmondian Constitutions*, tr. C. Pharr, Princeton, 1952, pp. 170, 172, 387, 544.

receive two solidi each for travel money. Especially, of course, do We urge this service upon the slaves of those persons who are retained in the armed imperial service, and likewise upon the slaves of federated allies and of conquered peoples, since it is evident that they are making war also along with their masters.

Emperors Theodosius II and Valentinian III Augustuses to the Roman People [A.D. 440]:

As often as the public welfare demands, We consider that the solicitude of all of you must be summoned as an aid, in order that the provisions which will profit all may be fulfilled by all, and We do not believe that it is burdensome to Our provincials that the regulation is made for the safety of all so that they shall undertake the responsibility of resisting brigands:

Genseric,[1] the enemy of Our Empire, is reported to have led forth from the port of Carthage a large fleet, whose sudden excursion and fortuitous depredation must be feared by all shores.

Although the solicitude of Our Clemency is stationing garrisons throughout various places and the army of the most invincible Emperor Theodosius, Our Father, will soon approach, and although We trust that the Most Excellent Patrician, Our Aëtius,[2] will soon be here with a large band and the Most Illustrious Master of Soldiers, Sigisvult,[3] does not cease to organize the guards of soldiers and federated allies for the cities and shores, nevertheless, because it is not sufficiently certain, under summertime opportunities for navigation, to what shore the ships of the enemy can come, We admonish each and all by this edict that, with the confidence in the Roman strength and the courage with which they ought to defend their own, with their own men against the enemy, if the occasion should so demand, they shall use those arms which they can, but they shall preserve the public discipline and the moderation of free birth unimpaired. Thus they shall guard Our provinces and their own fortunes with faithful harmony and with joined shields. Of course this hope for each man's exertions is published, namely, that whatever a victor takes away from an enemy shall undoubtedly be his own.

The Emperors Theodosius II and Valentinian III Augustuses to Maximus: [A.D. 440]:

Justice must be preserved both publicly and privately in all matters and transactions, and We must adhere to it especially in those matters that sustain the sinews of the public revenue, since such measures come to the aid of the diminished resources of Our loyal taxpayers with useful equity. Very many persons reject this idea, since they serve only their domestic profits and deprive the common good wherein is contained their true and substantial welfare, although

[1]Gaiseric in most sources; he was the leader of the Vandals who had by then occupied North Africa.

[2]Master of the Troops of the Western Empire.

[3]A Frank and Aëtius's lieutenant.

such welfare clearly comes better to each person when it profits all persons, especially since this necessity for tribute so demands, and without such tribute nothing can be provided in peace or in war. Nor can the continuity of such tax payments remain any further if there should be imposed on a few exhausted persons the burden which the more powerful man declines, which the richer man refuses, and which, since the stronger reject it, only the weaker man assumes.

Theodosius II, etc., to the Prefect of the east [A.D. 444]:

Valerianus, a curialis of Emesa, assumed for himself unjustly and surreptitiously the insignia of high office then, accompanied by a great horde of barbarians, he rushed into the private council chamber of the governor of the province and seated himself on the right of the man to whom We have committed the laws. When he had put to flight all the office staff of the governor, he left everything devastated and deserted. He placed a garrison of slaves in opposition to the tax collectors, contrary to public discipline, and thereby Our treasury suffered a great loss through his madness.

Valentinian III, Augustus, etc., to the provincials [A.D. 445]:

It shall also be the responsibility of the duke of the province that no one shall be allowed to have armed men, thus creating an opportunity of harassing others, except perhaps those persons who at their own risk with praiseworthy animosity against the enemy have promised their own bands of soldiers and their own forces for the common welfare.

READING 8

Priscus Describes a Roman Citizen Who Lives Among the Barbarians

Priscus (5th C.), Greek inhabitant of the fifth-century Roman Empire, served on an imperial ambassadorial mission to the court of Attila the Hun in 449. He tells here of his encounter with a Greek-speaking man who was living among the "Scythians"—a name applied very loosely at the time to barbarian tribes coming from southern Russia. Priscus's "Scythians" were a tributary tribe to the Huns and were settled in present-day Hungary. The Greek whom Priscus meets had once been a prosperous merchant of the Eastern Empire but had been taken prisoner in a barbarian raid. Having been granted his freedom, he chose not to return.

From Priscus of Panium, *An Embassy to the Huns*, in *Readings in European History*, ed. and tr. James H. Robinson; Boston, Ginn & Company, 1904, vol. 1, pp. 30-33.

He considered his new life among the Scythians better than his old life among the Romans, and the reasons he urged were as follows: "After war the Scythians live at leisure, enjoying what they have got, and not at all, or very little, disturbed. The Romans, on the other hand, are in the first place very liable to be killed, if there are any hostilities, since they have to rest their hopes of protection on others, and are not allowed, by their tyrants, to use arms. And those who do use them are injured by the cowardice of their generals, who cannot properly conduct war.

"But the condition of Roman subjects in time of peace is far more grievous than the evils of war, for the exaction of the taxes is very severe, and unprincipled men inflict injuries on others because the laws are practically not valid against all classes. A trangressor who belongs to the wealthy classes is not punished for his injustice, while a poor man, who does not understand business, undergoes the legal penalty—that is, if he does not depart this life before the trial, so long is the course of lawsuits protracted, and so much money is expended on them. The climax of misery is to have to pay in order to obtain justice. For no one will give a hearing to the injured man except he pay a sum of money to the judge and the judge's clerks."

In reply to this attack on the Empire, I asked him to be good enough to listen with patience to the other side of the question. "The creators of the Roman Republic," I said, "who were wise and good men, in order to prevent things from being done haphazardly, made one class of men guardians of the laws, and appointed another class to the profession of arms, who were to have no other object than to be always ready for battle, and to go forth to war without dread, as though to their ordinary exercise, having by practice exhausted all their fear beforehand. Others again were assigned to attend to the cultivation of the ground, to support themselves and those who fight in their defense by contributing the military corn supply.... To those who protect the interests of the litigants a sum of money is paid by the latter, just as a payment is made by the farmers to the soldiers. Is it not fair to support him who assists and requite him for his kindness? ....

"Those who spend money on a suit and lose it in the end cannot fairly put it down to anything but the injustice of their case. And as to the long time spent on lawsuits, that is due to anxiety for justice, that judges may not fail in passing accurate judgments by having to give sentence offhand; it is better that they should reflect, and conclude the case more tardily, than that by judging in a hurry they should both injure man and transgress against the Deity, the institutor of justice. ....

"The Romans treat their slaves better than the king of the Scythians treats his subjects. They deal with them as fathers or teachers, admonishing them to abstain from evil and follow the lines of conduct which they have esteemed honorable; they reprove them for their errors like their own children. They are not allowed, like the Scythians, to inflict death on their slaves. They have numerous ways of conferring freedom; they can manumit not only during life, but also by their wills, and the testamentary wishes of a Roman in regard to his property are law."

My interlocutor shed tears, and confessed that the laws and constitution of the Romans were fair, but deplored that the officials, not possessing the spirit of former generations, were ruining the state.

READING 9

Selections from *The Anglo-Saxon Chronicle*

This important historical source, written in the Anglo-Saxon
vernacular (rather than in Latin), reports on events that occurred
more than 400 years before the work's composition, although the
anonymous author may have had access to earlier records, now
lost. It tells the story, familiar in the late Empire, of Roman provincial leaders inviting Germanic warriors in to defend them. Similar
invitations—with similar results—brought the Burgundians to
Gaul, the Lombards to Italy, and the Arabs to Spain.

A. THE COMING OF THE ANGLO-SAXONS

446. In this year the Britons[1] sent across the sea to Rome and begged for help
against the Picts,[2] but they got none there, for the Romans were engaged in a
campaign against Attila, king of the Huns. And they then sent to the Angles, and
made the same request of the chieftains of the Angles.

449. Vortigern[3] invited the Angles hither, and they then came in three ships to
Britain at the place Ebbsfleet. King Vortigern gave them land in the south-east on
condition that they should fight against the Picts. They fought the Picts and had the
victory wherever they came. Then they sent to [their homeland of] Angeln,
bidding them more help, and had them informed of the cowardice of the Britons
and the excellence of the land. They then immediately sent hither a greater force
to help the others. Their leaders were two brothers, Hengest and Horsa,[4] who were
sons of Wihtgils.

455. In this year Hengest and Horsa fought against King Vortigern at the place
which is called Ægelsthrep, and his brother Horsa was killed there; and after that
Hengest and his son Æsc succeeded to the kingdom.

456. In this year Hengest and his son Æsc fought against the Britons in the place
called Creacanford and killed 4,000 men; and the Britons then deserted Kent and
fled with great fear to London.

465. In this year Hengest and Æsc fought against the Britons near Wippedesfleet,
and there slew twelve British chiefs, and a thane[5] of theirs was slain whose name
was Wipped.

473. In this year Hengest and Æsc fought against the Britons and captured
countless spoils and the Britons fled from the English as from fire.

[1]That is, the Romanized inhabitants of the island.

[2]From Scotland.

[3]"Vortigern" is not a name but a title meaning "king of the Britons."

[4]"Hengest" means stallion; "Horsa," horse: again, these are more likely descriptions than names.

[5]A warrior-nobleman.

B. THE SETTLEMENT OF WESSEX

495. In this year two princes, Cerdic and Cynric his son, came to Britain with five ships, arriving at the place called Cerdicesora, and the same day they fought against the Welsh.

501. In this year Port and his two sons, Bieda and Maegla, came with two ships to Britain at the place which is called Portsmouth, and immediately seized land and slew a young Briton, a very noble man.

508. In this year Cerdic and Cynric slew a Welsh king, whose name was Nazaleod, and 5,000 men with him.

514. In this year the West Saxons, Stuf and Whitgar, came to Britain with three ships, arriving at the place called Cerdicesora, and fought against the Britons and put them to flight.

519. In this year Cerdic and Cynric obtained the kingdom of the West Saxons, and the same year they fought against the Britons at a place now called Certicesford. And from that day on the princes of the West Saxons have reigned.

528. In this year Cerdic passed away, and his son Cynric continued to reign twenty-six more years.

597. In this year Ceowulf began to reign in Wessex, and ever after fought and made war either against the Angles, or against the Welsh, or the Picts, or the Scots. He was the son of Cuth, the son of Cynric, the son of Cerdic, the son of Elesa, the son of Elsa, the son of Gewis, the son of Wig, the son of Freawin, the son of Frithugar, the son of Brand, the son of Baeldaeg, the son of Woden.[6]

READING 10

Jordanes on the Fall of the Western Empire

Jordanes (6th C.), a Christian writer of partly Germanic ancestry, is using earlier sources to describe events that occurred between 60 and 75 years before he wrote. Jordanes exhibits a distinct pro-Gothic bias, and his sympathies have prompted him to exclude certain details from his account. We know from other sources, for example, that Emperor Zeno invited Theodoric to Constantinople and honored him there in order to halt a five-year plundering expedition that Theodoric had been conducting against the Eastern Empire. The Ostrogothic invasion of Italy resulted from a pact between Theodoric and Zeno to get rid of Odoacer. And Theodoric persuaded Odoacer to stop fighting by promising to

From *The Gothic History of Jordanes*, tr. Charles C. Mierow; Princeton, Princeton University Press, 1915, pp. 119-120, 134-139.

[6]A typical invented genealogy tracing the lineage of a Germanic ruler back to a god.

spare his life and share power with him. A few days later
Theodoric had Odoacer murdered along with all his soldiers and
their families. In short, this passage teaches us not only about the
later fifth century but also about the problem of dealing with
sources that are at once informative and biased. A biographer of
an American president would doubtlessly study the releases of his
press secretary but would be advised to seek other sources as well.

The passage begins with the appointment of the young Romulus
Augustulus, the last of the Western emperors.

Now when Augustulus had been appointed Emperor by his father Orestes in
Ravenna, it was not long before Odoacer, king of the Torcilingi, invaded Italy, as
leader of the Sciri, the Heruli and allies of various races. He put Orestes to death,
drove his son [Romulus] Augustulus from the throne and condemned him to the
punishment of exile in the Castle of Lucullus in Campania [A.D. 476]. Thus the
Western Empire of the Roman race, which Octavianus Augustus, the first of the
Augusti, began to govern in the seven hundred and ninth year from the founding of
the city, perished with this Augustulus in the five hundred and twenty-second year
from the beginning of the rule of his predecessors and those before them, and from
this time onward kings of the Goths held Rome and Italy. Meanwhile Odoacer,
king of nations, subdued all Italy and then at the very outset of his reign slew Count
Bracila at Ravenna that he might inspire a fear of himself among the Romans. He
strengthened his kingdom and held it for almost thirteen years, until the appearance
of Theodoric, of whom we shall speak hereafter.

When the [Eastern] Emperor Zeno heard that Theodoric had been appointed
king over his own people [the Ostrogoths], he received the news with pleasure and
invited him to come and visit him in Constantinople, sending an escort of honor.
Receiving Theodoric with all due respect, he placed him among the princes of his
palace. After some time Zeno increased his dignity by adopting him as his son-at-
arms and gave him a triumph[1] in the city at his expense. Theodoric was made
Consul Ordinary also, which is well known to be the supreme good and highest
honor in the world. Nor was this all, for Zeno set up before the royal palace an
equestrian statue to the glory of this great man.

Now while Theodoric was in alliance by treaty with the Empire of Zeno and was
himself enjoying every comfort in the city, he heard that his tribe, dwelling as we
have said in Illyricum, was not altogether satisfied or content. So he chose to seek
a living by his own exertions, after the manner customary to his race, rather than to
enjoy the advantages of the Roman Empire in luxurious ease while his tribe lived
apart.

---

[1]A ceremonial procession traditionally accorded victorious Roman military commanders.

Therefore Theodoric departed from the royal city and returned to his own people. In company with the whole tribe of the Goths, who gave him their unanimous consent, he set out for Hesperia. He went in straight march through Sirmium to the places bordering on Pannonia and, advancing into the territory of Venice as far as the bridge of the Sontius, encamped there. When he had halted there for some time to rest the bodies of his men and pack-animals, Odoacer sent an armed force against him, which he met on the plains of Verona and destroyed with great slaughter. Then he broke camp and advanced through Italy with greater boldness. Crossing the river Po, he pitched camp near the royal city of Ravenna, about the third milestone from the city in the place called Pineta. When Odoacer saw this, he fortified himself within the city. He frequently harassed the army of the Goths at night, sallying forth stealthily with his men, and this not once or twice, but often; and thus he struggled for almost three whole years. But he labored in vain, for all Italy at last called Theodoric its lord and the Empire obeyed his nod. But Odoacer, with his few adherents and the Romans who were present, suffered daily from war and famine in Ravenna. Since he accomplished nothing, he sent an embassy and begged for mercy. Theodoric first granted it and afterwards deprived him of his life.

It was in the third year after his entrance into Italy, as we have said, that Theodoric, by advice of the Emperor Zeno, laid aside the garb of a private citizen and the dress of his race and assumed a costume with a royal mantle, as he had now become the ruler over both Goths and Romans.

READING 11

From Gregory of Tours, *The History of the Franks*

Again we must contend with an account written several generations after the events it describes. Gregory, Bishop of Tours (c. 540-595), is, on the whole, a good historian although a bad Latinist. His discussions of the character of Clovis and his conversion to Catholic Christianity ring true. To Clovis, even more than to Constantine, the Christian God was a bringer of military victory. Clovis's conversion was of inestimable importance to the future history of Western Europe in that it eventually brought Classical-Christian culture, at least in attenuated form, to the Franks.

From Gregory of Tours, *The History of the Franks*, tr. E. Brehaut, New York, Columbia University Press, 1916, pp. 36-38, 45-50.

At that time many churches were despoiled by Clovis's army, since he was as yet involved in heathen error. Now the army had taken from a certain church a vase of wonderful size and beauty, along with the remainder of the utensils for the service of the church. And the bishop of the church sent messengers to the king asking that the vase at least be returned, if he could not get back any more of the sacred dishes. On hearing this the king said to the messengers: "Follow us as far as Soissons, because all that has been taken is to be divided there and when the lot assigns me that dish I will do what the bishop asks." Then when he came to Soissons and all the booty was set in their midst, the king said: "I ask of you, brave warriors, not to refuse to grant me in addition to my share, yonder dish," that is, he was speaking of the vase just mentioned. In answer to the speech of the king, those of more sense replied: "Glorious king, all that we see is yours, and we ourselves are subject to your rule. Now do what seems well-pleasing to you; for no one is able to resist your power." When they said this a foolish, envious and excitable fellow lifted his battle-axe and struck the vase, and cried in a loud voice: "You shall get nothing here except what the lot fairly bestows on you." At this all were stupefied, but the king endured the insult with gentleness of patience, and taking the vase he handed it over to the messenger of the church, nursing the wound deep in his heart. And at the end of the year he ordered the whole army to come with their equipment of armor, to show the brightness of their arms on the field of Mars. And when he was reviewing them all carefully, he came to the man who struck the vase, and said to him: "No one has brought armor so carelessly kept as you; for neither your spear nor sword nor axe is in serviceable condition." And seizing the man's axe he cast it to the earth, and when the other had bent over somewhat to pick it up, the king raised his hands and drove his own axe into the man's head. "This," he said, "is what you did at Soissons to the vase."

Upon the death of this man, he ordered the rest to depart, raising great dread of himself by this action.

It came about that as the armies of the Franks and the Alemanni were fighting fiercely, there was great slaughter, and Clovis's army was in danger of being destroyed. So with remorse in his heart he burst into tears and cried, "Jesus Christ, whom Clotilda [Clovis's wife] asserts to the son of the living God, and who is said to give aid to those in distress and victory to those who hope in you, I beg the glory of your aid, with the vow that if you grant me the victory over these enemies, I will believe in you and be baptized in your name." And when he said this the Alemanni turned their backs and fled; and their king was killed, and they submitted to the domination of Clovis. And he stopped the fighting, and after encouraging his men, retired in peace and told the queen how he had merit to win the victory by calling on the name of Christ. This happened in the fifteenth year of his reign. [500 if Gregory is right, but more likely 496.]

Then Clovis the king said to his people, "I take it very hard that these Arians[1] hold part of Gaul. Let us go with God's help and conquer them and bring the land

---

[1] Christians who denied the orthodox belief in the Trinity—the equality of the Father, Son, and Holy Spirit. The Visigoths, like many other Germanic peoples, were Arians.

under our control." Then Clovis met with Alaric II, king of the Visigoths, in the plain of Voillé, at the tenth milestone from Poitiers. And when the Goths had fled, as was their custom, King Clovis had the victory by God's aid. At that time there perished a very great number of the people of Auvergne, who had come with Apollinaris and the leading senators. Clovis sent his son to Clermont by way of Albi and Rodez. He went, and brought under his father's dominion the cities from the boundaries of the Goth [i.e., the Visigoths of Spain] to the limit of the Burgundians. When Clovis had spent the winter at Bordeaux and taken all the treasures of Alaric at Toulouse, he went to Angoulême. And the Lord gave him such grace that the walls fell down of their own accord when he gazed at them. Then he drove the Visigoths out and brought the city under his own dominion. Clovis received an appointment to the consulship from the emperor Anastasius, and in the church of the blessed St. Martin of Tours he clad himself in the purple tunic, and from that day he was called consul or Augustus. Leaving Tours he went to Paris, and there he established the seat of his kingdom.

CHAPTER 2

THE HEIRS OF CLASSICAL CIVILIZATION

With the collapse of the Western imperial regime in A.D. 476 and the establishment of Christian-Germanic kingdoms in its place, the cultures of the Eastern Empire and Western Europe began to drift apart. The vast lands that Rome had once ruled split into two distinct civilizations: Byzantium (East Rome) and Western Christendom. A third civilization emerged when the Arab conquests of the seventh and eighth centuries spread the religion and culture of Islam through much of the Middle East and westward across the formerly Roman lands of North Africa and Spain.

The three civilizations of medieval Western Eurasia—Byzantine, Western Christian and Islamic—were all influenced by the earlier Greco-Roman culture. All were, to some degree, heirs of Classical civilization. And all were committed to monotheistic religions that drew inspiration from ancient Judaism. Muhammad taught that Jesus, Moses, and the Old Testament prophets were, like himself, servants and spokesmen of the one God.

The sources in this chapter deal first with Byzantine civilization (documents 1-4), then with early Western Christendom through the seventh century (documents 5-9), and finally with Islam (documents 10-13). The Byzantine sources begin with an account of one of the holy men who functioned as spiritual heroes and foci of community devotion in early Byzantine society (document 1). There follows a selection from the *Corpus Juris Civilis* (The "Body of Civil Law"), assembled under the sixth-century emperor Justinian, which was to exert a commanding influence on medieval jurisprudence (document 2). We continue with an edict that demonstrates Byzantine imperial concern for the peasantry (document 3) and conclude with an account of the overwhelming Byzantine defeat at Manzikert in A.D. 1071, which crippled the Empire permanently (document 4).

The sources for the early medieval West (documents 5-9) all emphasize, in one way or another, the creative role of the popes and the Benedictine monks in preserving and expanding Classical-Christian culture in the Germanic kingdoms, beginning with one of the earliest assertions of papal supremacy. Our Islamic documents begin with an excerpt from the *Koran* (document 10), the holy book in which the Islamic faith is rooted. They continue with Muhammad's Constitution of Medina, the political-religious community that foreshadowed the future governance of the Islamic Empire (document 11). The final two additional Islamic sources demonstrate the vitality of the Moslem intellectual tradition. Alfarabi (document 12) was one of the most important political theorists of the Islamic world, and Al-Ghazali (document 13), anticipating Descartes' seventeenth-century philosophic inquiries based on doubt, provides an excellent example of Islamic theology.

READING 1

The Life of St. Daniel the Stylite

A disciple of the pillar-saint Simeon Stylites, St. Daniel was born in Syria in 409 and died near Constantinople in 493. He was a shrewd, uncomplicated man who gave practical advice to people of the neighborhood and travelers from afar. And he served as a living example of heroic Christian sanctity. The author of the *Life* was a younger contemporary of Daniel's, perhaps a disciple and certainly an eyewitness to many of Daniel's activities. Like the authors of other saints' lives throughout the Middle Ages, Daniel's biographer writes with the purpose of inspiring others to admire and emulate his spiritual hero. If Daniel had faults, we will not discover them here.

Daniel's career was paralleled by those of numerous Byzantine saints who, to a far greater extent than in the West, played intimate, unifying roles in their urban communities.

Before all things it is right that we should give glory to Jesus Christ our God, Who for us was made man and for our salvation endured all things according to the Dispensation; for His sake, too, prophets were killed, and just men crucified themselves because of this faith in Him and by His grace, after having kept patience under their sufferings unswervingly unto the end, they received a crown of glory. These men our Master and Saviour Christ gave us as an example that we might know that it is possible for a man by the patient endurance of his sufferings to please God and be called His faithful servant. . . .

The servant of God [St. Daniel] fell into an ecstasy, as it were, and saw a huge pillar of cloud standing opposite him and the holy and blessed Simeon [another famous pillar saint] standing above the head of the column and two men of goodly appearance, clad in white, standing near him in the heights. And he heard the voice of the holy and blessed Simeon saying to him, "Come here to me, Daniel." And he said, "Father, father, and how can I get up to that height?" Then the saint said to the young men standing near him, "Go down and bring him up to me." So the men came down and brought Daniel up to him and he stood there. Then Simeon took him in his arms and kissed him with a holy kiss, and then others called him away, and escorted by them he was borne up to heaven leaving Daniel on the column with the two men. When holy Daniel saw him being carried up to heaven he heard the voice of St. Simeon, "Stand firm and play the man." But he was confused by fear

From *Three Byzantine Saints*, ed. and tr. E. Dawes and N.H. Baynes; Crestwood, N.J., St. Vladmir's Seminary Press, 1948, pp. 7, 18-19, 29, 36, 43-44, 70-71.

and by that fearful voice, for it was like thunder in his ears. When he came to himself again he declared the vision to those around him. Then they said to the holy man, "You must mount on to a pillar and take up St. Simeon's mode of life and be supported by the angels." . . .

Now the blessed Emperor Leo [457-474] of pious memory had heard from many of these things and desired for a long time to see the man. Therefore he sent for the pious Sergius, who carried the saint's messages, and through him he asked that the saint would pray and beseech God to grant him a son. And Daniel prayed, and through God's good pleasure the emperor's wife, the Empress Verina, thereafter conceived and begot a son, whereupon the emperor immediately sent and had the foundations laid of a third column. . . .

It happened about the same time that Gubazius, the king of the Lazi, arrived at the court of the Emperor Leo, who took him up to visit the holy man. When he saw this strange sight Gubazius threw himself on his face and said, "I thank You, heavenly King, that by means of an earthly king You have deemed me worthy to behold great mysteries; for never before in this world have I seen anything of this kind." And these kings had a point in dispute touching the Roman policy; and they laid the whole matter open to the servant of God and through the mediation of the holy man they agreed upon a treaty which satisfied the claims of each. After this the emperor returned to the city and dismissed Gubazius to his native land, and when the latter reached his own country he related to all his folk what he had seen. Consequently the men who later on came up from Lazica to the city [of Constantinople] invariably went up to Daniel. Gubazius himself, too, wrote to the holy man and besought his prayers and never ceased doing so to the end of his life. . . .

At about that time the blessed Emperor Leo heard from many about a certain Titus, a man of vigor who dwelt in Gaul and had in his service a number of men well trained for battle; so he sent for him and honored him with the rank of count that he might have him to fight on his behalf if he were forced to go to war. This Titus he sent to the holy man for his blessing; on his arrival the saint watered him with many and diverse counsels from the holy writings and proved him to be an ever-blooming fruit-bearing tree; and Titus, beholding the holy man, marveled at the strangeness of his appearance and his endurance and just as good earth when it has received the rain brings forth much fruit, so this admirable man Titus was illuminated in mind by the teaching of the holy and just man and no longer wished to leave the enclosure, for he said, "The whole labor of man is spent on growing rich and acquiring possessions in this world and pleasing men; yet the single hour of his death robs him of all his belongings; therefore it is better for us to serve God rather than men." With these words he threw himself down before the holy man begging him to receive him and let him be enrolled in the brotherhood. And Daniel, the servant of the Lord, willingly accepted his good resolve. Thereupon that noble man Titus sent for all his men and said to his soldiers, "From now on I am the soldier of the heavenly King; aforetime my rank among men made me your captain and yet I was unable to benefit either you or myself, for I only urged you on to slaughter and bloodshed. From today, however, and henceforth I bid farewell to all such things; therefore those of you who wish it, remain here with me, but I do not compel any one of you, for what is done under compulsion is not acceptable. See, here is the money, take some, each of you, and go to your homes." Then he brought much gold and he took and placed it in front of the column and gave to each according to his rank. Two of them, however, did not choose to take any, but remained with him. All the rest embraced Titus and went their ways.

When the emperor heard this he was very angry and sent a messenger up to the holy man to say to Titus, "I brought you up from your country because I wanted to have you quite near me and I sent you to the holy man to pray and receive a blessing, but not that you should separate yourself from me." Titus replied to the messenger, "From now on, since I have listened to the teaching of this holy man, I am dead to the world and to all the things of the world. Whatever the just man says about me to you, tell to the emperor, for Titus your servant is dead." Then the messengers went outside into the enclosure to the holy man and told him everything. And the holy man sent a letter of counsel by them to the emperor, beseeching him and saying, "You yourself need no human aid; for owing to your perfect faith in God you have God as your everlasting defender; do not therefore covet a man who today is and tomorrow is not; for the Lord does all things in accordance with His will. Therefore dedicate your servant to God Who is able to send your Piety in his stead another still braver and more useful; without your approval I never wished to do anything."

And the emperor was satisfied and sent and thanked the holy man and said, "To crown all your good deeds there yet remained this good thing for you to do. Let the man, then, remain under your authority, and may God accept his good purpose." Not long afterwards they were deemed worthy of the holy robe, and both made progress in the good way of life; but more especially was this of Titus, the former count. . . .

Let us now in a short summary review his whole life down to the end of his time on earth.

Our all-praiseworthy father Daniel said good-bye to his parents when he was twelve years old, then for twenty-five years he lived in a monastery; after that during five years he visited the fathers and from each learned what might serve his purpose, making his anthology from their teachings. At the time when the crown of his endurance began to be woven the saint had completed his forty-second year, and at that age he came by divine guidance, as we have explained above, to this our imperial city. He dwelt in the church for nine years, standing on the capital of a column, thus training himself beforehand in the practice of that discipline which he was destined to bring to perfection. For he had learned from many divine revelations that his duty was to enter upon the way of life practiced by the blessed and sainted Simeon.

For three and thirty years and three months he stood for varying periods on the three columns, as he changed from one to another, so that the whole span of his life was a little more than eighty-four years.

During these he was deemed worthy to receive "the prize of his high calling"; he blessed all men, he prayed on behalf of all, he counseled all not to be covetous, he instructed all in the things necessary to salvation, he showed hospitality to all, yet he possessed nothing on earth beyond the confines of the spot on which the enclosure and religious houses had been built. And though many, amongst whom were sovereigns and very distinguished officials occupying the highest posts, wished to present him with splendid possessions he never consented, but he listened to each one's offer and then prayed that he might be recompensed by God for his pious intention.

READING 2
From the Institutes of Justinian

During the early years of the reign of the Byzantine emperor Justinian (reigned 527-565), a commission of imperial lawyers headed by Tribonian carried out the emperor's order to systematize and produce official texts of the whole of Roman law still in effect. The result of this immense effort, the *Corpus Juris Civilis,* included all valid imperial statutes since the time of Hadrian (the *Codex*) along with a synthesis of the authoritative writings of Roman legal officials (the *Digest)* and an introductory textbook on the fundamental principles of Roman law (the *Institutes).* It is from the *Institutes,* completed in 533, that the following passages are drawn.

PROLOGUE

In the name of our Lord Jesus Christ. The emperor Caesar Flavius Justinian, conqueror of the Alamanni, Goths, Franks, Germans, Antes, Alani, Vandals and Africans, rightly fortunate and renowned, victorious and triumphant, ever Augustus, to the young [scholars] desirous of legal knowledge.

The imperial majesty should not only be embellished with arms but also strengthened by laws, so that the times of both war and peace can be ordered correctly and that the Roman emperor *[princeps]* may emerge not only victorious

From *Corpus Juris Civilis,* ed. Paul Krueger, vol. 1, Berlin, 1882, pp. 2-4; tr. Marc Anthony Meyer.

in battle with enemies but also, eliminating the iniquities of villains through legal means, may be as solicitous of the law as he is triumphant over conquered foes.

1. We have reached each of these objectives through the greatest vigilance and foresight, and by the will of God.   And the barbarian nations brought under our subjection know of our military achievements, and Africa as well and many other provinces have been restored after a very long time to Roman domination through our victories, and with divine guidance we have achieved and proclaimed our empire.   Truly, all of the people are now also governed by laws that have been promulgated or compiled by us.

2. And after bringing the revered constitutions, previously in a confused state, into lucid harmony, we turned our attention to the great mass of venerable jurisprudence and, as if crossing the open sea, we completed—by the favor of heaven—a nearly hopeless task.

3. And when, with God's help, this had been done, we called together Tribonian, a great man and teacher and ex-quaestor of our sacred palace, and Theophilus and Dorotheus, both illustrious men—all of whose ingenuity and legal expertise and tried obedience to our orders we have had ample proof.   We issued a special mandate that by our authority and with our encouragement they should compose the *Institutes* so that you might acquire your first knowledge of the law not from old stories but through the splendor of the emperor [and] that your ears and minds might receive nothing useless or false but that which is deemed proper in these matters.   And whereas in the past at least four years would go by before the imperial constitutions were read, you can now do this from the beginning, meriting such honor and discovering with such happiness that the beginning and the end of your legal studies proceed from the mouth of the emperor.

7. Therefore, with all endeavor and eager study, receive these our laws and show yourselves so learned that you may cherish the marvelous hope that, at the end of your legal studies, you may even be able to order our state *[res publica]* in that part given over to you. . . .

ON JUSTICE AND LAW

Justice is the constant and perpetual desire to give to each person his own due right *[ius]*.

1. Jurisprudence *[iurisprudentia]* is the acquaintance with both human and divine things, the knowledge of what is just and what unjust.

3. These are the precepts of law *[ius]*: to live honestly, not to injure another, and to render to each his own.

4. The two aspects of this study are public and private: public law is that which pertains to the Roman state, private is that which concerns the benefit of the individual.   This is to say, therefore, that private law has three parts—indeed, it consists of natural precepts or either those of nations or of states.

ON NATURAL LAW, THE LAW OF NATIONS AND CIVIL LAW

Natural law *[ius naturale]* is that which nature has instilled in all animals, because this law is not characteristic of humankind but of all animals which are born on land and in the air and in the sea. From this derives the association of man and woman which we call marriage, as well as procreation and the rearing of off-spring because we see that animals are imbued with the experience of this law.

1. Civil law *[ius civile]* and the law of nations *[ius gentium],* however, are divided in this way: all peoples who are governed by laws *[leges]* and customs *[mores]* use law which is in part particular to themselves and in part common to all men. The law that each people has established for itself is particular to that state and is called civil law as being specifically of that state. Yet, what natural reason has established among all men is kept equally by all peoples and is called the law of nations, as it were, the law common to all peoples. And hence, the Roman people observe partly their own particular law [and] partly that which is common to all peoples. . . .

3. Our law is derived from written or unwritten [sources], just as among the Greeks: some laws are written, others unwritten. . . .

4. A 'law' *[lex]* is that which the Roman people commanded on a question submitted by a senatorial magistrate, like a consul. A 'plebiscite' *[plebiscitum]* is that which the plebs ordered put by a plebian magistrate, like a tribune. The plebs, however, differ from the people as a 'species' is distinguished from a 'genus' because the term 'people' means all the citizens, including as well patricians and senators, while the name 'plebians' signifies the other citizens, excluding the patricians and the senators. Yet, with the passing of the *lex Hortensia*[1] the plebiscites came to be no less valid than the laws.

5. A '*senatus consultum*' is that which the senate orders and directs, for when the Roman people had increased in its number, it became difficult to call it together in one place for the enactment of a law, [and thus,] it seemed best instead to invoke the senate in place of the people.

6. The emperor's voice has the force of law as well since, by the 'law of kings' *[lex regia]* which regulated his authority *[imperium],* the people conceded to him and placed in him all their power and authority. Thus, whatever the emperor directed by letter or decreed in a hearing or ordered by edict is to be conceived as law: these are what are called "constitutions." Some of these, of course, are special cases which are not to be used as precedents, for the emperor did not intend this to go beyond the individual because he views one person favorably because of merits or inflicts a penalty on another or offers relief to another. Others, however, when general in intent, undoubtedly apply to everyone.

---

[1] In 287 B.C. the "struggle of the orders" culminated in the promulgation of the *lex Hortensia,* which decreed that plebiscites were to be as fully valid as laws *[leges]* proper.

7. Furthermore, praetorian[2] edicts have no ordinary authority as law. We normally call this the law of honor because those who bear honor, that is a magistrate, have given their authority to this law. And *curule aediles,*[3] as well issued edicts concerning certain cases and that kind of edict is part of honorary law.

8. The responses of the learned [jurists] are sentences and opinions of those to whom it was permitted to lay down the law; for in ancient times it was instituted that there were those who publicly interpreted the law—who are called jurisconsults—to whom the right of responding [in legal matters] was given by the caesar. All of their sentences and opinions [when unanimous] held such authority that judges were not permitted to differ from their responses, so that it is a constitution.

9. Unwritten law is that which usage has approved, for long-observed customs take on the effect of law by consent of those who observe them. . . .

11. And, natural laws, which are followed by all nations alike, deriving from divine providence, remain always firm and unchangeable: truly, those which each state constitutes for itself often subject to alteration whether by the tacit approval of the people or else by subsequent legislation.

READING 3

Basil II on the Protection of Peasants' Lands, 996

Basil II (957-1025) was a great Byzantine emperor known affectionately as 'the Bulgar Slayer'. Like their counterparts in the medieval west, Byzantine rulers faced a problem when great landholders encroached on the lands of poor, for the great landlords were better able to evade taxes and imperial dues then were lesser landholders. Basil II attempted to address the problem in this law. But the emperor is not necessarily the friend of the poor that this passage might suggest: on one occasion he had 14,000 war captives blinded (though, very charitably, he left one out of every hundred with one eye intact to lead the others home).

From D.J. Geanakoplos, *Byzantium, Church Society and Civilization as Seen through Contemporary Eyes,* University of Chicago Press, 1984, pp. 245-47.

[2] The *praetor* was responsible for the administration of justice in both the Republic and Empire periods, but the authority of this high office was restricted by the superior authority of the consul. When Roman authority was established outside the boundaries of Italy, the praetors acted as provincial governors of the Senate; but with the dictatorship of Sulla in the first century B.C., these officers were required to remain in the capital to preside over criminal courts.

[3] In their capacity as market officers the *curule aediles* were responsible for important features of the Roman law of sale.

1. Whereas our imperial majesty, by the grace of God from whom we have received the imperial authority, has undertaken to scrutinize the legal cases initiated by both rich and poor, we have found that those powerful *dynatoi*[1] who desire to aggrandize [their lands] have a legitimate excuse for their personal covetousness, that is, the prescription of up to forty years [e.g., a kind of statute of limitations], and that they anxiously await to pass through this period either by means of bribes and gifts or through the power they possess and then to enjoy in full ownership whatever they have wrongly appropriated at the expense of the poor. Therefore we have promulgated the present legislation, which on the one hand rectifies what has previously occurred but, on the other hand, also curbs the present-day *dynatoi* and forbids those in the future from undertaking such things [to attack the poor], since they now have the knowledge that they will get no assistance from this quarter. Not only will they themselves be stripped of the property belonging to others, but so also will their children and whomever else they leave it to as heirs. From this we wish it to be clear that our imperial majesty does not without purpose or investigation overturn ownership [based upon] prescription of long-standing, but takes pity on the poor and watches out for the common welfare and conditions and embraces justice and provides a remedy against this fearful passion of desire for aggrandizement. Because of this circumstance we have been very disturbed on behalf of the poor, and we have observed with our own eyes (when we traversed the themes[2] of our empire and set out on campaigns) the avarice and injustices every day perpetrated against the poor. Indeed how can time be of any assistance at all since, as has happened, the *dynatoi*, who is powerful and prosperous and aggrandizes himself at the expense of the poor man, will profit from the passage of time and will bequeath to his heirs his power and wealth? . . .

Therefore, we decree by our present enactment, that those properties which have been acquired by the *dynatoi* in communities of peasant villages up to the initial law of our great-grandfather Emperor Romanus the Elder and which derive their validity from written documents or supporting witnesses, be preserved and kept in their owner's hands, as has been declared in earlier laws. For this reason we seek written privileges and supporting witnesses to be adduced, so that the *dynatoi* might not by means of subterfuge allege that the lands recently acquired by them carry over to them by written documents from a long time ago. But from that time when the written prescription was issued through the law published by our great-grandfather Emperor Romanus the Elder, until the present (which is the first of January, of the year 996 and also into the future), [we declare] that in no way at all can time [elapsed] have [legal] validity or be made use of against the poor, when they have dealings with the *dynatoi*, but their possessions should be given back to the poor, nor [should anything be brought up] concerning the return of any costs [paid] or necessary improvements made by the *dynatoi*, because they have been

---

[1] Member of the landed nobility.

[2] Administrative and military districts.

discovered to transgress the aforementioned law and are indeed liable to be called to account. For when the aforesaid emperor, our great grandfather Emperor Romanus the Elder, wrote and said: 'From now I forbid the *dynatoi* to acquire property among lands in peasant villages,' he meant that he forbade them forever and for eternity, and he did not give them [a prescription of] time as a method of assistance. . . .

2. Since we have found many [of our] subjects listed in [imperial] surveys recorded in chrysobulls,[3] and many such cases have been brought before our tribunal, we decree that those surveys which are adduced [as evidence] have no validity, nor shall those utilizing them derive any legal benefit from the ambiguity which may exist in these documents. For the surveys are not issued with imperial knowledge or assent but for the benefit of those receiving them. Moreover, the chief secretaries who draw up the chrysobulls are neither present nor do they observe when the [actual] measuring [of the property] or the notification [of the results] occurs. For this reason, as has been made clear, we wish that those surveys in which ambiguity exists be considered invalid and have no effect. But if such surveys happen to be among the archives of the imperial treasury or in some other [legally] substantiating documents, we command that they be heeded and obeyed.

READING 4
Michael Psellus Describes the Battle of Manzikert, 1071

In August 1071 a Byzantine army led by Emperor Romanus Diogenes was routed by the invading Seljuk Turks under their sultan, Alp Arslan. As a result of the Turkish victory the Byzantines lost Asia Minor, which had for many centuries been the Empire's best source of revenues and soldiers. Having captured Emperor Romanus, the Turks released him in return for a tremendous ransom and an annual tribute.

The author of this account, Michael Psellus, was a contemporary though not an eyewitness. He was a master of philosophy at the academy at Constantinople and one of the most celebrated and influential scholars of the age, whose keen intellect was matched only by his vanity and ambition. Psellus died a few years after the battle.

From Michael Psellus, *Chronographica*, in *Fourteen Byzantine Rulers*, tr. E.R.A. Sewter; New York, Penguin Books, 1966, pp. 353-356.

[3] Manuscripts written in gold ink.

With his usual contempt of all advice, whether on matters civil or military, [Romanus] at once set out with his army and hurried to Caesarea. Having reached that objective, he was loath to advance any further and tried to find excuses for returning to Byzantium, not only for his own sake but for the army's. When he found the disgrace involved in such a retreat intolerable, he should have come to terms with the enemy and put a stop to their annual incursions. Instead, whether in desperation, or because he was more confident than he should have been, he marched to the attack without taking adequate measures to protect his rear. The enemy, seeing him advance, decided to lure him on still farther and ensnare him by cunning. They therefore rode on ahead of him and then retired again, as though the retreat was planned. By carrying out this maneuver several times, they succeeded in cutting off some of our generals, who were taken captive.

Now I was aware—though he was not—that the Sultan himself, the king of the Persians and Kurds [Alp Arslan, the Seljuk leader], was present in person with his army, and most of their victories were due to his leadership. Romanus refused to believe anyone who detected the Sultan's influence in these successes. The truth is, he did not want peace. He thought he would capture the barbarian camp without a battle. Unfortunately for him, through his ignorance of military science, he had scattered his forces; some were concentrated round himself, others had been sent off to take up some other position. So, instead of opposing his adversaries with the full force of his army, less than half were actually involved.

Although I cannot applaud his subsequent behavior, it is impossible for me to censure him. The fact is, he bore the whole brunt of the danger himself. His action can be interpreted in two ways. My own view represents the mean between these two extremes. On the one hand, if you regard him as a hero, courting danger and fighting courageously, it is reasonable to praise him; on the other, when one reflects that a general, if he conforms to the accepted rules of strategy, must remain aloof from the battle-line, supervising the movements of his army and issuing the necessary orders to the men under his command, then Romanus's conduct on this occasion would appear foolish in the extreme, for he exposed himself to danger without a thought of the consequences. I myself am more inclined to praise than to blame him for what he did.

However that may be, he put on the full armor of an ordinary soldier and drew sword against his enemies. According to several of my informants he actually killed many of them and put others to flight. Later, when his attackers recognized who he was, they surrounded him on all sides. He was wounded and fell from his horse. They seized him, of course, and the Emperor of the Romans was led away, a prisoner, to the enemy camp, and his army was scattered. Those who escaped were but a tiny fraction of the whole. Of the majority some were taken captive, the rest massacred.

I do not intend at this moment to write of the time spent by the emperor in captivity, or of the attitude adopted towards him by his conqueror. That must wait till later. A few days after the battle, one of those who escaped, arriving before his comrades, brought the terrible news to the city. He was followed by a second messenger, and by others. The picture they painted was by no means distinct, for each explained the disaster in his own fashion, some saying that Romanus was dead, others that he was only a prisoner; some again declared that they had seen him wounded and hurled to the ground, while others had seen him being led away in chains to the barbarian camp. In view of this information, a conference was held in the capital, and the empress considered our future policy. The unanimous decision of the meeting was that, for the time being, they should ignore the emperor, whether he was a prisoner, or dead, and that Eudocia and her sons should carry on the government of the Empire.

READING 5

Pope Leo I on the Authority of St. Peter

Pope Leo the Great (440-461), who won fame by facing down Attila the Hun and persuading him to turn back from Rome, was one of the earliest proponents of papal supremacy over the Church. He here uses the argument, to be advanced countless times by future popes, that St. Peter was singled out by Jesus Christ as his chief apostle. Originally named "Simon," the apostle was renamed Peter (in Aramaic, "Rock") by Jesus, who said, "Upon this rock I will build my Church." Peter was believed to be the first bishop of Rome—the first pope—and his bones are believed, to this day, to lie beneath the great papal basilica in Rome that bears his name. In this passage, Leo places the papacy in the tradition of the superiority of Peter over the other apostles.

Although we be found both weak and slothful in fulfilling the duties of our office, because we are hindered by the very frailty of our condition; yet we worthily and piously rejoice over His dispensation, whereby, though He has delegated the care of His sheep to many shepherds, yet He has not abandoned the guardianship of His flock. And the strength of the foundation, on which the whole superstructure of the Church is raised, is not weakened by the weight of the temple that rests upon it.

The dispensation of Truth therefore abides, and the blessed Peter has not abandoned the helm of the Church. For he was ordained before the rest in a special way that from his being called the "rock" (i.e., "Peter") from his being pronounced the foundation, from his being constituted the doorkeeper of the kingdom of

From *The Sermons of Leo the Great*, tr., C.L. Feltoe, *Library of the Nicene and Post-Nicene Fathers*, vol. 12, New York, 1895, p. 117.

heaven, from his being set as the judge to bind and loose, from all these mystical titles we might know the nature of his association with Christ. And still today he performs what is entrusted to him, and carries out every part of his duty and charge in Him and with Him, through whom he has been glorified. And so if anything is won from the mercy of God by our daily prayers, it is of His work and merits whose power lives and whose authority prevails in His see.

READING 6

Pope Gelasius I on Priestly and Royal Power

In 494 Pope Gelasius I (492-496) set forth, in this letter to the East Roman emperor, the classic papal argument on the superiority of priestly to royal power—the so-called "doctrine of the two swords." Gelasius' words would be repeated by popes and other churchmen throughout the Middle Ages.

. . . Two there are, august emperor, by which this world is chiefly ruled, the sacred authority [auctoritas] of the priesthood and the royal power [potestas]. Of these the responsibility of the priests is more weighty in so far as they will answer for the kings of men themselves at the divine judgment. You know, most clement son, that, although you take precedence over all mankind in dignity, nevertheless you piously bow the neck to those who have charge of divine affairs and seek from them the means of your salvation, and hence you realize that, in the order of religion, in matters concerning the reception and right administration of the heavenly sacraments, you ought to submit yourself rather than rule, and that in these matters you should depend on their judgment rather than seek to bend them to your will. For if the bishops themselves, recognizing that the imperial office was conferred on you by divine disposition, obey your laws so far as the sphere of public order is concerned lest they seem to obstruct your decrees in mundane matters, with what zeal, I ask you, ought you obey those who have been charged with administering the sacred mysteries? Moreover, just as no light risk attends pontiffs who keep silent in matters concerning the service of God, so too no little danger threatens those who show scorn—which God forbid—when they ought to obey. And if the hearts of the faithful should be submitted to all priests in general

From Pope Gelasius' letter to Emperor Anastasius, in *The Crisis of Church and State*, 1050-1300, ed. Brian Tierney; Englewood, N.J., Prentice-Hall, Inc., 1964, pp. 13-14. Reprinted by permission.

who rightly administer divine things, how much more should assent be given to the bishop of that see which the Most High wished to be pre-eminent over all priests, and which the devotion of the whole church has honored ever since. As your piety is certainly well aware, no one can ever raise himself by purely human means to the privilege and place of him whom the voice of Christ has set before all, whom the Church has always venerated and held in devotion as its primate. The things which are established by divine judgment can be assailed by human presumption; they cannot be overthrown by anyone's power.

READING 7

From the Rule of St. Benedict

The Rule of St. Benedict (c. 480-544), based in part on earlier models, spread throughout Western Christendom to govern the lives of countless monks and nuns of the Middle Ages and beyond. The excerpts that follow stress two fundamental elements in Benedictine monasticism: humility and poverty.

PROLOGUE

Hear, my son, the precept of your master, and incline the ear of your heart, willingly receive and faithfully fulfill the admonition of your loving Father, that you may return by the labor of obedience to Him from Whom you had departed through the sloth of disobedience. Therefore, my little speech is now addressed to you—whoever you are—that, renouncing your own will, you take up the strong and bright weapons of obedience to fight for the Lord Christ, our true King. In the first place, whatever good work you begin to do, beg Him with most earnest prayer to perfect it; that He Who has now vouchsafed to count us in the number of His sons may not be grieved at any time by our evil deeds. For we must always serve Him with the good things he has given us, that not only may He never, as an angry father, disinherit His children, but may never, as an irate lord, incensed by our sins, deliver us to everlasting punishment, as most wicked servants who would not follow Him to glory. . . .

If we wish to dwell in the tabernacle of His kingdom, we will not reach it unless we approach by our good deeds. But let us ask the Lord with the prophet, saying to Him: "Lord, who will dwell in Your tabernacle, or who will rest upon Your holy mountain?" After this question, brothers, let us hear the lord answering, and

From *Patrologiae Cursis Completus, sive Latinorum*, ed. J.P. Migre, vol. 66, columns 215-218, 371-376, 551-552, 839-840, tr. Marc Anthony Meyer.

showing us the way to His tabernacle, and saying: "He who walks without stain and works justice; he who speaks the truth in his heart [and] has not spoken wickedly with his tongue; he who has done no evil to his neighbor and has not taken up a reproach against his neighbor." He who has brought the malignant one to nothing, casting him out of his heart with all his suggestions, and has taken his evil thoughts, while still new, and dashed them down on Christ. These are the ones who, fearing the Lord, are not puffed up with their own good works, but knowing that the good which is in them comes not from themselves but from the Lord, they magnify the Lord Who works in them, saying with the prophet: "Not to us, Lord, not to us but to Your name give the glory. . . ."

Therefore, a school of the Lord's service has been instituted by us, in which institution we hope will be ordered nothing harsh or nothing rigorous. But if anything is somewhat strictly laid down, according to the dictates of equity, for the amendment of vices or the preservation of charity, do not on account of this flee in dismay from the road of salvation, whose beginning cannot but be straight. But as we go forward in our life and faith, we will, with hearts enlarged and with unspeakable sweetness of love, run in the way of God's commandments; so that never departing from His guidance, but persevering in His teaching in the monastery until death, we may by patience share in the sufferings of Christ, that we may deserve to be consorts of His kingdom.

CHAPTER SEVEN: ON HUMILITY

The Holy Scripture cries out to us, brothers, saying: "Everyone who exalts himself will be humbled, and he who humbles himself shall be exalted." In saying this, it teaches us all exaltation is a kind of pride, against which the prophet shows himself to be on his guard when he says: "Lord, my heart is not excited nor my eyes lifted up; nor have I walked in great things, nor in wonders above me." And why? "If I did not think humbly, but exalted my soul, like a child who is weaned from his mother, so will you requite my soul." Hence, brothers, if we wish to arrive at the highest point of humility and quickly reach that heavenly exaltation to which we can only ascend by the humility of this present life, we must by our ever-ascending actions erect such a ladder as that which Jacob beheld in his dream, by which the angels appeared to him descending and ascending [*Genesis* 28]. This descent and ascent signify nothing else but that we descend by exaltation and ascend by humility. And the ladder thus erected is our life in the world which, if the heart is humble, is lifted up by the Lord to heaven. The sides of the same ladder we understand to be our body and soul, in which the call of God has placed various degrees of humility or discipline, which we must ascend.

The first degree of humility, then, is that a man must always keep the fear of God before his eyes [and] avoid all forgetfulness; and that he must remember all that God has commanded and that those who despise God will be consumed in hell for their sins; and that he must consider that life everlasting is prepared for those who fear Him.   And keeping himself at all times from sin and vice, whether of the thoughts, the tongue, the eyes, the hands, the feet, or his own will, let him quickly hasten to cut off the desires of the flesh. Let him consider that he is always seen from heaven by God, and that his actions are everywhere seen by the eye of the Divine Majesty and are every hour reported to Him by His angels. . . . Since, therefore, the eyes of the Lord see good and evil, and the Lord is always looking down from the heavens upon the children of men to see who has understanding or is seeking God, and since the works of our hands are reported to Him, Maker and Creator, day and night by the angels appointed to watch over us, we must always be on guard, brothers, lest, as the prophet says in the psalm, God should see us at any time descending into evil and become unprofitable, and lest, though He would spare us now, because He is merciful and expects our conversion, He should say to us in the future: "These things you did and I held my peace."

The second degree of humility is that a man should not love his own will, nor delight in gratifying his own desires; but should carry out in his own deeds that saying of the Lord: "I came not to do my own will, but the will of Him who sent me." And again, Scripture says "Self-will has punishment, but necessity wins a crown."

The third degree of humility is that for the love of God a man should surrender himself in all obedience to his superior, imitating the Lord of whom the apostle says: "He was made obedient even to death."

The fourth degree of humility is that if in this very obedience hard and contrary things, or even injuries, are done to him, he should embrace them patiently with silent consciousness, and not grow weary or submit, as the Scripture says: "He who will persevere to the end will be saved." And again: "Let your heart take courage and wait for the Lord. . . . "

The fifth degree of humility is to hide from one's abbot none of the evil thoughts that beset one's heart, nor the sins committed in secret, but humbly confess them. Concerning which the Scripture exhorts us, saying: "Make known the way to the Lord, and hope in Him." And again: "Confess to the Lord, for He is good, for His mercy endures forever." The prophet also says: "I have made known to You my offence, and my iniquities I have not hidden. I said I will confess against myself my iniquities to the Lord, and You have forgiven the wickedness of my heart."

The sixth degree of humility is for a monk to be contented with the vilest and worst of everything and in all that is enjoined him to esteem himself a bad and worthless laborer, saying with the prophet: "I have been brought to nothing, and I knew it not; I have become like a beast before You, yet I am always with You."

The seventh degree of humility is that he should not only call himself with his tongue lower and viler than all else, but also believe himself with intimate affection of the heart to be so, humbling himself, and saying with the prophet: "I am a worm and no man, the shame of men and the outcast of the people; I have been exalted, and cast down and confounded." And again: "It is good for me that You have humbled me so that I may learn Your commandments."

The eighth degree of humility is for a monk to do nothing except what is authorized by the common rule of the monastery or by the example of his seniors.

The ninth degree of humility is that a monk should refrain his tongue from speaking, keeping silence until a question is asked him, as the Scripture shows: "In much talking you will not avoid sin" and "The talkative man will not be directed upon the earth."

The tenth degree of humility is that he should not be easily or quickly moved to laughter, because it is written: "The fool lifts up his voice in laughter."

The eleventh degree of humility is that when a monk speaks he should do so gently and without laughter, humbly and with gravity, or with few words and reasonable speech, as it is written: "A wise man is known in a few words."

The twelfth degree of humility is that a monk, not only in his heart but also in his very body, should always show his humility to all who see him, that is, in work, in the oratory, in the monastery, in the garden, on the road, in the field, or wherever he may be, whether sitting, walking or standing, with head always bent down, and eyes fixed on the earth; that he always thinks of the guilt of his sins and imagines himself already present before the terrible judgment of God, always saying in his heart what the publican said with his eyes fixed on earth: "Lord, I am a sinner and am not worthy to raise my eyes to heaven." And again with the prophet: "I am bowed down and humbled on every side."

Therefore, having ascended all these degrees of humility, the monk will presently arrive at the love of God which, being perfect, casts out fear; whereby he will begin to keep, without labor, and as it were naturally and by custom, all those precepts which he had once observed only out of fear; no longer through dread of hell, but for the love of Christ, and of a good habit and a delight in virtue, which God will deem to make manifest by the Holy Spirit in His laborer, now cleansed from sin and vice.

CHAPTER THIRTY THREE: IF MONKS SHOULD HAVE ANYTHING OF THEIR OWN

Above all let the vice of private ownership be cut off from the monastery by the roots. Let no one presume to give or receive anything without leave of the abbot, or to keep anything as their own—either book or writing tablet or pen or anything whatsoever—since they are permitted to have neither body nor will in their own power. But let them hope to receive all necessities from the abbot of the monastery; nor let them keep anything which the abbot has not given or permitted. Let all things be common to all, as it is written; nor let anyone say or assume that anything is his own. But if anyone shall be found to indulge in this most horrible vice, and after one or two admonitions he does not make amends, let him be subjected to correction.

READING 8

Selected Letters of Pope Gregory the Great

St. Gregory I "the Great" (590-604) was one of the most learned popes of the early Middle Ages and perhaps the ablest. His letter to John bishop of Ravenna (letter A), better known as *The Book of Pastoral Care,* was written shortly after his accession to the papacy. A wise and authoritative guide to the responsibilities of bishops, it achieved tremendous popularity across Western Christendom. Gregory's letter to Emperor Maurice (letter B), echoing Pope Gelasius' two-swords doctrine, discloses the precarious semi-independent position of the papacy in central Italy. Rome and the lands around it were under Byzantine rule in Gregory's time as a result of Justinian's reconquest (535-555), but imperial authority was being undermined by the attacks of Lombard warriors. Despite the unsettled conditions in Rome, Gregory worked effectively toward the reform and expansion of Western Christendom. The monks whom he sent to pagan England in 596 (letters C–E) succeeded in converting the southern kingdom of Kent, thereby launching a missionary process that would eventually bring all of England into the Christian fold.

A.   THE BOOK OF PASTORAL CARE

With kind and humble intent you reprove me, dearest brother, for having wished by hiding myself to flee from the burdens of pastoral care; as to which, lest to some they should appear light, I express with my pen in the book before you all my own estimate of their heaviness, in order both that he who is free from them may not unwarily seek them, and that he who has freely sought them may tremble for having gotten them. . . .

What manner of man ought to come to rule? A man ought by all means be drawn to be an example of good living who already lives spiritually, dying to all passions of the flesh; who disregards worldly prosperity; who is afraid of no adversity; who desires only inward wealth; whose intention the body, in good accord with it, thwarts not at all by its frailness, nor the spirit greatly by its disdain—one who is not led to covet the things of others but gives freely of his own; who through the bowels of compassion is quickly moved to pardon, yet is never bent down from the fortress of rectitude by pardoning more than is necessary; who perpetrates no

From Letters of Pope Gregory the Great, Tr. James Barmby, in *Library of Nicene and Post-Nicene Fathers,* vol. XII, pp. 1, 7, 24-25, 71, 175-177, 202-203, 205-206.

unlawful deeds, yet deplores those perpetrated by others as though they were his own; who out of affection of the heart sympathizes with another's infirmity and so rejoices in the good of his neighbor as though it were his own advantage; who so insinuates himself as an example to others in all he does that among them he has nothing, at any rate of his own past deeds, to blush for; who studies so to live that he may be able to water even dry hearts with the streams of sacred learning; who has already by the use and trial of prayer that he can obtain what he has requested from the Lord, having already been told, as it were, through the voice of experience, "While you are still speaking, I will say, here am I." For if by chance anyone should come to us asking us to intercede for him with some great man, who was incensed against him, but unknown to us, we should at once reply, we cannot go to intercede for you since we have no familiar acquaintance with that man. If, then, a man blushes to become an intercessor with another man on whom he has no claim, with what idea can anyone grasp the duty of intercession with God for the people, who does not know himself to be in favor with Him through the merit of His own life? And how can he ask pardon of Him for others while ignorant whether towards himself He is appeased? And in this matter there is still another thing to be more anxiously feared; namely, lest one who is supposed to be competent to appease wrath should himself provoke it on account of guilt of his own. For we all know well that when one who is in disfavor is sent to intercede with an incensed person the mind of the latter is provoked to greater severity. Wherefore, let one who is still tied and bound with earthly desires beware lest by more grievously incensing the strict Judge, while he delights himself in his place of honor, he becomes the cause of ruin to his subordinates. . . .

How the ruler, while living well, ought to teach and admonish those who are placed under him: Since, then, we have shown what manner of man the pastor ought to be, let us now set forth after what manner he should teach. For as long before us Gregory Nazianzen[2] of reverend memory has taught, one and the same exhortation does not suit all, since all people are not bound together by similarity of character. For the things that profit some often hurt others; seeing that also for the most part herbs which nourish some animals are fatal to others; and the gentle hissing that quiets horses incites puppies; and the medicine which abates one disease aggravates another; and the bread which invigorates the life of the strong kills little children. Therefore, according to the quality of the listeners the discourse ought to be fashioned by teachers to suit all and each for their different needs, and yet never deviate from the art of common edification. For what are the intent minds of listeners but, so to speak, a kind of tight tension of strings in a harp, which the skillful player strikes variously that he may produce a tune not at variance with itself? And for this reason the strings render back a consonant

---

[2]Gregory of Nazianzus (d. 389) is one of the four great Greek doctors of the Church and is associated with the final defeat of the Arian heresy in the East. Gregory was made bishop of Constantinople in 380, but the difficulties he encountered forced him to resign within a few weeks and he ended his life in contemplation near Arianzus in Iona.

modulation, that they are struck indeed with one quill, but not with one kind of stroke. Whence every teacher also, that he may edify all in the one virtue of charity, ought to touch the hearts of his listeners out of one doctrine, but not with one and the same exhortation. . . . Differently, then, men and women are to be admonished because on the former heavier injunctions and on the latter lighter ones are to be laid so that [men] may be exercised by great things, but women overwhelmingly converted by light ones. Differently to be admonished are young and old men because for the most part severity of admonition directs the former to improvement, while kind remonstrance disposes the latter to better deeds. . . .

How the preacher, when he has accomplished his task, should return to himself lest either his life or his preaching puff him up. But since often, when preaching is abundantly poured forth in fitting ways, the mind of the preacher is elevated in itself by a hidden delight in self-display, great care is necessary that he may gnaw himself with the laceration of fear, lest he who recalls the diseases of others to health by remedies should himself swell through neglect of his own; lest in helping others he deserts himself, lest in lifting up others he falls. For some the greatness of their virtue has often been the occasion of their perdition, causing them, while inordinately secure in confidence of strength, to die unexpectedly through negligence. For virtue strives with vice—the mind flatters itself with a certain delight in it—and it comes to pass that the soul of a well intentioned man casts aside the fear of its circumspection and rests secure in self-confidence; and to it, now torpid, the cunning seducer enumerates all things that it has done well, and exalts it in swelling thoughts as though super-excellent beyond all beside it. Whence it is brought about that before the eyes of the just Judge the memory of virtue is a pitfall of the soul; because, in calling to mind what it has done well, while it lifts itself up in its own eyes, it falls before the Author of humility.

B. TO THE EMPEROR MAURICE, C. 591-592.

The piety of my lords in their most serene commands, while set on refuting me on certain matters, in sparing me have by no means spared me. For by the use therein of the word "simplicity" they politely call me silly. It is true indeed that in Holy Scripture, when simplicity is used in a good sense, it is often carefully associated with prudence and uprightness. . . .

Indeed if the captivity of my land were not increasing day by day, I would gladly pass over in silence contempt and ridicule of myself. But this does afflict me exceedingly, that from my bearing the charge of falsehood it ensues also that Italy is daily led captive under the yoke of the Lombards. And, while my representations are not believed, the strength of the enemy is increasing. This, however, I suggest to my most pious lord, that he would think anything that is bad of me, but with regards to the advantage of the Republic and the cause of the rescue of Italy, not easily lend his pious ears to anyone, but believe facts rather than words. Moreover, let our lord, in virtue of his earthly power, not too hastily disdain priests, but with excellent consideration, on account of Him Whose servants they are, so rule over them as also to pay the reverence that is due to them. For in Holy Scripture priests are sometimes called gods and sometimes angels. For even through Moses it is said of him who is to be put upon his oath, "Bring him unto the gods"—that is "unto the priests. . . ." Why, then, should it be strange if your piety were to condescend to honor those to whom even God Himself in His word gives honor, calling them angels or gods? Ecclesiastical history also testifies that when accusations in writing against bishops had been given to the emperor Constantine of pious memory, he received the written accusations; but calling together the bishops who had been accused, he burnt before their eyes the documents he had received, saying, "You are gods, constituted by the true God. Go and settle your causes among yourselves, for it is not fit that we should judge gods." Yet in this sentence, my pious lord, he conferred more on himself by his humility than on them by the reverence paid to them. For before him there were pagan princes in the Republic who knew not the true God but worshipped gods of wood and stone; and yet they paid the greatest honor to their priests. What wonder then if a Christian emperor should condescend to honor the priests of the true God, when pagan princes, as we have already said, knew how to bestow honor on priests who served gods of wood and stone?

These things, then, I suggest to the piety of my lords, not in my behalf but in behalf of all priests. For I am a man who is a sinner. And since I offend against Almighty God incessantly every day, I surmise that there will be some amends for this at the tremendous judgment, that I am stricken incessantly every day by blows. And I believe that you appease the same Almighty God all more as you more severely afflict me who serve Him badly. For I had already received many blows, and when the commands of my lords came in addition, I found consolations that I was not hoping for. For if I can, I will briefly enumerate these blows.

First, the peace which without any cost to the Republic I had made with the Lombards who were in Tuscany was withdrawn from me. Then, the peace having been broken, the [imperial] soldiers were removed from the Roman city. And indeed some were slain by the enemy, but others were placed at Narni and Perugia, and Rome was left that Perugia might be held. After this a still heavier blow was the arrival of Agilulph,[3] so that I saw with my own eyes Romans tied by the neck with ropes like dogs to be taken to Gaul for sale. And, because we who were in the city under the protection of God escaped his hand, a reason was then sought for making us look culpable—particularly because corn ran short, which cannot by any means be kept for long in large quantities in this city, as I have written more fully in another letter. On my own account, I was in no way disturbed since I declare, my conscience bearing witness, that I was prepared to suffer any adversity whatever so long as I came out of all these things with the safety of my soul. But

---

[3]Agilulph of Turin succeeded the great Lombard king Authari in c. 591 and also took the dead king's Catholic wife, Theodolinda of Bavaria, as his queen. Many of Gregory's letters are addressed to the powerful Theodolinda, who was herself partly responsible for the conversion of the Lombards to Catholicism.

for the glorious men, Gregory the praefect and Castorius the military commander, I have been distressed to a great degree, seeing that they did not neglect to do all that could be done and endured most severe toil in watching and guarding the city during the siege; and after all this were smitten by the heavy indignation of my lord. As to them, I clearly understand that it is not their conduct but my person that goes against them. For having along with me labored in trouble, they are alike troubled after labor.

Now as to the piety of my lord holding over me the formidable and terrible judgment of Almighty God, I ask you by the same Almighty God to do this no more. . . . [And] this I say briefly, that, unworthy sinner as I am, I rely more on the mercy of Jesus when He comes than on the justice of your piety. And there are many things that men are ignorant of with regards to this judgment; for perhaps He will blame what you praise and praise what you blame. Therefore, among all these uncertainties I return to tears only, praying that the same Almighty God may both direct our most pious lord with His hand and in that terrible judgment find him free of all defaults. And may He make me so to please men, if need be, as not to offend His eternal grace.

C. TO THE MISSIONARIES GOING TO ENGLAND, DATED AUGUST 596

Gregory, servant of the servants of God, to the servants of our Lord Jesus Christ.

Since it had been better not to have begun what is good than to return from it when begun, you must, most beloved sons, fulfill the good work which you have started with the help of the Lord. Let, then, neither the toil of the journey nor the tongues of evil-speaking men deter you; but with all constancy and fervor go on with what under God's guidance you have begun, knowing that great toil is followed by the glory of an eternal reward. Humbly obey in all things your leader Augustine[4] who is returning to you [and] whom we have appointed your abbot, knowing that whatever may be fulfilled in you through his admonition will in all ways profit your souls. May Almighty God protect you with his grace, and grant to me to see the fruit of your work in the eternal country, that I may be found together with you in the joy of the reward, for in truth I desire to labor. God keep you safe, most beloved sons.

D. TO QUEEN BRUNECHILD, DATED 596

Gregory to Brunechild, etc.

The Christianity of your excellence had long been so truly known to us that we do not in the least doubt your goodness but rather hold it to be in all ways certain that you will devoutly and zealously concur with us in the case of faith and supply most abundantly the succour of your religious sincerity. Being for this reason well

---

[4]Augustine became the first archbisop of Canterbury in 597 and died *c.* 604 and was succeeded by other members of the original mission to England.

assured and greeting you with paternal charity, we inform you that it has come to your knowledge how the nation of the English, by God's authority, is anxious to become Christian, but that the priests who are in their neighborhood have no pastoral solicitude with regards to them. And lest their souls should by chance perish in eternal damnation, it has been our care to send to them the bearer of these presents, Augustine, the servant of God, whose zeal and earnestness are well known to us, with other servants of God, that through them we might be able to learn their wishes, and as far as possible, you also striving with us, to take thought to their conversion. We have also charged them that for carrying out this design they should take with them preachers from the neighboring regions. Therefore, your excellency, habitually prone to good works [and] on account of our request as well as with regards to the fear of God, deign to hold him in all ways as commended to you and earnestly bestow on him the favor of your protection, and lend the aid of your patronage to his labor, and, that he may have the fullest fruit thereof, provide for his going secure under your protection to the above-mentioned nation of the English to the end that our God, who has adorned you in this world with good qualities well pleasing to Him, may cause you to give thanks here and in eternal rest with his saints. . . .

E. TO ABBOT MELLITUS[5]

Since the departure of our congregation [to convert England] we have been in a great state of suspense, having heard nothing of your success. But when almighty God shall have brought you to our most reverend brother bishop Augustine [leader of the mission to the Anglo-Saxons and the first archbishop of Canterbury], tell him that I have long been considering the case of the Angles, to wit, that the temples of the idols in that nation should not be destroyed, but that the idols that are in them should be. If these temples are well-built, it is necessary that they should be transferred to the service of the true God; and so that, when the people see that these temples are not destroyed, they may put away error from their heart and, knowing and adoring the true God, may have recourse to the familiar places they have been accustomed to. And since they are wont to kill many oxen in sacrifice to demons, they should have some ceremony of this kind but in a changed form, so that on the anniversaries of the holy martyrs they may make for themselves tents of the branches of trees around these temples that have been changed into churches. And do not let them sacrifice animals to the devil, but slay animals to the praise of God for their own eating, and return thanks to the Giver for all their fullness. For it is undoubtedly impossible to cut away everything at once from hard hearts, since one who strives to ascend to the highest place must rise by steps or paces and not by leaps.

---

[5]A French abbot who later became Bishop of London. Gregory I's wise advice to the missionaries sent to England should bring delight to modern anthropologists and ethnographers.

READING 9

A Description of the Synod of Whitby, 664

As Pope Gregory's monks and their successors spread Roman Christianity through England, they encountered rival missionaries from the Celtic monasteries of Ireland and southern Scotland. Celtic Christians, isolated from Rome and the Continent by the barbarian invasions, had developed distinctive customs and modes of organization: they used a different formula for calculating the date of Easter, they employed a different tonsure (below, note 2), and their church was organized around monasteries rather than bishoprics. Celtic and Roman-Benedictine missionaries had both been active in the conversion of the kingdom of Northumbria (northern England and southeastern Scotland). In 664, King Oswiu (or Oswy) of Northumbria summoned a council to meet at the Benedictine nunnery of Whitby to decide between the two forms of Christian practice. Although much of the argument at Whitby turned on the seemingly minor issue of the Easter date, far more was actually at stake. Northumbria had become the most power-ful kingdom in England, and the decision at Whitby brought Northumbria out of the Celtic backwater into the papal-Benedictine mainstream. The champion of the papal cause at Whitby was the celebrated Benedictine missionary, Wilfrid of Hexham, better known as Wilfrid of Ripon. The account below was written by Eddius, one of his disciples and perhaps an eyewit-ness, shortly after Wilfrid's death.

On a certain occasion while Colman was bishop of York and metropolitan archbishop, during the reign of Oswiu and Alhfrith,[1] abbots, priests, and clerics of every rank gathered at Whitby Abbey in the presence of the most holy abbess Hilda, the two kings, and bishops Colman and Agilberht [of the West Saxons], to discuss the proper time for celebrating Easter: whether the practice of the British, Irish and the northern province of keeping it on the Sunday between the fourteenth and twenty-second day of the moon was correct or whether they ought to give way to the Roman plan for fixing it for the Sunday between the fifteenth and twenty-

From Eddius, "The Life of St. Wilfred of Hexham," in *Lives of the Saints*, tr. J.F. Webb; New York, Penguin Books, 1965, pp. 141-143.

[1] King Oswiu and his son, King Alhfrith, ruled jointly for a time. Oswiu controlled the entire kingdom of Northumbria, of which Deira, Alhfrith's area of jurisdiction, was a part. The young king died shortly after the synod of Whitby and his father Oswiu survived another six years, dying in 670.

first days of the moon. Bishop Colman, as was proper, was given the first chance to state his case. He spoke with complete confidence, as follows: "Our fathers and theirs before them, clearly inspired by the Holy Spirit, as was Columba, stipulated that Easter Sunday should be celebrated on the fourteenth day of the moon if that day were a Sunday, following the example of St. John the Evangelist 'who leaned on the Lord's breast at supper,' the disciple whom Jesus loved. He celebrated Easter on the fourteenth day of the moon, as did his disciples, and Polycarp and his disciples, and as we do on their authority. Out of respect to our fathers we dare not change, nor do we have the least desire to do so. I have spoken for our party. Now let us hear your side of the question."

Agilberht, the foreign prelate, and his priest Agatho bade St. Wilfrid, priest and abbot [of Hexham], use his winning eloquence to express in his own words the case of the Roman Church and Apostolic See. His speech was, as usual, humble. "This question has already been admirably treated by a gathering of our most holy and learned fathers, three hundred and eighteen strong, at Nicaea, a city in Bithynia. Among other things they decided upon a lunar cycle recurring every nineteen years. This cycle gives no room for celebrating Easter on the fourteenth day of the moon. This is the rule followed by the Apostolic See and by nearly the whole world. At the end of the decrees of the fathers of Nicaea come these words: 'Let him who condemns any one of these decrees be anathema.'"

At the end of Wilfrid's speech Oswiu asked them, with a smile on his face, "Tell me, which is greater in the Kingdom of Heaven, Columba or the apostle Peter?"

Then the whole synod with one voice and one accord cried: "The Lord Himself settled this question when He declared, 'Thou art Peter and upon this rock I will build my Church and the gates of hell shall not prevail against it. And I will give you the keys of the Kingdom of Heaven; and whatsoever thou shalt bind on earth shall be bound in Heaven and whatsoever thou shalt loose on earth shall be loosed in Heaven.' " To this the king added, showing his wisdom: "He is the keeper of the door and the keys. I will neither enter into strife and controversy with him, nor will I condone any who do. As long as I live I shall abide by his every decision."

Bishop Colman was told that if, out of respect for his own country's customs, he should reject the Roman tonsure[2] and method of calculating Easter, he was to resign his see in favor of another and better candidate. This he did.

---

[2] The Roman method of tonsure, the shearing of the hair upon entry into the monastic or clerical order, provided for a bald spot on the top of the head, whereas the Irish method simply extended the length of the forehead.

READING 10

From "The Cow" (Sura 2) of *The Koran*

Muhammad (d. 632) makes it clear that Allah, the God of Islam, is also the God of the Old and New Testaments, and that the new religion is actually the fulfillment of Judaism and Christianity. He respects Jews and Christians as "People of the Book" (the Bible) but chides those among them who reject the teachings of God's final prophet. The passage concludes with a summary of Islamic ethics as revealed by Allah to Muhammad.

In the Name of Allah, the Compassionate, the Merciful. This Book is not to be doubted. It is a guide to the righteous, who have faith in the unseen and are steadfast in prayer; who bestow in charity a part of what We have given them; who trust what has been revealed to you [Muhammad] and to others before you, and firmly believe in the life to come. These are rightly guided by their Lord; these shall surely triumph. . . .

Believers, Jews, Christians, and Sabaeans—whoever believes in Allah and the Last Day and does what is right—shall be rewarded by their Lord; they have nothing to fear or to regret. . . .

When Moses said to his people; "Allah commands you to sacrifice a cow," they replied: "Are you making game of us?" "Allah forbid that I should be so foolish!" he rejoined. "Call on your Lord," they said, "to make known to us what kind of cow she shall be." Moses replied: "Your Lord says: 'Let her be neither an old cow nor a young heifer, but in between.' Do, therefore as you are bidden." "Call on your Lord," they said, "to make known to us what her color shall be." Moses replied: "Your Lord says: 'Let the cow be yellow, a rich yellow pleasing to the eye.'" "Call on your Lord," they said, "to make known to us the exact type of cow she shall be; for to us cows look all alike. If Allah wills we shall be rightly guided." Moses replied: "Your Lord says: 'Let her be a healthy cow, not worn out with ploughing the earth or watering the field; a cow free from any blemish.'" "Now you have told us all," they answered. And they slaughtered a cow, after they had almost succeeded in evading the sacrifice. . . .

To Moses We gave the Scriptures and after him We sent other apostles. We gave Jesus the son of Mary veritable signs and strengthened him with the Holy Spirit. Will you then scorn each apostle whose message does not suit your fancies, charging some with imposture and slaying others? They say: "Our hearts are sealed." But Allah has cursed them for their unbelief. They have but little faith.

From *The Koran*, tr. N.J. Dawood; New York, 1968, pp. 326-356. Reprinted by permission of Penguin Books, Ltd.

And now that a Book confirming their Scriptures has been revealed to them by Allah, they deny it, although they know it to be the truth and have long prayed for help against the unbelievers. May Allah's curse be upon the infidels! Evil is that for which they have bartered away their souls. To deny Allah's own revelation, grudging that He should reveal His bounty to whom He chooses from His servants! They have incurred Allah's most inexorable wrath. An ignominious punishment awaits the unbelievers. . . .

The unbelievers among the People of the Book, and the pagans, resent that any blessings should have been sent down to you from your Lord. But Allah chooses whom He will for His mercy. His grace is infinite.

If We abrogate any verse or cause it to be forgotten We will replace it by a better one or one similar. Do you not know that Allah has power over all things? Do you not know that it is to Allah that the kingdom of heaven and the earth belongs and that there is none besides Him to protect or help you? . . .

Who but a foolish man would renounce the faith of Abraham? We chose him in this world, and in the world to come he shall dwell among the righteous. When his Lord said to him: "Submit," he answered: "I have submitted to the Lord of the Creation."

Abraham enjoined the faith on his children, and so did Jacob, saying: "My children, Allah has chosen for you the true faith. Do not depart this life except as men who have submitted to Him." . . .

They say: "Accept the Jewish or the Christian faith and you shall be rightly guided." Say: "By no means! We believe in the faith of Abraham, the upright one. He was no idolater." Say: "We believe in Allah and that which is revealed to us; we believe in what was revealed to Abraham, Ishmael, Isaac, Jacob, and the tribes; to Moses and Jesus and the other prophets. We make no distinction between any of them, and to Allah we have surrendered ourselves." . . .

Your God is one God. There is no god but Him. He is the Compassionate, the Merciful. . . .

Righteousness does not consist in whether you face towards the east or the west. The righteous man is he who believes in Allah and the Last Day, in the angels and the Scriptures and the prophets; who for the love of Allah gives his wealth to his kinsfolk, to the orphans, to the needy, to the wayfarers, and to the beggars, and for the redemption of captives; who attends to his prayers and pays the alms-tax; who is true to his promises and steadfast in trial and adversity and in times of war. Such are the true believers; such are the Godfearing. . . .

Believers, fasting is decreed for you as it was decreed for those before you; perchance you will guard yourselves against evil. Fast a certain number of days, but if any one of you is ill or on a journey let him fast a similar number of days later on; and for those that can afford it there is a ransom: the feeding of a poor man. He that does good of his own accord shall be well rewarded; *but to fast is better for you, if you but knew it.* . . .

Fight for the sake of Allah those that fight against you, but do not attack them first. Allah does not love the aggressors.

Kill them wherever you find them. Drive them out of the places from which they drove you. Idolatry is worse than carnage. But do not fight them within the precincts of the Holy Mosque unless they attack you there; if they attack you put them to the sword. Thus shall the unbelievers be rewarded: but if they mend their ways, know that Allah is forgiving and merciful. . . .

Give generously for the cause of Allah and do not with your own hands cast yourselves into destruction. Be charitable; Allah loves the charitable.

Make the pilgrimage and visit the Sacred House [the Ka'ba at Mecca] for His sake. If you cannot, send such offerings as you can afford and do not shave your heads until the offerings have reached their destination. But if any of you is ill or suffers from an ailment of the head, he must pay a ransom either by fasting or by alms-giving or by offering a sacrifice.

You shall not wed pagan women, unless they embrace the faith. A believing slave-girl is better than an idolatress, although she may please you. Nor shall you wed idolaters, unless they embrace the faith. A believing slave is better than an idolater, although he may please you. These call you to Hell-fire; but Allah calls you, by His will, to Paradise and to forgiveness. He makes plain His revelations to mankind, so that they may take heed. . . .

Women are your fields: go, then, into your fields as you please. Do good works and fear Allah. Bear in mind that you shall meet Him. Give good news to the believers. . . .

Women shall with all justice have rights similar to those exercised against them, although men have a status above women. Allah is mighty and wise. . . .

Attend regularly to your prayers, including the middle prayer, and stand up with all devotion before Allah. When you are exposed to danger pray while riding or on foot; and when you are restored to safety remember Allah, as He has taught you what you did not know. . . .

There shall be no compulsion in religion. True guidance is now distinct from error. He that renounces idol-worship and puts his faith in Allah shall grasp a firm handle that will never break. Allah hears all and knows all.

Allah is the Patron of the faithful. He leads them from darkness to the light. As for the unbelievers, their patrons are false gods who lead them from light to darkness. They are the Heirs of Hell and shall abide in it forever. . . .

Fear the day when you shall all return to Allah; when every soul shall be requited according to its deserts. None shall be wronged. . . .

The Apostle [Muhammad] believes in what has been revealed to him by his Lord, and so do the faithful. They all believe in Allah and His angels, His scriptures, and His apostles: We discriminate against none of His apostles. They say: "We hear and obey. Grant us your forgiveness, Lord; to You we shall all return. Allah does not charge a soul with more than it can bear. It shall be requited for whatever good and whatever evil it has done. Lord, do not be angry with us if we forget or lapse into error. Lord, do not lay on us the burden You laid on those before us. Lord, do not charge us with more than we can bear. Pardon us, forgive us our sins, and have mercy upon us. You alone are our Protector. Give us victory over the unbelievers."

READING 11

The "Constitution of Medina," 622

In 622, Muhammad left his home city of Mecca, where he had won only a small following, to become the civil and religious leader of the city of Yathrib—later renamed Medina, "the Prophet's City." From Medina, Muhammad's followers made war on Mecca—raiding its caravans, blockading its commerce, and eventually accepting its submission. The sacred community that Muhammad forged in Medina, at once a state and a church, foreshadowed the later organization of the Islamic Empire under the caliphs. The Constitution of Medina, the first official document of the Islamic political community, also foreshadowed the relatively tolerant policy of the Islamic Empire toward its Jewish inhabitants.

The Prophet wrote a document concerning the emigrants and the helpers in which he made a friendly agreement with the Jews and established them in their religion and their property, and stated the reciprocal obligations, as follows:

In the name of God the Compassionate, the Merciful. This is a document from Muhammad the prophet [governing the relations] between the believers and Muslims of Quraysh and Yathrib [Medina], and those who followed them and joined them and labored with them. They are one community [*umma*] to the exclusion of all other men. The Quraysh emigrants according to their present custom shall pay the blood-price within their company and shall redeem their prisoners with the kindness and justice common among believers. . . . Believers shall not leave anyone destitute among them by not paying his redemption money or blood-price in kindness.

A believer shall not take as an ally the freedman of another Muslim against him. The God-fearing believers shall be against the rebellious or him who seeks to spread injustice, or sin or enmity, or corruption between believers; the hand of every man shall be against him even if he be a son of one of them. A believer shall not slay a believer for the sake of a believer nor shall he aid an unbeliever against a believer. God's protection is one, the least of them may give protection to a stranger on their behalf. Believers are friends one to the other to the exclusion of outsiders. To the Jew who follows us belong help and equality. He shall not be wronged nor shall his enemies be aided. The peace of the believers is indivisible.

From Ibn Ishaq's "Life of the Prophet," in *The Life of Mohammed, a Translation of Ishaq's Sirat Rasul Allah*, ed. and tr. A. Guillaume; New York, 1955, pp. 231-233. By permission of Oxford University Press.

No separate peace shall be made when believers are fighting in the way of God. Conditions must be fair and equitable to all. In every foray a rider must take another behind him. The believers must avenge the blood of one another shed in the way of God. The God-fearing believers enjoy the best and most upright guidance. No polytheist [the heathen Arabs of Medina] shall take the property or person of Quraysh under his protection nor shall he intervene against a believer. Whosoever is convicted of killing a believer without good reason shall be subject to retaliation unless the next of kin is satisfied [with blood-money], and the believers shall be against him as one man, and they are bound to take action against him.

It shall not be lawful to a believer who holds by what is in this document and believes in God and the last day to help an evil-doer *[muhdith]* or to shelter him. The curse of God and His anger on the day of resurrection will be upon him if he does, and neither repentance nor ransom will be upon him if he does, and neither repentance nor ransom will be received from him. Whenever you differ about a matter it must be referred to God and to Muhammad.

The Jews shall contribute to the cost of war so long as they are fighting alongside the believers. The Jews of the Bani Auf are one community with the believers [the Jews have their religion and the Muslims have theirs], their freedmen and their persons except those who behave unjustly and sinfully, for they hurt but themselves and their families. . . . Loyalty is a protection against treachery. The freedmen of Tha'laba are as themselves. The close friends of the Jews are as themselves. None of them shall go out to war save with the permission of Muhammad, but he shall not be prevented from taking revenge for a wound. He who slays a man without warning slays himself and his household, unless it be one who has wronged him, for God will accept that. The Jews must bear their expenses and the Muslims their expenses. Each must help the other against anyone who attacks the people of this document. They must seek mutual advice and consultation, and loyalty is a protection against treachery. A man is not liable for his ally's misdeeds. The wronged must be helped. The Jews must pay with the believers so long as war lasts. Yathrib shall be a sanctuary for the people of this document. A stranger under protection shall be as his host doing no harm and committing no crime. A woman shall only be given protection with the consent of her family. If any dispute or controversy likely to cause trouble should arise it must be referred to God and to Muhammad the prophet of God. God accepts what is nearest to piety and goodness in this document. Quraysh and their helpers shall not be given protection. The contracting parties are bound to help one another against any attack on Yathrib. If they are called to make peace and maintain it they must do so; and if they make a similar demand on the Muslims it must be carried out except in the case of a holy war. Every one shall have his portion from the side to which he belongs; the Jew of al-Aus, their freedmen and themselves have the same standing with the people of this document in pure loyalty from the people of this document.

Loyalty is a protection against treachery: He who acquires it ought to acquire it for himself. God approves of this document. This deed will not protect the unjust and the sinner. The man who goes forth to fight and the man who stays at home in the city is safe unless he has been unjust and sinned. God is the protector of the good and God-fearing man and Muhammad is the prophet of God.

READING 12
Alfarabi's The Political Regime

The Political Regime written by the great Moslem scholar Alfarabi (d. 950 A.D.) was immensely popular throughout the tenth century, and is usually cited by Moslem authors as one of his fundamental works. Indeed, it was said by the exceptional Jewish scholar Maimonides that a man need not read any other books on logic except that composed by "the wise man Abu Nasr al-Farabi." Although the first section of the treatise deals with the principles on which the natural world is based and is Aristotelian in perspective, the second part of the work serves as an introduction to and preparation for Alfarabi's views on political life and the classification of political regimes.

Man belongs to the species that cannot accomplish their necessary affairs or achieve their best state except through the association of many groups of them in a single dwelling-place. Some human societies are large, others are of a medium size, still others are small. The large societies consist of many nations that associate and cooperate with one another; the medium ones consist of a nation; the small are the ones embraced by the city. These three are the perfect societies. Hence, the city represents the first degree of perfection. . . .

Happiness is the good without qualification. Everything useful for the achievement of happiness or by which it is attained, is good too, not for its own sake, but because it is useful with respect to happiness; and everything that obstructs the way to happiness in any fashion is unqualified evil. The good that is useful for the achievement of happiness may be something that exists by nature or that comes into being by the will, and the evil that obstructs the way to happiness may be something that exists by nature or that comes into being by the will. . . .

From Ralph Lerner and Muhsin Mahdi, eds., *Medieval Political Philosophy: A Sourcebook*, The Free Press, New York: 1963, pp. 32, 34, 36-8.

As to voluntary good and evil, which are the noble and the base respectively, they have their origin specifically in man. Now there is only one way in which the voluntary good can come into being. That is because the faculties of the human soul are five: the theoretical-rational, the practical-rational, the appetitive, the imaginative, and the sensitive. Happiness, which only man can know and perceive, is known by the theoretical-rational faculty and by none of the remaining faculties. Man knows it when he makes use of the first principles and the primary knowledge given to him by the Active Intellect [the last of the 'intelligences' associated with the Aristotelian spheres that produces the world of generation and corruption]. When he knows happiness, desires it by the appetitive faculty, deliberates by the practical-rational faculty upon what he ought to do in order to attain it, uses the instruments of the appetitive faculty to do the actions he has discovered by deliberation, and his imaginative and sensitive faculties assist and obey the rational and aid it in arousing man to do the actions with which he attains happiness, then everything that originates from man will be good. It is only in this way that the voluntary good comes into being. . . .

Since what is intended by man's existence is that he attain supreme happiness, he—in order to achieve it—needs to know what happiness is, make it his end, and hold it before his eyes. Then, after that, he needs to know the things he ought to do in order to attain happiness, and then do these actions. In view of what has been said about the differences in the natural dispositions of individual men, not everyone is disposed to know happiness on his own, or the things that he ought to do, but needs a teacher and a guide for this purpose. Some men need little guidance, others need a great deal of it. In addition, even when a man is guided to these two [that is, happiness and the actions leading to it], he will not, in the absence of an external stimulus and something to arouse him, necessarily do what he has been taught and guided to. This is how most men are. Therefore they need someone to make all this known to them and to arouse them to do it. . . .

The supreme ruler without qualification is he who does not need anyone to rule him in anything whatever, but has actually acquired the sciences and every kind of knowledge, and has no need of a man to guide him in anything. He is able to comprehend well each one of the particular things that he ought to do. He is able to guide well all others to everything in which he instructs them, to employ all those who do any of the acts for which they are equipped, and to determine, define, and direct these acts toward happiness. This is found only in the one who possesses great and superior natural dispositions, when his soul is in union with the Active Intellect. He can only attain this [union with the Active Intellect] succeeding them. Hence the pleasure felt by the very ancient ones will continue to increase indefinitely. Such is the state of every group of them. This, then, is true and supreme happiness, which is the purpose of the Active Intellect.

READING 13

Al-Ghazali's Deliverance from Error

More than a half millennium before René Descartes wrote his celebrated *Discourse on Method*, with its exploration of "systematic doubt,"Al-Ghazali (1058-1111) engaged in the same process. The great problem with systematic doubt is that the moment you doubt the validity of your own reason you are stuck. Descartes tried to reason his way out of the dilemma, to the satisfaction of few. Al-Ghazali sought a different, perhaps more plausible, refuge which is described here.

You must know—and may God most high perfect you in the right way and soften your hearts to receive the truth—that the different religious observances and religious communities of the human race and likewise the different theological systems of the religious leaders, with all the multiplicity of sects and variety of practices, constitute ocean depths in which the majority drown and only a minority reach safety. . . .

From my early youth, since I attained the age of puberty before I was twenty, until the present time when I am over fifty, I have ever recklessly launched out into the midst of these ocean depths, I have ever bravely embarked on this open sea, throwing aside all craven caution; I have poked into every dark recess, I have made an assault on every problem, I have plunged into every abyss, I have scrutinized the creed of every sect, I have tried to lay bare the inmost doctrines of every community. All this have I done that I might distinguish between true and false, between sound tradition and heretical innovation. . . .

To thirst after a comprehension of things as they really are was my habit and custom from a very early age. It was instinctive with me, a part of my God-given nature, a matter of temperament and not of my choice or contriving. Consequently as I drew near the age of adolescence the bonds of mere authority ceased to hold me and inherited beliefs lost their grip upon me . . . I therefore said within myself: "To begin with, what I am looking for is knowledge of what things really are, so I must undoubtedly try to find what knowledge really is." It was plain to me that sure and certain knowledge is that knowledge in which the object is disclosed in such a fashion that no doubt remains along with it, that no possibility of error or illusion accompanies it, and that the mind cannot even entertain, such a supposition. Certain knowledge must also be infallible. . . . After these reflections I knew that whatever I do not know in this fashion and with this mode of certainty is not reliable and infallible knowledge; and knowledge that is not infallible is not certain knowledge.

From W. Montgomery Watt, *The Faith and Practice of Al-Ghazali*, Kazi Publications, Chicago, Ill. , 1982, pp. 19-26.

Thereupon I investigated the various kinds of knowledge I had, and found myself destitute of all knowledge with this characteristic of infallibility except in the case of sense-perception and necessary truths. . . . I proceeded therefore with extreme earnestness to reflect on sense-perception and on necessary truths, to see whether I could make myself doubt them. The outcome of this protracted effort to induce doubt was that I could no longer trust sense-perception [and necessary truths] . . . .

When these thoughts had occurred to me and penetrated my being, I tried to find some way of treating my unhealthy condition; but it was not easy. Such ideas can only be repelled by demonstration; but a demonstration needs a combination of first principles; since this is not admitted, however, it is impossible to make the demonstration. The disease was baffling, and lasted almost two months, during which I was a skeptic in fact though not in theory nor in outward expression. At length God cured me of the malady; my being was restored to health and an even balance; the necessary truths of the intellect became once more accepted, as I regained confidence in their certain and trustworthy character.

This did not come about by systematic demonstration or marshalled argument, but by a light which God most high cast into my breast. That light is the key to the greater part of knowledge. Whoever thinks that the understanding of things Divine rest upon strict proofs has in his thought narrowed down the wideness of God's mercy. When the Messenger of God (peace be upon him) was asked about 'enlarging' and its meaning in the verse, "Whenever God wills to guide a man, He enlarges his breast for *Islam*" [Koran 6:125], he said, "It is a light which God most high casts into the heart.". . . From that light must be sought an intuitive under-standing of things Divine. That light at certain times gushes from the spring of Divine generosity, and for it one must watch and wait—as Muhammad (peace be upon him) said: "In the days of your age your Lord has gusts of favour; then place yourselves in the way of them."

CHAPTER 3

CAROLINGIAN EUROPE

The eighth century witnessed a revival of Classical-Christian culture among the papal missionaries and in the kingdom of the Franks under a powerful new dynasty, the Carolingians. The papacy broke more and more from its ties with the Byzantine Empire (document 1) and drew closer to English Benedictine missionary scholars such as St. Boniface, who labored to convert pagan Germanic tribes to the northeast of Christian Francia, and to reform the Frankish Church itself. Like the monks whom Pope Gregory the Great had sent to England more than a century before, St. Boniface worked under the supervision of the papacy (document 2).

It was Boniface, acting as a representative of Pope Zacharias, who anointed the first Carolingian king, Pepin the Short, bringing to an end the rule of the Merovingian dynasty (document 3). King Pepin reciprocated by leading an army into Italy, at the papacy's urging, to rescue Rome from the Lombard menace. Defeating the Lombards in battle, Pepin granted the papacy authority over extensive territories in central Italy known thereafter as the Papal States, or the Patrimony of St. Peter. The papacy justified its claim to these lands by asserting that they had been given originally to Pope Sylvester I by the Emperor Constantine back in the early fourth century. Happily, an imperial letter known as the "Donation of Constantine" conveniently materialized in just the nick of time to provide documentary authority for the papal position (document 4).

Charlemagne (768-814), Pepin's son and successor, extended the boundaries of the Carolingian realm by military conquests (document 5). He appointed loyal dukes and counts as regional governors throughout his dominions, established close relations with the papacy (document 6), and was crowned Roman Emperor by Pope Leo III on Christmas Day, A.D. 800, under circumstances that are disputed to this day (document 7). He supervised his lands in Francia through traveling agents called *missi dominici, or* "envoys of the lord" (document 8).

Charlemagne's patronage and encouragement gave rise to an intellectual and cultural revival centering on major bishoprics and Benedictine abbeys (document 9) and on the royal court, where Charlemagne assembled a group of scholars from the length and breadth of Western Christendom. This "Carolingian Renaissance," which continued through the reigns of Charlemagne's successors, contributed much to solidifying Europe's Classical-Christian foundations.

READING 1

Pope Gregory II's Letter to Emperor Leo III, 727

The papacy grew up in the Roman world and long maintained its allegiance to the Roman—that is, Byzantine—Empire. By the mid-eighth century the papacy will have broken with Byzantium and allied with the Carolingian Franks. Even a generation earlier, as this letter from the feisty Pope Gregory II (715-731) makes clear, relations between the papacy and the Byzantine Empire were not warm.

You know that the dogmas of the holy Church are not the concern of emperors but of pontiffs, who ought to teach securely. The pontiffs who preside over the Church do not meddle in affairs of state, and likewise the emperors ought not to meddle in ecclesiastical affairs, but to administer the things committed to them.

The Lombards and Sarmatians and others who live in the north have attacked the wretched Decapolis and occupied Ravenna itself. They have deposed your governors and appointed governors of their own, and they have determined to do the same at other imperial cities in this neighborhood and even at Rome itself, since you are unable to defend us.

All this is the result of your imprudence and stupidity. But you wish to strike terror into them, and you say, "I will send to Rome and destroy the image of St. Peter, and having overcome Pope Gregory, will carry him off." You ought rather to know and to hold for certain that the pontiffs who have ruled at Rome preside there in order to maintain peace, like a wall joining east and west, occupying the middle ground between them, and that they are arbitrators and promoters of peace. If you insolently threaten and insult us there is no need for us to descend to fighting with you. The Roman pontiff will withdraw for a few miles into Campania; then you may go and chase the wind.

Would that I might, by God's gift, tread the same path as Pope Martin [who died in exile during the reign of Constantine (d. 337)]. And yet I wish to survive and to live for the sake of the people, since the whole western world has turned its eyes upon our humility and the people greatly trust in us and in him whose statue you threaten to cast down and destroy, namely St. Peter, whom all the kingdoms of the west regard as an earthly god.

From *The Crisis of Church and State*, edited by Brian Tierney, Prentice Hall, Inc., Englewood Cliffs, NJ, 1964, pp. 19-20.

READING 2

Letters of St. Boniface

These three documents show Boniface (680-754) first as a servant of the pope and of Catholic orthodoxy (document A), next as a missionary among Germanic pagans (document B), and finally as a pastoral adviser (document C). They reveal something of the communications network connecting the churches of Rome, England, Francia, and pagan Germany—and, in the letter to Abbess Bugga, the hazards of travel within Christendom. The letter of Bishop Daniel of Winchester (A.D. 723-24), with its deep-set confidence in the intellectual plausibility of Christianity as against the "idol worship" of rival religions, will help to explain the eventual success of Christian missions to central and eastern Europe.

A.   OATH OF BONIFACE TO POPE GREGORY II, DATED 30 NOVEMBER, 722.

In the name of the Lord God and of our Savior Jesus Christ. In the sixth year of Leo, by the grace of God emperor, in the sixth year of his consulship and in the fourth year of his son, the Emperor Constantine, in the sixth indiction:

I, Boniface, by the grace of God bishop, promise to you, blessed Peter, chief of the Apostles, and to your vicar, the blessed Pope Gregory [II] and to his successors, in the name of the Father, the Son, and the Holy Spirit, the indivisible Trinity, and of this, thy most sacred body, that I will show entire faith and sincerity toward the holy catholic doctrine and will persist in the unity of the same, so God help me— that faith in which, beyond a doubt, the whole salvation of Christians consists. I will in no wise agree to anything which is opposed to the unity of the Church Universal, no matter who shall try to persuade me; but I will, as I have said, show in all things a perfect loyalty to you and to the welfare of your Church, to which the power to bind and loose is given by God, and to your vicar and his successors.

But, if I shall discover any bishops who are opponents of the ancient institutions of the holy Fathers, I will have no part nor lot with them, but so far as I can will restrain them or, if that is impossible, will make a true report to my apostolic master. But if (which God forbid!) I should be tempted into any action contrary to this my promise, in any way or by any device or pretext whatsoever, may I be found guilty at the last judgment and suffer punishment of Ananias and Sapphira, who dared to defraud you by making a false declaration of their property.

From *The Letters of St. Boniface*, tr. E. Emerton; New York, Columbia University Press, 1940, nos. viii, xv, xix.

This text of my oath, I, Boniface, a humble bishop, have written with my own hand and laid above thy most sacred body. I have taken this oath, as is prescribed, in the presence of God, my witness and my judge, and I pledge myself to observe it.

B. LETTER OF BISHOP DANIEL OF WINCHESTER, ENGLAND, TO BONIFACE

To the venerable and beloved prelate Boniface, Daniel, servant of the people of God.

I rejoice, beloved brother and fellow priest, that you are deserving of the highest prize of virtue. You have approached the hitherto stony and barren hearts of the pagans, trusting in the plenitude of your faith, and have labored untiringly with the plowshare of Gospel preaching, striving by your daily toil to change them into fertile fields. To you may well be applied the Gospel saying: "The voice of one crying in the wilderness," etc. Yet a part of the second prize shall be given, not unfittingly, to those who support so pious and useful a work with what help they can give and supplement the poverty of those laborers with means sufficient to carry on zealously the work of preaching which has already been begun and to raise up new sons to Christ.

And so I have with affectionate good will taken pains to suggest to Your Prudence a few things that may show you how, according to my ideas, you may most readily overcome the resistance of those uncivilized people. Do not begin by arguing with them about the origin of their gods, false as those are, but let them affirm that some of them were begotten by others through the intercourse of male with female, so that you may at least prove that gods and goddesses born after the manner of men are men and not gods and, since they did not exist before, must have had a beginning.

Then, when they have been compelled to learn that their gods had a beginning since some were begotten by others, they must be asked in the same way whether they believe that the world had a beginning or was always in existence without beginning. If it had a beginning, who created it? Certainly they can find no place where begotten gods could dwell before the universe was made. I mean by "universe" not merely this visible earth and sky, but the whole vast extent of space, and this the heathen too can imagine in their thoughts. But if they argue that the world always existed without beginning, you should strive to refute this and to convince them by many documents and arguments. Ask your opponents who governed the world before the gods were born, who was the ruler? How could they bring under their dominion or subject to their law a universe that had always existed before them? And whence, or from whom or when, was the first god or goddess set up or begotten? Now, do they imagine that gods and goddesses still go on begetting others? Or, if they are no longer begetting, when or why did they cease from intercourse and births? And if they are still producing offspring, then the number of gods must already be infinite. Among so many and different gods, mortal men cannot know which is the most powerful, and one should be extremely careful not to offend that most powerful one.

Do they think the gods are to be worshiped for the sake of temporal and immediate good or for future eternal blessedness? If for temporal things, let them tell in what respect the heathen are better off than Christians. What gain do the heathen suppose accrues to their gods from their sacrifices, since the gods already possess everything? Or why do the gods leave it in the power of their subjects to say what kind of tribute shall be paid? If they are lacking in such things, why do they not themselves choose more valuable ones? If they have plenty, then there is no need to suppose that the gods can be pleased with such offerings of victims.

These and many similar things which it would take long to enumerate you ought to put before them, not offensively or so as to anger them, but calmly and with great moderation. At intervals you should compare their superstitions with our Christian doctrines, touching upon them from the flank, as it were, so that the pagans, thrown into confusion rather than angered, may be ashamed of their absurd ideas and may understand that their infamous ceremonies and fables are well known to us.

This point is also to be made: if the gods are all-powerful, beneficent, and just, they not only reward their worshipers but punish those who reject them. If, then, they do this in temporal matters, how is it that they spare us Christians who are turning almost the whole earth away from their worship and overthrowing their idols? And while these, that is, the Christians, possess lands rich in oil and wine and abounding in other resources, they have left to those, that is, the pagans, lands stiff with cold where their gods, driven out of the world, are falsely supposed to rule. They are also frequently to be reminded of the supremacy of the Christian world, in comparison with which they themselves, very few in number, are still involved in their ancient errors.

If they boast that the rule of the gods over those peoples has been, as it were, lawful from the beginning, show them that the whole world was once given over to idol-worship, until by the grace of Christ and through the knowledge of one God, its Almighty Founder and Ruler, it was enlightened, brought to life, and reconciled to God. For what is the daily baptism of the children of believing Christians but purification of each one from the uncleanness and guilt in which the whole world was once involved?

I have been glad to call these matters to your attention, my brother, out of my affection for you, though I suffer from bodily infirmities so that I may well say with the Psalmist: "I know, Oh Lord, that thy judgments are right and that thou in faithfulness hast afflicted me." Wherefore I earnestly pray Your Reverence and all those who serve Christ in spirit to make supplication for me that the Lord Who gave me to drink of the wine of remorse, may be swift in mercy, that He who was just in condemnation may graciously pardon, and by His mercy enable me to sing in gratitude the words of the Prophet: "In the multitude of my thoughts within me thy comforts delight my soul."

I pray for your welfare in Christ, my very dear colleague, and beg you to bear me in mind.

C. LETTER OF BONIFACE TO ABBESS BUGGA, DATED PRE-738.

To the beloved lady, Abbess Bugga, sister and dearest of all women in Christ, Boniface, a humble and unworthy bishop, wishes eternal salvation in Christ.

I desire you to know, dearest sister, that in the matter about which you wrote asking advice of me, unworthy though I am, I dare neither forbid your pilgrimage on my own responsibility nor rashly persuade you to it. I will only say how the matter appears to me. If, for the sake of rest and divine contemplation, you have laid aside the care for the servants and maids of God and for the monastic life which you once had, how could you now subject yourself with labor and wearing anxiety to the words and wishes of men of this world? It would seem to me better, if you can in no way have freedom and a quiet mind at home on account of worldly men, that you should obtain freedom of contemplation by means of a pilgrimage, if you so desire and are able, as our sister Wiethburga did. She has written me that she has found at the shrine of St. Peter the kind of quiet life which she had long sought in vain. With regard to your wishes, she sent me word, since I had written to her about you, that you would do better to wait until the rebellious assaults and threats of the Saracens who have recently appeared about Rome should have subsided. God willing, she will then send you an invitation. To me also this seems the best plan. Make ready what you will need for the journey, wait for word from her, and then act as God's grace shall command.

In regard to the writings which you have requested of me, you must excuse my remissness, for I have been prevented by pressure of work and by my continual travels from completing the book you ask for. When I have finished it, I shall see that it is sent to you.

In return for the gifts and garments you have sent me, I offer my grateful prayers to God that he may give you a reward with the angels and the archangels in the highest heavens. I exhort you, then, in God's name, my very dear sister—nay mother and most sweet lady—to pray earnestly for me, since for my sins I am wearied with many sorrows and am far more disturbed by anxiety of mind than by the labor of my body. May you rest assured that the long-tried friendship between us shall never be found wanting.

Farewell in Christ.

READING 3

The Coronation of Pepin the Short, 751

The abbey of Lorsch in southern Germany, like many other abbeys across Christendom, compiled brief, year-by-year records of events that seemed particularly important. These records, known as annals, reflect the perspectives and biases of their respective monasteries. The events they include might range from eclipses, storms, and the births of two-headed cows to matters of major political importance such as the one recorded here.

By 751 the Merovingian dynasty of Frankish kings had become impoverished and politically impotent. Actual power was exercised by the chief official of the royal household, the *Major Domus*. This office was in the hereditary control of a great Frankish aristocratic family known later as the "Carolingians." Pepin the Short (741-768), the Carolingian *Major Domus* in 751, hungered for the crown. But the Merovingians, even though powerless, were an ancient and revered royal dynasty, and Pepin therefore needed potent spiritual backing for his coup d'etat. Pope Zacharias was harassed by hostile Byzantines and rampaging Lombards and viewed Pepin as a potential military supporter who might rescue the papacy from its predicament. Pepin and Zacharias were thus well-placed to help each other, as these douments describe.

In the year [751] of the Lord's incarnation Pepin sent ambassadors to Rome to Pope Zacharias [741-752], to inquire concerning the kings of the Franks who, though they were of the royal line and were called kings, had no power in the kingdom, except that charters and privileges were drawn up in their names. They had absolutely no kingly authority, but did whatever the *Major Domus* of the Franks desired. But on the first day of March in the Campus Martius, according to ancient custom, gifts were offered to these kings by the people, and the king himself sat in the royal seat with the army standing round him and the *Major Domus* in his presence, and he commanded on that day whatever was decreed by the Franks; but on all other days thenceforth he remained quietly at home. Pope Zacharias, therefore, in the exercise of his apostolic authority, replied to their

From *The Lesser Annals of Lorsch*, in *A Sourcebook of Medieval History*, ed. F.A. Ogg; New York, American Book Company, 1907, pp. 106-107. Reprinted by permission.

inquiry that it seemed to him better and more expedient that the man who held power in the kingdom should be called king and be king, rather than he who falsely bore the name. Therefore the aforesaid pope commanded the king and people of the Franks that Pepin, who was exercising royal power, should be called king, and should be established on the throne. This was therefore done by the anointing of the holy archbishop Boniface in the city of Soissons. Pepin was proclaimed king, and Childeric, who was falsely called king, was shaved[1] and sent into a monastery.

READING 4

The Donation of Constantine

King Pepin expressed his gratitude by defeating the Lombards and granting the papacy large portions of central Italy. Since the Lombards had only recently seized this territory from the Byzantine Empire, the Byzantines regarded Pepin's grant as a usurpation of imperial lands. The papacy responded by pointing to the legend, current in Rome, that Constantine I had long ago granted the papacy perpetual dominion over Italy and all the West. The papal court evidently accepted this tale as historically accurate but the documentary proof was lacking. Accordingly, the "Donation of Constantine" was forged, with the intent not of rewriting history but of supplying the missing documentation. Such was the intent of a great number of forged grants throughout the Middle Ages. The "Donation of Constantine" was exposed as a forgery first around A.D. 1000 by court scholars of the Emperor Otto III, and then, more decisively, by the fifteenth-century Italian humanist, Lorenzo Valla. Notice the logical inconsistency in the two references to Constantinople.

    In the name of the Holy and Undivided Trinity. The emperor Caesar Flavius Constantinus in Christ . . . to the most holy and blessed Father of fathers, Sylvester, Bishop of the city of Rome and Pope, and to all his successors, who shall forever sit on the throne of Saint Peter until the end of time. . . .

From *The Medieval World, 300-1300*, ed. Norman Cantor, 2nd ed., New York, 1968, pp. 132-139. Reprinted with permission of Macmillan Publishing Co., Inc.

[1] I.e., his head was shaved. Uncut hair was a mark of royalty among male members of the Merovingian dynasty.

On the first day, then, after receiving the mystery of holy Baptism and after the cure of my body from the filth of leprosy[2], I recognized that there was no other God except the Father and the Son and the Holy Spirit, whom the most blessed Pope Sylvester preaches, Trinity in Unity, Unity in Trinity. For all the gods of the heathen which up to now I have worshipped, have been proved to be demons, the hand-made work of men. That same venerable father told very plainly to us the great power in heaven and earth which our Saviour had committed to the blessed Apostle Peter when, finding him faithful under questioning, he said: "Thou art Peter and upon this rock I will build my Church and the gates of hell shall not prevail against it." Take note, Oh mighty sovereigns, and incline the attention of your heart to what the good Master and Lord gave in addition to His disciple when He said: "And I will give unto you the keys of the kingdom of heaven; whatsoever thou shall bind on earth shall be bound also in heaven and whatsoever thou shall loose on earth shall be loosed also in heaven." It is a very wonderful and glorious thing to bind and loose on earth and to have that sentence of binding and loosing carried out in heaven.

While the blessed Sylvester was preaching these things I understood them and found that I was restored to full health by the beneficence of the same blessed Peter. So we, together with all our satraps and the whole Senate and all the nobles and the whole Roman people which is subject to the glory of our Empire, judged it in the public interest that, because St. Peter was made Vicar of the Son of God on earth, the Pontiffs also, who are the successors of the same Prince of the Apostles, may obtain from us and our Empire greater governmental power than the earthly clemency of our Imperial serenity has so far conceded to them; thus we chose the same Prince of the Apostles and his Vicar to be our powerful patrons with God. And because our Imperial power is earthly, we have decided to honor reverently his most holy Roman Church, and to exalt the most holy See of blessed Peter in glory above our own Empire and earthly throne, ascribing to it power and glorious majesty and strength and Imperial honor.

And we command and decree that he should have primacy over the four principal Sees of Antioch, Alexandria, Constantinople and Jerusalem, as well as over all the Churches of God throughout the whole world; and the Pontiff who occupies at any given moment the See of that same most holy Roman Church shall rank as the highest and chief among all the priests of the whole world and by his decision all things are to be arranged concerning the worship of God or the security of the faith of Christians. For it is just that the holy law should have its center of government at the place where the institutor of the holy laws, our Saviour, commanded blessed Peter to set up the chair of his apostolate. . . .

Let every people and the nations of the Gentiles in all the world rejoice therefore with us; we exhort you all that you return thanks abundantly to our God and

---

[2] The "Donation" begins with an elaborate statement concerning Constantine's conversion to Christianity and a theological part explaining the Christian Creed. Constantine was believed (incorrectly) to have been miraculously cured of leprosy by Pope Sylvester I.

Saviour Jesus Christ, because he is God in Heaven above and on earth beneath, Who, visiting us through His holy Apostles made us worthy to receive the holy Sacrament of Baptism and bodily health. In recompense for this we concede to those same holy Apostles, my lords the most blessed Peter and Paul and through them also to blessed Sylvester our father, Supreme Pontiff and Universal Pope of the City of Rome, and to all his successors, the Pontiffs who will preside over the See of blessed Peter until the end of the world, and by this present document we confer, our Imperial palace of the Lateran, which surpasses and excels all palaces in the whole world, then a diadem which is the crown of our head, and at the same time the tiara; also the shoulder covering, that is the strap which is wont to surround our Imperial neck; also the purple cloak and the crimson tunic and all our Imperial garments. They shall also receive the rank of those who preside over the Imperial cavalry. We confer on them also the Imperial scepters and at the same time the spears and standards, also the banners and various Imperial decorations and all the prerogatives of our supreme Imperial position and the glory of our authority.

We decree that those very reverend men, the clerics who serve the most holy Roman Church in various orders, shall have the same dignity, distinction, power and preeminence, by the glory of which our Senate is decorated; and we decree that the clergy of the most holy Roman Church shall be adorned as are the soldiers of the Empire. . . . Above all, in addition, we grant to the same our most holy father Sylvester, Bishop of the City of Rome and Pope, and to all the most blessed Pontiffs who shall come after him in succession for ever, for the honor and glory of Christ our God, to add to the numbers in that same great Catholic and Apostolic Church of God any one from our court who shall wish of his own free choice to become a cleric, and to add any to the number of monastic clergy. Let no one presume to act arrogantly in all these matters. . . .

To correspond to our own Empire and so that the supreme Pontifical authority may not be dishonored, but may rather be adorned with glorious power greater than the dignity of any earthly empire, behold, we give to the often-mentioned most holy Pontiff, our father Sylvester, the Universal Pope, not only the above-mentioned palace, but also the city of Rome and all the provinces, districts and cities of Italy and the Western regions, relinquishing them to the authority of himself and his successors as Pontiffs by a definite Imperial grant. We have decided that this should be laid down by this our divine, holy and lawfully framed decree and we grant it on a permanent legal basis to the holy Roman Church.

Therefore we have seen it to be fitting that our Empire and the power of the kingdom should be transferred and translated to the Eastern regions and that in the province of Byzantium in the most suitable place a city should be built in our name and our Empire established there; because it is not just that an earthly Emperor should exercise authority where the government of priests and the Head of the Christian religion have been installed by the heavenly Emperor.

We decree also that all the things, which we have established and approved by this our holy Imperial edict and by other divine decrees shall remain uninjured and unbroken until the end of the world; so, in the presence of the living God, Who ordered us to reign, and in the presence of His terrible judgment, we solemnly warn, by this our Imperial enactment, all our successors as Emperors and all our nobles, the satraps, the most honorable Senate and all people throughout the world, now and in the future and in all times previously subject to our Empire, that none of them will be permitted in any way to oppose or destroy or to take away any of these privileges, which have been conceded by our Imperial decree to the most holy Roman Church and to its Pontiffs.

READING 5

From Einhard's Life of Charlemagne

Einhard (c. 770-840) was reared in the monastery of Fulda, founded by St. Boniface, and joined Charlemagne's court in the early 790s. He served Charlemagne as an administrative official and knew him well. Einhard wrote his biography a few years after Charlemagne's death (814). As secretary to Charlemagne's son and heir, Louis the Pious, Einhard had easy access to court annals and official records. He also drew on his own intimate knowledge of the great emperor. Modeling his work on *The Lives of the Caesars* by the ancient Roman historian Suetonius, Einhard borrowed a number of descriptive passages from Suetonius' life of Augustus. Later medieval biographers, using a similar methodology, borrowed heavily from Einhard. But Einhard borrowed cautiously and intelligently, and his *Life*, despite its Suetonian echoes and admiring tone, brings us closer to the historical Charlemagne than does any other source. Later biographies portray Charlemagne as a legendary hero performing impossible deeds. The Gascon attack on Charlemagne's rearguard as his army withdrew from Spain was expanded and embroidered in later centuries into the great epic poem, the "Song of Roland."

When [the war in Aquitaine] was ended the Saxon war, which seemed dropped for a time, was taken up again. Never was there a war more prolonged nor more cruel than this, nor one that required greater efforts on the part of the Frankish peoples. For the Saxons, like most of the races that inhabit Germany, are by nature

From *Early Lives of Charlemagne,* ed. and tr. A.J. Grant; London, Chatto & Windus, Ltd., 1922, part 1, chaps. 7, 8, 9, 11.

fierce, devoted to the worship of demons and hostile to our religion, and they think it no dishonor to confound and transgress the laws of God and man. There were reasons, too, which might at any time cause a disturbance of the peace. For our boundaries and theirs touch almost everywhere on the open plain, except where in a few places large forests or ranges of mountains are interposed to separate the territories of the two nations by a definite frontier; so that on both sides murder, robbery, and arson were of constant occurrence. The Franks were so irritated by these things that they thought it was time no longer to be satisfied with retaliation but to declare open war against them.

So war was declared, and was fought for thirty years[1] continuously with the greatest fierceness on both sides, but with heavier loss to the Saxons than the Franks. The end might have been reached sooner had it not been for the perfidy of the Saxons. It is hard to say how often they admitted themselves beaten and surrendered as suppliants to King Charles; how often they promised to obey his orders, gave without delay the required hostages, and received the ambassadors that were sent to them. Sometimes they were so cowed and broken that they promised to abandon the worship of devils and willingly to submit themselves to the Christian religion. But though sometimes ready to bow to his commands they were always eager to break their promise, so that it is impossible to say which course seemed to come more natural to them, for from the beginning of the war there was scarcely a year in which they did not both promise and fail to perform.

But the high courage of the King and the constancy of his mind, which remained unshaken by prosperity and adversity, could not be conquered by their changes nor forced by weariness to desist from his undertakings. He never allowed those who offended in this way to go unpunished, but either led an army himself, or sent one under the command of his counts, to chastise their perfidy and inflict a suitable penalty. So that at last, when all who had resisted had been defeated and brought under his power, he took ten thousand of the inhabitants of both banks of the Elbe, with their wives and children, and planted them in many groups in various parts of Germany and Gaul. And at last the war, protracted through so many years, was finished on conditions proposed by the King and accepted by them; they were to abandon the worship of devils, to turn from their national ceremonies, to receive the sacraments of the Christian faith and religion, and then, joined to the Franks, to make one people with them.

In this war, despite its prolongation through so many years, he did not himself meet the enemy in battle more than twice,[2] once near the mountain called Osning, in the district of Detmold, and again at the river Haase, and both these battles were fought in one month, with an interval of only a few days.[3] In these two battles the

---

[1] The Saxon wars lasted from 772 until 804.

[2] In addition to the two battles mentioned by Einhard, Charlemagne also met the Saxons at a battle near Lübeck in 775 and one at Bochult in 779.

[3] These engagements were fought in 783.

enemy were so beaten and cowed that they never again ventured to challenge the King nor to resist his attack unless they were protected by some advantage of ground.

In this war many men of noble birth and high office fell on the side both of the Franks and Saxons. But at last it came to an end in the thirty-third year, though in the meanwhile so many and such serious wars broke out against the Franks in all parts of the world, and were carried on with such skill by the King, that an observer may reasonably doubt whether his endurance of toil or his good fortune deserves the greater admiration. For the war in Italy began two years before the Saxon war [in 770], and though it was prosecuted without intermission no enterprise in any part of the world was dropped, nor was there anywhere a truce in any struggle, however difficult. For this King, the wisest and most high-minded of all who in that age ruled over the nations of the world, never refused to undertake or prosecute any enterprise because of the labor involved, nor withdrew from it through fear of its danger. He understood the true character of each task that he undertook or carried through, and thus was neither broken by adversity nor misled by the false flatteries of good fortune.

While the war with the Saxons was being prosecuted constantly and almost continuously he placed garrisons at suitable places on the frontier, and attacked Spain with the largest military expedition that he could collect. He crossed the Pyrenees, received the surrender of all the towns and fortresses that he attacked, and returned with his army safe and sound, except for a reverse which he experienced through the treason of the Gascons on his return through the passes of the Pyrenees. For while his army was marching in a long line, suiting their formation to the character of the ground and the defiles, the Gascons placed an ambuscade on the top of the mountain—where the density and extent of the woods in the neighborhood rendered it highly suitable for such a purpose—and then rushing down into the valley beneath threw into disorder the last part of the baggage train and also the rearguard which acted as a protection to those in advance. In the battle which followed the Gascons slew their opponents to the last man.[4] Then they seized upon the baggage, and under cover of the night, which was already falling, they scattered with the utmost rapidity in different directions. The Gascons were assisted in this feat by the lightness of their armor and the character of the ground where the affair took place. In this battle Eggihard, who was in charge of the King's table, Anselm, the count of the Palace, and Roland, lord of the Breton frontier, were killed along with very many others. Nor could this assault be punished at once, for when the deed had been done the enemy so completely disappeared that they left behind them not so much as a rumor of their whereabouts. . . .

Then the Bavarian war broke out suddenly, and was swiftly ended. It was caused by the pride and folly of Tassilo, Duke of Bavaria.[5] For upon the instigation

---

[4] The Gascons, more properly the Basques, engaged the rearguard on 15 August 778 in the Battle of Roncevaux, so-called since the composition of the "Song of Roland" in the late eleventh century.

[5] This war took place in 787-788.

of his wife—who thought that she might revenge through her husband the banishment of her father Desiderius, King of the Lombards—Tassilo made an alliance with the Huns,[6] the eastern neighbors of the Bavarians, and not only refused obedience to King Charles but even dared to challenge him in war. The high courage of the King could not bear his overweening insolence, and he forthwith called a general levy for an attack on Bavaria, and came in person with a great army to the river Lech, which separates Bavaria from Germany. He pitched his camp upon the banks of the river, and determined to make trial of the mind of the Duke before he entered the province. But Duke Tassilo saw no profit either for himself or his people in stubbornness, and threw himself upon the King's mercy. He gave the hostages who were demanded, his own son Theodo among the number, and further promised upon oath that no one should ever persuade him again to fall away from his allegiance to the King. And thus a war which seemed likely to grow into a very great one came to a most swift ending. But Tassilo was subsequently summoned into the King's presence, and was not allowed to return,[7] and the province that he ruled was for the future committed to the administration not of dukes but of counts.

READING 6
Charlemagne's Letter to Pope Leo III, 796

This letter, written about four years before Pope Leo III (795-816) crowned Charlemagne (768-814) Roman Emperor, shows not only Charlemagne's policy towards the papacy but also his ideas about the proper functions of spiritual and secular power. The idea persists, from the conversation of Constantine and of Clovis, that the Christian God is the god of military victory.

As I have done with your predecessors, I desire to establish with your blessedness an inviolable covenant of faith and charity so that divine mercy obtained by the prayers of your apostolic holiness and your apostolic blessing may follow me everywhere while, God willing, the most holy See of the Roman Church will always be defended by our devotion. Indeed, it is our task with divine help to shield everywhere with our arms the Holy Church of Christ from all her enemies abroad,

From S. Ehler and J.B. Morral, *Church and State through the Centuries*, Bilbo and Tannen, Inc., New York; 1967, p. 12.

[6] More properly the Avars, yet Einhard continually refers to them as the "Huns."
[7] Duke Tassilo was forcibly placed in the monastery at Jumièges.

from the incursions of the heathen and the devastations of the infidel, and to fortify her from within by the profession of the Catholic faith. It is your part, holy father, to assist the success of our arms with your hands raised in prayer to God, as Moses did, so that by your intervention, God willing and granting, the Christian people will forever achieve victory over the enemies of His name, and the name of our Lord Jesus Christ will be glorified throughout the world.

READING 7

Documents Relating to the Imperial Coronation of Charlemagne

All historians are agreed that Pope Leo III crowned Charlemagne Roman Emperor on Christmas Day, A.D. 800, thereby reviving the Western Empire after a hiatus of nearly 325 years. They are not agreed, however, on whether the initiative was Leo's or Charlemagne's. These sources bear on the issue, but they do not resolve it.

A. ALCUIN'S LETTER TO CHARLEMAGNE, DATED JUNE, 799

To this day three persons have held the highest positions in this world: The apostolic sublimity who as the vicar of the blessed Peter, prince of the apostles, occupies his See. Thanks to your care I have been informed of the fate of the last incumbent [*i.e.*, Leo III] of this See.[1] The second is the imperial dignity and the secular power of the Second Rome. The rumor of the impious fashion in which the present head of the empire was deposed not by foreigners but by relatives and fellow citizens has spread everywhere. The third person is the royal dignity to the peak of which you have been exalted as the ruler of the Christian people: it excels the two others in power, renowned for wisdom, and sublime royal dignity. The welfare of the Church is now in danger and rests on you alone: you are the avenger of evil deeds, the guide of those who go astray, the comforter of those who mourn, the glory of the good. . . .

From S.C. Easton and H. Wieruszowski, *The Era of Charlemagne*, Van Nostrand, Inc., New York, 1961, pp. 126-127, 127-128, 128, 129.

[1] Leo III was accused of wrongdoing by hostile Roman townspeople and in 799 was forced to flee Rome and take refuge at Charlemagne's court.

B. FROM THE *ANNALS OF LORSCH*, C. 800

And as the title of an emperor had then come to an end among the Greeks, since they had a woman [Irene] on the imperial throne, it seemed to Pope Leo[2] and the holy fathers assembled at the council as well as to the rest of the Christian people that they should give the title of emperor to Charles, King of the Franks, since he held not only Rome itself, where the Caesars used to reside, but the other seats in Italy, Gaul, and Germany as well. Since the almighty God had given into his possession all these places, they deemed it right that with the assistance of God and according to the request of the whole Christian people he should bear the title also. King Charles was not able to refuse this demand: in all humility he submitted to God and to the request of the whole Christian people and on the day of the nativity of our Lord Jesus Christ he assumed the title of an emperor and was consecrated by Pope Leo.

C. FROM THE *LIFE* OF POPE LEO III, DATED 812

After this [the purgation oath of Leo taken in the Basilica of St. Peter] all convened again on the day of the nativity in the abovementioned Basilica of the blessed apostle Peter. And then the venerable and peaceful pontiff crowned him with his own hands with that most precious crown. Then all the faithful Romans who saw how he was eager to defend and how he loved the Holy Roman Church and its vicar, cried out with one voice—and this was the will of God and of the blessed Peter, the key-holder to the kingdom of heaven: To Charles, the most pious Augustus, crowned by God, the great and peaceful emperor, life and victory! This was announced three times before the holy confession of the Blessed Apostle Peter while they were invoking various saints; and he was established by all as Emperor of the Romans.

Thereupon the most holy prelate and pontiff anointed King Charles, his most excellent son, with the holy oil on that very day of the nativity of our Lord Jesus Christ.

D. FROM EINHARD'S *LIFE OF CHARLEMAGNE*, DATED 814

Although [Charlemagne] held [the Roman Church] in great respect, he only traveled to Rome to fulfill his vows and make his supplications four times during the forty-seven years of his reign.

But for his last journey there was still another reason. The Romans had inflicted many injuries upon Pope Leo, tearing out his eyes and cutting out his tongue so that he felt compelled to implore the help of the king. Therefore he went to Rome to restore order in the much disturbed affairs of the Church, and stayed

---

[2] Leo cleared himself of the charges against him by publicly swearing his innocence.

there for the whole winter. At this time he received the titles of Emperor and Augustus. But at first he disliked this act so much that he declared that, had he anticipated the intention of the pontiff, he would not have entered the church on that day when it happened, although it was a great feast day. But he endured very patiently the jealousy of the emperors who were indignant about his assuming these titles. By sending them frequent embassies and letters in which he addressed them as brothers, he overcame their contempt with his magnanimity, in which he was undoubtedly their superior.

READING 8

The General Capitulary for the Missi, Spring, 802

This imperial ordinance (capitulary), issued shortly after Charlemagne's coronation as Roman emperor, provides valuable evidence regarding the administration of the Carolingian realm. It discloses, among other things, the way in which the *missi dominici* were employed, the importance of oaths of loyalty (to the emperor as distinct from the empire), the workings of the Germanic-based legal system, the intimate connection between empire and church, and—by implication—the high incidence of crime and violence within Charlemagne's dominions. What the document does not reveal is the degree to which Charlemagne's commands were actually carried out.

1. Concerning the commission dispatched by our lord the emperor. Our most serene and most Christian lord and emperor, Charles, has selected the most prudent and wise from among his leading men, archbishops and bishops, together with venerable abbots and devout laymen, and has sent them out into all his kingdom, and bestowed through them on all his subjects the right to live in accordance with a right rule of law. Wherever there is any provision in the law that is other than right or just he has ordered them to inquire most diligently into it and bring it to his notice, it being his desire, with God's help, to rectify it. And let no one dare or be allowed to use his wit and cunning, as many do, to subvert the law as it is laid down or the emperor's justice, whether it concerns God's churches, or poor people and widows and orphans, or any Christian person. Rather should all men live a good

From *The Reign of Charlemagne*, ed. H. R. Loyn and J. Percival; London, 1975, pp. 74-79. Reprinted by permission of Edward Arnold, Ltd.

and just life in accordance with God's commands, and should with one mind remain and abide each in his appointed place or profession: the clergy should live a life in full accord with the canons without concern for base gain, the monastic orders should keep their life under diligent control, the laity and secular people should make proper use of their laws, refraining from ill-will and deceit, and all should live together in perfect love and peace. And the *missi*[1] themselves, as they wish to have the favor of Almighty God and to preserve it through the loyalty they have promised, are to make diligent inquiry wherever a man claims that someone has done him an injustice; so everywhere, and amongst all men, in God's holy churches, among poor people, orphans and widows, and throughout the whole people they may administer law and justice in full accordance with the will and the fear of God. And if there be anything which they themselves, together with the counts of the provinces, cannot correct or bring to a just settlement, they should refer it without any hesitation to the emperor's judgment along with their reports. And in no way, whether by some man's flattery or bribery, or by the excuse of blood relationship with someone, or through fear of someone more powerful, should anyone hinder the right and proper course of justice.

2. Concerning the promise of fealty to our lord the emperor. He has given instructions that in all his kingdom all men, both clergy and laity, and each according to his vows and way of life, who before have promised fealty to him as king, should now make the same promise to him as Caesar; and those who until now have not made the promise are all to do so from twelve years old and upwards. And that all should be publicly informed, so that each man may understand how many important matters are contained in that oath—not only, as many have thought until now, the profession of loyalty to our lord the emperor throughout his life, and the undertaking not to bring any enemy into his kingdom for hostile reasons, nor to consent to or be silent about anyone's infidelity towards him, but also that all men may know that the oath has in addition the following meaning within it.

3. First, that everyone on his own behalf should strive to maintain himself in God's holy service, in accordance with God's command and his own pledge, to the best of his ability and intelligence, since our lord the emperor himself is unable to provide the necessary care and discipline to all men individually.

4. Second, that no man, through perjury or any other craft or deceit, or through anyone's flattery or bribery, should in any way withhold or take away or conceal our lord the emperor's serf, or his landmark, or his land, or anything that is his by right of possession; and that no one should conceal the men of his fisc[2] who run away and unlawfully and deceitfully claim to be free men, nor take them away by perjury or any other craft.

---

[1] The closest modern equivalent of "missus" or "missi" is "commissioner," but neither it nor "envoy" conveys its full meaning.

[2] The "fisc" *[fiscus]* is an administrative unit of the royal estates that can be translated "crown lands" or "crown estate," though at times it means, as in this case, the "royal purse."

5. That no one should presume to commit fraud or theft or any other criminal act against God's holy churches or against widows or orphans or pilgrims; for the lord emperor himself, after God and his saints, has been appointed their protector and defender.

6. That no one should dare neglect a benefice [land granted on condition of service] held of our lord the emperor, and build up his own property from it.

7. That no one should presume to ignore a summons to the host from our lord the emperor, and that no count should be so presumptuous as to dare to excuse any of those who ought to go with the host, either on the pretext of kinship or through the enticement of any gift.

8. That no one should presume to subvert in any way any edict or any order of our lord the emperor, nor trifle with his affairs nor hinder nor weaken them, nor act in any other way contrary to his will and his instructions. And that no one should dare to be obstructive about any debt or payment that he owes.

9. That no one in court should make a practice of defending another man in an unlawful manner, by arguing the case weakly through a desire for gain, by hampering a lawful judgment by showing off his skill in pleading, or by presenting a weak case in an attempt to do his client harm. Rather should each man plead for himself, be it a question of tax or debt or some other case, unless he is infirm or unacquainted with pleading; for such men the *missi* or the chief men who are in the court or a judge who knows the case can plead it before the court, or if necessary a man can be provided to plead, who is approved by all parties and has a good knowledge of the case at issue; this, however, should only be done at the convenience of the chief men or *missi* who are present. At all events, it must be done in accordance with justice and the law; and no one should be allowed to impede the course of justice by offering a reward or a fee, by skillful and ill-intentioned flattery, or by the excuse of kinship. And let no one make an unlawful agreement with anyone, but let all men be seriously and willingly prepared to see that justice is done.

25. That the counts and *centenarii*[3] should strive to see that justice is done, and should have as assistants in their duties men in whom they can have full confidence, who will faithfully observe justice and the law, will in no wise oppress the poor, and will not dare, for flattery or a bribe, to conceal in any manner of concealment any thieves, robbers or murderers, adulterers, evil-doers and performers of incantations and auguries, and all other sacrilegious people, but rather will bring them to light, that they may receive correction and punishment according to the law, and that with God's indulgence all these evils may be removed from among our Christian people.

26. That the justices should give right judgment according to the written law, and not according to private opinions.

---

[3] "Centenarii" were subordinates of a count with administrative and judicial functions within the territorial divisions of a county.

27. We ordain that no one in all our kingdom, whether rich or poor, should dare to deny hospitality to pilgrims: that is, no one should refuse a roof, a hearth and water to any pilgrims who are traveling the country in the service of God, or to anyone who is journeying for love of God or for the salvation of his soul. And if a man should be willing to offer any further benefit to such people, let him know that God will give him the best reward, as he himself said: "Whoever shall receive one such little child in my name receiveth me"; and in another place, "I was a stranger, and ye took me in" [Matthew 18.5; 25.35].

28. Concerning the commissions coming from our lord the emperor: The counts and the *centenarii* should, as they are desirous of the favor of our lord the emperor, provide for the *missi* who are sent upon them with all possible attention, that they may go about their duties without any delay; and he has given instructions to all men that it is their duty to make such provision, that they suffer no delay to occur anywhere, and that they help them to go upon their way with all haste, and make such provision for this as our *missi* may require.

29. Concerning those poor men who owe payment of the royal fine and to whom the lord emperor in his mercy has given remission: the counts or the *missi* are not to have the right for their part to bring constraint upon people so excused.

30. Concerning those whom the lord emperor wishes, with Christ's blessing, to have peace and protection in his kingdom, that is, those who have thrown themselves upon his mercy, those who, whether Christians or pagans, have desired to offer any information, or who from poverty or hunger have sought his intervention: let no one dare to bind them in servitude or take possession of them or dispose of them or sell them, but rather let them stay where they themselves choose, and live there under the lord emperor's protection and in his mercy. If anyone should presume to transgress this instruction, let him know that a man so presumptuous as to despise the lord emperor's orders must pay for it with the loss of his life.

31. For those who administer the justice of our lord the emperor let no one dare to devise harm or injury, nor bring any hostility to bear upon them. Anyone who presumes to do so must pay the royal fine; and if he is guilty of a greater offence, the orders are that he be brought to the king's presence.

32. Murder, by which a great multitude of our Christian people perish, we ordain should be shunned and avoided by every possible means; Our Lord himself forbade hatred and enmity among his faithful, and murder even more. How can a man feel confident that he will be at peace with God, when he has killed the son most close to himself? Or who can believe that Christ Our Lord is on his side, when he has murdered his brother? It is, moreover, a great and unacceptable risk with God the Father and Christ the ruler of heaven and earth to arouse the hostility of men. With men, we can escape for a time by hiding, but even so by some chance of fortune we fall into our enemy's hands; but where can a man escape from God, from whom no secrets are hid? What rashness to think to escape his anger! For this reason we have sought, by every kind of precept, to prevent the people entrusted to us for ruling from perishing as a result of this evil; for he who feels no dread at the

anger of God should not receive mild and benevolent treatment from us; rather would we wish a man who had dared to commit the evil act of murder to receive the severest of punishments.   Nevertheless, in order that the crime should not increase further, and in order that serious enmity should not arise among Christians when they resort to murders at the persuasion of the devil, the guilty person should immediately set about making amends, and should with all possible speed pay the appropriate recompense to the relatives of the dead man for the evil he has done to them.   And this we firmly forbid, that the parents of the dead man should dare in any way to increase the enmity arising from the crime committed, or refuse to allow peace when the request is made; rather, they should accept the word given to them and the compensation offered, and allow perpetual peace, so long as the guilty man does not delay payment of the compensation.   And when a man sinks to such a depth of crime as to kill his brother or a relative, he must betake himself immediately to the penance devised for him, and do so as his bishop instructs him and without any compromising.   He should strive with God's help to make full amends, and should pay compensation for the dead man according to the law and make his peace in full with his kinsmen; and once the parties have given their word let no one dare to arouse further enmity on the matter.   And anyone who scorns to pay the appropriate compensation is to be deprived of his inheritance pending our judgment.

33.   We forbid absolutely the crime of incest.   If anyone is stained by wicked fornication he must in no circumstances be let off without severe penalty, but rather should be punished for it in such a way that others will be deterred from committing the same offence, that filthiness may be utterly removed from our Christian people, and that the guilty person himself may be fully freed from it through the penance that is prescribed for him by his bishop.   The woman concerned should be kept under her parents' supervision subject to our judgment.   And if such people are unwilling to agree to the bishop's judgment concerning their improvement they are to be brought to our presence, mindful of that exemplary punishment for incest imposed by Fricco upon a certain nun.

34.   That all should be fully and well prepared for whenever our order or announcement may come.   And if anyone then maintains that he is not ready and disregards our instructions he is to be brought to the palace—and not he alone, but all those who presume to go against our edict or our orders.

35.   That all bishops and their priests should be accorded all honor and respect in their service to God's will.   They should not dare to stain themselves or others with incestuous unions.   They should not presume to solemnize marriages until the bishops and priests, together with the elders of the people, have carefully inquired to see if there be any blood relationship between the parties, and should only then give their blessing to the marriage.   They should avoid drunkenness, shun greediness, and not commit theft; disputes and quarrels and blasphemies, whether in normal company or in a legal sense, should be entirely avoided; rather, they should live in love and unity.

36. That all men should contribute to the full administration of justice by giving their agreement to our *missi*. They should not in any way give their approval to the practice of perjury, which is a most evil crime and must be removed from among our Christian people. And if anyone after this is convicted of perjury he should know that he will lose his right hand; but he is also to be deprived of his inheritance subject to our judgment.

37. That those who commit patricide or fratricide, or who kill an uncle or a father-in-law or any of their kinsmen, and who refuse to obey and consent to the judgment of bishops, priests, and other justices, are for the salvation of their souls and for the carrying out of the lawful judgment to be confined by our *missi* and counts in such custody that they will be safe, and will not pollute the rest of the people, until such time as they are brought to our presence. And in the meantime they are not to have any of their property.

38. The same is to be done with those who are arraigned and punished for unlawful and incestuous unions, and who refuse to mend their ways or submit to their bishops and priests, and who presume to disregard our edict.

39. That no one should dare to steal our beasts in our forests; this we have forbidden already on many occasions, and we now firmly ban it again, that no one should do it any more and should take care to keep the faith which everyone has promised to us and desires to keep. And if any count or *centenarius* or vassal of ours or any of our officials should steal our game he must at all costs be brought to our presence to account for it. As for the rest of the people, anyone who steals the game in this way should in every case pay the appropriate penalty, and under no circumstances should anyone be let off in this matter. And if anyone knows that it has been done by someone else, in accordance with the faith he has promised to us to keep and has now to promise again he should not dare to conceal this.

40. Finally, therefore, from all our decrees we desire it to be known in all our kingdom through our *missi* now sent out: among the clergy, the bishops, abbots, priests, deacons, clerks, and all monks and nuns, that each one in his ministry or profession should keep our edict or decree, and when it is right should of his good will offer thanks to the people, give them help, or if need be correct them in some way. Similarly for the laity, in all places everywhere, if a plea is entered concerning the protection of the holy churches, or of widows or orphans or less powerful people, or concerning the host [army], and is argued on these cases, we wish them to know that they should be obedient to our order and our will, that they maintain observance of our edict, and that in all these matters each man strive to keep himself in God's holy service. This in order that everything should be good and well-ordered for the praise of Almighty God, and that we should give thanks where it is due; that where we believe anything to have gone unpunished we should so strive with all earnestness and willingness to correct it that with God's help we may bring it to correction, to the eternal reward both of ourselves and of all our faithful people. Similarly concerning the counts and *centenarii*, our officers *[ministerialibus]*, we wish all the things above mentioned in our deliberations to be known. So be it.

READING 9

Charlemagne's Letter to Abbot Baugulf, Late 700s

Although undated, this letter must have been written before Charlemagne's imperial coronation in 800 because he titles himself patrician rather than emperor of the Romans. The letter reflects Charlemagne's policy of using the bishoprics and monasteries of his realm to advance literacy and learning. It also reflects, by implication, the sorry state of learning at the time. Although addressed to Abbot Baugulf of Fulda, the letter was intended for all bishops and abbots—as its conclusion makes clear. One can only hope that they possessed sufficient learning and patience to decipher the tangled sentence that follows the address clause.

Charles, by the grace of God, king of the Franks and Lombards and patrician of the Romans, to Abbot Baugulf and to all the congregation, also to the faithful committed to you, we have directed a loving greeting by our ambassadors in the name of omnipotent God.

Be it known, therefore, to your devotion pleasing to God, that we, together with our faithful, have considered it useful that the bishoprics and monasteries entrusted by the favor of Christ to our control, in addition to the order of monastic life and the intercourse of holy religion, in the culture of letters also ought to be zealous in teaching those who by the gift of God are able to learn, according to the capacity of each individual, so that just as the observance of the rule imparts order and grace to honesty of morals, so also zeal in teaching and learning may do the same for sentences, so that those who desire to please God by living rightly should not neglect to please him also by speaking correctly. For it is written: "Either from thy words thou shalt be justified or from thy words thou shalt be condemned." For although correct conduct may be better than knowledge, nevertheless knowledge precedes conduct. Therefore, each one ought to study what he desires to accomplish, so that so much the more fully the mind may know what ought to be done, as the tongue hastens in the praises of omnipotent God without the hindrances of errors. For since errors should be shunned by all men, so much the more ought they to be avoided as far as possible by those who are chosen for this very purpose alone, so that they ought to be the especial servants of truth. For when in the years just passed, letters were often written to us from several monasteries in which it was stated that the brethren who dwelt there offered up in our behalf sacred and pious

From *Translations and Reprints from Original Sources of European History,* ed. and tr. D. C. Munro; Philadelphia, University of Pennsylvania Press, 1897, vol. VI, no. 5, pp. 12-14.

prayers, we have recognized in most of these letters both correct thoughts and uncouth expressions; because what pious devotion dictated faithfully to the mind, the tongue, uneducated on account of the neglect of study, was not able to express in the letter without error. Whence it happened that we began to fear lest perchance, as the skill in writing was less, so also the wisdom for understanding the Holy Scriptures might be much less than it rightly ought to be. And we all know well that, although errors of speech are dangerous, far more dangerous are errors of the understanding. Therefore, we exhort you not only not to neglect the study of letters, but also with most humble mind, pleasing to God, to study earnestly in order that you may be able more easily and more correctly to penetrate the mysteries of the divine Scriptures. Since, moreover, images, tropes and similar figures are found in the sacred pages, no one doubts that each one in reading these will understand the spiritual sense more quickly if previously he shall have been fully instructed in the mastery of letters. Such men truly are to be chosen for this work as have both the will and the ability to learn and a desire to instruct others. And may this be done with a zeal as great as the earnestness with which we command it. For we desire you to be, as it is fitting that soldiers of the church should be, devout in mind, learned in discourse, chaste in conduct and eloquent in speech, so that whosoever shall seek to see you out of reverence for God, or on account of your reputation for holy conduct, just as he is edified by your appearance, may also be instructed by your wisdom, which he has learned from your reading or singing, and may go away joyfully giving thanks to omnipotent God. Do not neglect, therefore, if you wish to have our favor, to send copies of this letter to all your suffragans and fellow bishops and to all the monasteries.

CHAPTER 4

ORDEAL AND SURVIVAL

The materials in this chapter illustrate how various regions of Western Christendom responded to the breakdown of the Carolingian Empire and the attacks of the Vikings and Hungarians.

When Charlemagne's son and heir, Louis the Pious, died in 840 after a reign marred by internal upheavals and Viking raids, his three sons—Lothar, Louis the German, and Charles the Bald—struggled with one another over the division of the Empire (document 1). A truce between Louis and Charles, recorded in the oaths of Strasbourg of A.D. 842 (document 2), illustrates the linguistic difference between the Frankish and Germanic parts of the former empire (the Germanic ruler, Louis, gave his oath in Frankish so that his brother's troops could understand it; and Charles the Bald, for the same reason, did the reverse).

The eventual settlement between the three brothers—the Treaty of Verdun of 843—partitioned the former Carolingian Empire into a western kingdom (France), an eastern kingdom (Germany), and an unstable middle kingdom stretching from the Netherlands to Italy. Under continued Viking pressure, the kingdom of France broke up into smaller units as the counts and dukes of Carolingian officialdom converted their former administrative offices into hereditary lordships and acquired increasing numbers of sworn followers (documents 3, A-D). These followers—"vassals"—often received lands from their lords in return for their service and loyalty, and sometimes granted portions of these lands to their own oath-bound retainers. The process resulted in a tenurial chain commonly described as "feudalism," which was complemented by what historians refer to as "manorialism" (document 3, E and F).

Amid the political confusion and incessant warfare of late-Carolingian Europe there gradually emerged a strong movement of resistance against the invaders. In England, after a century of Viking raids and conquests, the kings of the West Saxons managed to reverse the Danish tide (document 4), and eventually to unite all England under their rule. A movement for Church reform and social order emerged in France, centering on the Burgundian Abbey of Cluny and gradually spreading across Christendom (document 5). Germany saw a revival of royal power under a new Saxon dynasty whose ablest member, Otto the Great, routed the Hungarians in 955 at the battle of the Lechfeld (document 6). Bringing northern Italy under his control, Otto the Great was crowned "Roman Emperor" in 962—the first of a long line of king-emperors who reigned over both Germany and northern Italy (document 7). The relative stability that Otto and his successors brought to northern Italy provided an encouraging environment for the development of Italian commerce and urban life (document 8). Italy's cities were to play a commanding role in the commercial revolution that would transform Europe in the High Middle Ages.

In the course of the eleventh century, the revival of Europe's commerce and political order brought the invasions to an end. The Vikings and Hungarians were themselves converted to Christianity and were incorporated into European civilization. The final document demonstrates that the seafaring Vikings had much to contribute to Europe's landbound culture—that their activities were by no means limited to murder and devastation. With Christopher Columbus so deeply etched in our minds, it is too easy to forget that Europe's first discovery of America occurred not in 1492 but toward the end of the early Middle Ages (document 9).

READING 1

Nithard's Account of the Year 840

Nithard (d. 844) was one of the few lay historians of the early
Middle Ages. An illegitimate son of one of Charlemagne's daughters, he was reared and educated at the Carolingian court and
subsequently joined the following of King Charles the Bald, the
youngest of Louis the Pious's three surviving sons. On Louis'
death in 840, Charles and his two royal brothers—Lothar and
Louis the German—struggled over the division of the Carolingian
Empire. Having fought for Charles the Bald on more than one
occasion, Nithard was well placed to report the fraternal struggle
but quite unable to mask his own sympathies.

When Lothar [840-855] heard of his father's [Louis the Pious] death, he
immediately sent emissaries everywhere, especially all over Francia. They proclaimed that he was coming into the empire which had once been given to him. He
promised that he wished to grant everyone the benefices which his father had given
and that he would make them even bigger. He gave orders also that oaths of fealty
should be exacted from those who were still uncommitted. In addition, he ordered
that all should join him as fast as they could; those who were unwilling to appear
he threatened with death. He himself advanced slowly since he wanted to find out
how the wind was blowing before he crossed the Alps.

Presently, men from everywhere joined him, driven by either greed or fear.
When Lothar saw that, his prospects and power made him bold, and he began to
scheme about how he might best seize the whole empire. He decided to send an
army against Louis [the German] first, since this would not take him out of his way,
and to devote himself with all his might to the destruction of Louis' forces. In the
meantime he was shrewd enough to send emissaries to Charles [the Bald] in
Aquitaine, informing Charles that he was friendly toward him, as their father had
demanded and as was proper for one to feel toward a godchild. But he begged him
to spare their nephew, Pepin's son [Pepin II of Aquitaine], until he had spoken to
him. Having settled this, he turned to the city of Worms.

At that time [June 840] Louis had left part of his army as a garrison in Worms
and had gone to meet the Saxons who were in revolt. But after a small skirmish
Lothar put the defenders to flight and, crossing the Rhine with his entire army,
headed for Frankfurt. Here they suddenly came upon each other, Lothar approaching from one side and Louis from the other. After peace had been arranged for the

From *Carolingian Chronicles,* ed. and tr. Bernhard W. Schloz; Ann Arbor, 1970, pp. 141-
145, 174. Reprinted by permission of the University of Michigan Press.

night, they pitched their camps, not exactly in brotherly love, Lothar right at the place where they had met and Louis at the point where the Main flows into the Rhine. Since Louis' opposition was vigorous and his brother was not sure that he could make him give in without a fight, Lothar thought it might be easier to get the better of Charles first. He therefore put off battle with the understanding that he would meet Louis again at the same place on November 11. Unless an agreement could be negotiated beforehand, they would settle by force what each of them was going to get. And so, giving up his initial schemes, Lothar set out to subdue Charles.

At this time [July 840] Charles had come to Bourges to the assembly which Pepin [II] was going to attend, as his men had sworn. When Charles had learned what he could from everybody, he selected as ambassadors Nithard and Adalgar[1] and dispatched them as speedily as possible to Lothar, enjoining and entreating him to remember the oaths they had sworn each other and to preserve what their father had arranged between them. He also reminded him that he, Charles, was his brother and godson. Lothar should have what belonged to him; but should also permit Charles to have without a fight what his father had granted him with Lothar's consent. Charles pledged, if Lothar should do this, that he was willing to be loyal and subject to him, as it is proper to behave toward one's first-born brother. Besides, Charles promised that he would wholeheartedly forgive whatever Lothar had done to him up to that time. He implored him to stop stirring up his people and disturbing the kingdom committed to him by God, and sent word to Lothar that peace and harmony should rule everywhere. This peace he and his people considered most desirable and were willing to preserve. If Lothar did not believe this, Charles promised to give him whatever assurances he wanted.

Lothar pretended to receive this message kindly, but permitted the emissaries to return with greetings only and the reply that he would answer fully through his own envoys. Moreover, he deprived Charles' emissaries of the benefices which his father had given them because they did not want to break their fealty and join him. In this way he unwittingly betrayed his designs against his brother. Meanwhile, all men living between the Meuse and the Seine sent to Charles, asked him to get there before the land was taken over by Lothar, and promised to wait for his arrival. Charles quickly set out with only a few men and marched from Aquitaine to Quierzy. There he received graciously those who had come from the Charbonnière and the land on this side of it.[2] Beyond the Charbonnière, however, Herefrid, Gislebert, Bovo, and the others duped by Odulf[3] disregarded their sworn fealty and defected.

---

[1] This Nithard is the author of the *Histories* and Adalgar was a count of Charles the Bald's court party.

[2] This territory constitutes the frontier between Neustria and Austrasia.

[3] Ordulf was the lay-abbot of St.-Josse in northern France.

At the same time [August 840] a messenger coming from Aquitaine announced that Pepin and his partisans wanted to attack Charles' mother. Charles left the Franks at Quierzy by themselves, but ordered them to move his way if his brother should attempt to subdue them before his return. In addition, he dispatched Hugo, Adalhard, Gerard, and Hegilo to Lothar. Repeating everything that he had said before, he entreated Lothar again for God's sake not to subvert Charles' men and further to whittle away at the kingdom which God and his father had given to Charles with Lothar's consent. After making this appeal to Lothar he rushed into Aquitaine, fell upon Pepin and his men, and put them to flight.

Meanwhile [October 840], Lothar was returning from the confrontation with Louis and being joined by every man on this side of the Charbonnière. He thought it best to cross the Meuse and advance as far as the Seine. On his way there Hilduin, abbot of St. Denis, and Gerard, count of the city of Paris, came and met him. They had broken their fealty and defected from Charles. When Pepin, son of Bernard, king of the Lombards, and others saw this treachery, like slaves they also chose to break their word and disregard their oaths rather than give up their holdings for a little while. That is why these men broke faith, followed the example of those we mentioned already, and submitted to Lothar. Then Lothar became bold and crossed the Seine, sending ahead, as he always did, to the inhabitants between the Seine and the Loire men who were to make them defect by threats and promises. He himself followed slowly, as usual, heading for the city of Chartres. When he learned that Theodoric and Eric were on the way with the rest who had decided to join him, he resolved to proceed as far as the Loire, putting his confidence in his great numbers. Charles returned from the pursuit in which he had dispersed Pepin and his followers, and since he had no place where he could safely leave his mother, they both hastily departed for Francia.

In the meantime Charles heard of all these defections and that Lothar was determined to hound him to the death with an immense army, while Pepin on one side and the Bretons on the other had raised arms against him. So he and his men sat down to think about all these troubles. They easily found a simple solution. Since they had nothing left but their lives and their bodies, they chose to die nobly rather than betray and abandon their king.

They headed [in November 840] in Lothar's direction, and both sides thus approached the city of Orléans. They pitched camps at a distance of barely six Gallic miles from each other, and both parties dispatched emissaries. Charles only asked for peace and justice, but Lothar tried to think of a way he could deceive and get the better of Charles without a fight. This scheme came to nothing because of strong resistance on the other side. Then Lothar hoped that his own forces would continue to grow from day to day, and he thought he might be able to conquer his brother more easily when Charles' following had further dwindled.

But he was disappointed in the hope and refrained from battle. The condition of the truce was that Charles should be granted Aquitaine, Septimania, Provence, and ten counties between the Loire and the Seine, with the stipulation that he should be satisfied with them and remain there for the time being until they met again at Attigny on May 8.[4] Lothar promised that he was indeed willing to talk over and settle the interests of both parties by mutual consent. The leaders of Charles' party also realized that the problems at hand were more than they could handle. They feared, if it came to a battle, that they might be hard put to save the king in view of their small numbers, and all of them set great store by his talents. So they consented to the stipulations if only Lothar from now on would be as loyal a friend to Charles as a brother should be, permit him to hold peacefully the lands he had allotted to him, and in the meantime also refrain from hostilities against Louis. Otherwise, they should be absolved from the oath they had sworn.

By this device they both rescued their king from danger and soon freed themselves from an oath. For those who had sworn this had not yet left the house when Lothar tried to seduce some of them from Charles and by the next day in fact he received a few defectors. He immediately sent into the lands which he had assigned to his brother, to stir up trouble so that they would not submit to Charles. Then he moved on in order to receive homage from those coming to him out of Provence and tried to think of ways to overcome Louis by force or deception. . . .

From this history, everyone may gather how mad it is to neglect the common good and to follow only private and selfish desires, since both sins insult the Creator, so much in fact that He turns even the elements against the madness of the sinner. I shall easily prove this by examples still known to almost everyone. In the times of Charles the Great [d. 814] of good memory, who died almost thirty years ago, peace and concord ruled everywhere because our people were treading the one proper way, the way of the common welfare, and thus the way of God. But now since each goes his separate way, dissension and struggle abound. Once there was abundance and happiness everywhere, now everywhere there is want and sadness. Once even the elements smiled on everything and now they threaten, as scripture . . . testifies: "And the world will wage war against the madness."

READING 2
The Oaths of Strasbourg, 842

The bilingual versions of these oaths, which record an alliance between Louis the German (840-876) and Charles the Bald (840-877) against their older brother Lothar, illustrate the linguistic split between the western and eastern halves of the former Carolingian Empire. Not only are these among the earliest documents in French and German, they also show the strong ethnic differences that undermined centralized Carolingian administration.

From *Monumenta Germania Historica, Scriptores: 'Nithardi Historiarum' Libri IV, iii, 5*, pp. 38-39. G.H. Pertz, ed. (Hannover, 1870), trans. J.W. Leedom.

[4] Of the lands assigned to Charles at Worms in 839, one-third, which included Burgundy, were now left out.

THE FRENCH VERSION

"Pro Deo amur et pro Christian poblo et nostro commun salvament dist di in avant, in quant Deus savir et podir me dunat, si salvarai eo cist meon fradre Karlo et in adiudha et in cadhuna cosa, si cum om per driet son fradre salvar dist, in o quid il mi altresi fazet; et ab Ludher nul plaid numquam prindrai, qui meon vol cist meon fradre Kario in damno sit."

THE GERMAN VERSION

"In Godes minna ind in thes Christianes folches ind unser bedhero gealtnissi, fon thesemo dage frammordes, so fram so mir God gewizci indi madh furgibit, so haldih thesan minan broudher so man mit rehtu sinan broudher scal, in thiu, thaz er mig so sama duo; indi mit Ludheren in nohheiniu thing ne gegango, the minan willon imo ce scadhen werben."

ENGLISH TRANSCRIPTION

For the love of God and for the Christian people and our common salvation, it is decreed from this day forward that, so long as God grants me the knowledge and ability, I will aid my brother just as one should by right aid a brother—so long as he does the same for me—and I will enter into no compact or concord with Lothar through which my brother may be harmed.

READING 3
Select Feudal Documents

The following sources illustrate the evolution of lord-vassal relationships and hereditary tenures from pre-Carolingian to post-Carolingian times. The element of reciprocal rights and obligations between lord and vassal is particularly evident in the letter of Fulbert bishop of Chartres (1002-28), a celebrated scholar and school master. Reciprocity also characterized the relationships between aristocratic benefactors and the religious houses that they

A. "Frankish Commendation," from *Translations and Reprints of Original Sources of European History*, ed. and tr. E. P. Cheyney; Philadelphia, 1897, vol. 4, no. 3, pp, 3-4. B. "Capitulary of Mersen," from *ibid., p.* 5. C. "Capitulary of Quierzy," *from ibid.,* p. 14. D. Letter of Fulbert of Chartres, from *ibid.,* p. 23-24. E. "Survey of the Manor of Neuillay" from Georges Duby, *Rural Economy and Country Life in the Medieval West*, Charleston, 1972, pp. 204-5. F. "The Rights and Ranks of People" from D.C. Douglas and G.W. Greenaway, ed. and tr., *English Historical Documents*, volume 2, Oxford University Press, Oxford, 1953, pp. 813-14.

founded; monks were normally expected to serve benefactors, with prayers for their souls and, often, with knights who were granted lands on the monastic estates.

A. A SEVENTH-CENTURY COMMENDATION FORMULA

To that magnificent lord [blank], I, [blank]. Since it is known familiarly to all how little I have whence to feed and clothe myself, I have therefore petitioned your piety, and your good will has decreed to me that I should hand myself over or commend myself to your guardianship, which I have thereupon done; that is to say in this way, that you should aid and succor me as well with food as with clothing, according as I shall be able to serve you and deserve it.

And so long as I shall live I ought to provide service and honor to you, suitably to my free condition; and I shall not during the time of my life have the ability to withdraw from your power or guardianship; but must remain during the days of my life under your power or defense. Wherefore it is proper that if either of us shall wish to withdraw himself from these agreements, he shall pay [blank] shillings to the other party, and this agreement shall remain unbroken.

B. THE CAPITULARY OF MERSEN, 847

We [Emperor Lothar and Kings Lewis the German and Charles the Bald] will moreover that each free man in our realms shall choose a lord, from us or our faithful, such a one as he wishes.

We command moreover that no man shall leave his lord without just cause, nor should any one receive him, except in such a way as was customary in the time of our predecessors.

And we wish you to know that we want to grant right to our faithful subjects and we do not wish to do anything to them against reason. Similarly we admonish you and the rest of our faithful subjects that you grant right to your men and do not act against reason toward them.

And we will that the man of each one of us in whosoever kingdom he is, shall go with his lord against the enemy, or in his other needs unless there shall have been (as may there not be) such an invasion of the kingdom as is called a *landwer*, so that the whole people of that kingdom shall go together to repel it.

C. THE CAPITULARY OF QUIERZY, 877

If a count of this kingdom, whose son is with us, shall die, our son with the rest of our faithful shall appoint some one of the nearest relatives of the same count, who, along with the officials of his province and with the bishop in whose diocese the same province is, shall administer that province until announcement is made to us, so that we may honor his son who is with us with his honors.

If, however, he had a minor son, this same son, along with the officials of that province and with the bishop in whose diocese it is, shall make provision for the same province until the notice of the death of the same count shall come to us, that his son may be honored, by our concession, with his honors.

If, however, he had no son, our son along with the rest of the faithful, shall take charge, who, along with the officials of the same province and with the proper bishop shall make provision for the same province until our order may be made in regard to it. Therefore, let him not be angry who shall provide for the province if we give the same province to another whom it pleases us, rather than to him who has so far provided for it.

Similarly also shall this be done concerning our vassals. And we will and command that as well the bishops as the abbots and the counts, and any others of our faithful also, shall study to preserve this toward their men.

D.   LETTER OF FULBERT OF CHARTRES, 1020

To William most glorious duke of the Aquitanians, Bishop Fulbert the favor of his prayers.

Asked to write something concerning the form of fealty, I have noted briefly for you on the authority of books the things which follow. He who swears fealty to his lord ought always to have these six things in memory; what is harmless, safe, honorable, useful, easy, practicable. Harmless, that is to say that he should not be injurious to his lord in his body; safe, that he should not be injurious to him in his secrets or in the defenses through which he is able to be secure; honorable, that he should not be injurious to him in his justice or in other matters that pertain to his honor; useful, that he should not be injurious to him in his possessions; easy or practicable, that that good which his lord is able to do easily, he make not difficult, nor that which is practicable he make impossible to him.

However, that the faithful vassal should avoid these injuries is proper, but not for this does he deserve his holding; for it is not sufficient to abstain from evil, unless what is good is done also. It remains, therefore, that in the same six things mentioned above he should faithfully counsel and aid his lord, if he wishes to be looked upon as worthy of his benefice and to be safe concerning the fealty which he has sworn.

The lord also ought to act toward his faithful vassal reciprocally in all these things. And if he does not do this he will be justly considered guilty of bad faith, just as the former, if he should be detected in the avoidance of or the doing of or the consenting to them, would be perfidious and perjured. . . .

E.   SURVEY OF THE MANOR OF NEUILLAY, C. 860

There is in Neuillay a seigneurial manor amply equipped with other buildings. There are 10 fields, which can be sown with 200 muids of oats. There are 9 arpents [nearly 3 acres] of meadow, from which 10 loads of hay can be harvested. There is forest there; it is estimated to be 3 leagues long and 1 league wide. In it 800 pigs can find forage.

Electeus a slave and his wife a "colona" [a type of serf], Landina. They are dependents of St. Germain. They live in Neuillay. He holds half a farm, which has in arable land 19 acres, in meadow 1/2 arpent [less than a third of an acre]. He plows in the winter field 4 perches [a small measurement of land] and in the spring field 13. He carts manure to the lord's field, and performs no other service nor pays anything in addition.

Abrahil a slave and his wife, a "lida" [a public slave], by the name of Berthildis. They are dependents of St. Germain. And Ceslinus a lidus and his wife a lida, named Leutberga. And Godalbertus a lidus. These three families live in Neuillay. They hold a farm, which has in arable land 47 1/2 acres and in meadow 4 arpents. They do carting to Anjou, and in the month of May to Paris. They pay for the army tax 2 muttons, 8 chickens, 30 eggs, 100 planks and as many shingles, 12 staves, 6 hoops, and 12 torches. They bring 2 loads of wood to Sutre. They enclose, in the lord's court, 4 perches with a palisade, in the meadow 4 perches with a fence, and at the harvest as much as is necessary. They plow in the winter field 8 perches and in the spring field 26 perches. Along with their corvees [public taxes payable in labor] and labor services, they cart manure into the lord's field. Each pays a poll tax of 4 pennies.

There are in Neuillay 6 and 1/2 inhabited farms, and 1/2 not occupied. They are distributed among 16 families. They pay to the army tax 12 muttons; in poll tax, 5 shillings and 4 pennies; 48 chickens, 160 eggs, 600 planks and as many shingles, 54 staves and as many hoops, and 72 torches. They make two cartings for wine, and during May, 2 and 1/2 cartings, and give 1/2 an ox.

F.   THE RIGHTS AND RANKS OF PEOPLE, C. 1050

. . . The Cottar's right is according to the custom of the estate: in some he must work for his lord each Monday throughout the year, or 3 days each week at harvest-time. . . . He does not make land payment. He should have 5 acres: more if it be common on the estate; and it is too little if it ever be less; because his work must be frequent. Let him give his hearth-penny [Peter's pence] on Ascension Day even as each freeman ought to do. Let him also perform services on his lord's demesne-land if he is ordered, by keeping watch on the sea-coast and working at the king's deer fence and such things according to his condition. Let him pay his church dues at Martinmas.

The boor's duties are various, in some places heavy and in others light. On some estates the custom is that he must perform week-work for 2 days in each week of the year as he is directed, and 3 days from the Feast of the Purification to Easter. If he perform carrying service he need not work while his horse is out. At Michaelmas he must pay 10 pence for rent, and at Martinmas 23 sesters of barley, and 2 hens, and at Easter a young sheep or 2 pence. And he must lie from Martinmas to Easter at his lord's fold as often as it falls to his lot; and from the time when ploughing is first done until Martinmas he must each week plough 1 acre, and himself present the seed in the lord's barn. Also [he must plough] 3 acres as boon-work, and 2 for pasturage. If he needs more grass, let him earn it as he may be permitted. Let him plough 3 acres as his tribute land [the lord's demesne strips of the open fields] and sow it from his own barn, and pay his hearth-penny. And every pair of boors must maintain 1 hunting dog, and each boor must give 6 loaves to the herdsman of the lord's swine when he drives his herd to the mast-pasture. On the same land to which the customs apply a farmer ought to be given for his occupation of the land 2 oxen, 1 cow, 6 sheep and 7 acres sown on his rood of land. [During] that year let him perform all the dues that fall to him, and let him be given tools for his work and utensils for his house. When death befalls him let the lord take charge of what he leaves. . . . [The text continues by listing the duties and rights of people and slaves who perform specific functions on the manor.]

About men's provisioning. Every slave ought to have as provisions 12 pounds of good corn and 2 carcasses of sheep and 1 good cow for food and the right of cutting wood according to the custom of the estate.

About women's provisioning. For a female slave 8 pounds of corn for food, 1 sheep or 3 pence for winter food, 1 sester of beans for lenten food, whey in summer or 1 penny.

All slaves belonging to the estate ought to have food at Christmas and Easter, a strip of land for ploughing and a "harvest-handful" besides their dues. . . .

READING 4

More Selections from the Anglo-Saxon Chronicle

The *Anglo-Saxon Chronicle*, which we have already encountered, is an unusual and diabolically complex document. Unlike most of our sources, it was written not in Latin but in the Old English vernacular, a distant ancestor of modern English and indecipher-able without special training. From the 890s onward, copies of the *Anglo-Saxon Chronicle* were circulated to a number of English monasteries, at a few of which they were kept up to date more or less year by year. Thus, the so-called "Chronicle" is actually a series of interrelated annals varying in content between one

From *Two of the Anglo-Saxon Chronicles Parallel*, ed. Charles Plummer and John Earle; Oxford, The Clarendon Press, 1899, vol. 1, pp. 54, 62-76. tr. Marc Anthony Meyer.

manuscript and another. The "Parker Version," translated here, is the oldest of them. All its year-entries through 891 were transcribed in a single hand by an anonymous monk who was probably writing at Winchester, the chief city of the kingdom of Wessex. The entries after 891 occur in a variety of hands, suggesting that the writers were contemporary with the events described. But the annals translated here run from about 789 to 878, and the monk who transcribed them must therefore have been depending in part on earlier sources, now lost. His point of view is suggested by the fact that he was writing toward the end of the reign of Alfred the Great and probably at Alfred's capital.

789. In this year . . . three [of the Norsemen's] ships came [to Portland, Dorset] for the first time; and then the reeve rode there and tried to force them to go to the king's manor because he did not know who they were; and they slew him. These ships were the first of the Danes that attacked the English.

836. In this year King Ecgbert fought with thirty-five ships' crews at Carhampton, and great slaughter was made there, and the Danes had possession of the place of slaughter. . . .

838. In this year a large hostile army came into west Wales [Cornwall], and [the Britons] joined forces with them and continued to fight against King Ecgbert of Wessex. When the king heard this, he and his levies fought against them at Hingston Down and there put to flight both the Britons and the Danes.

840. In this year the ealdorman[1] Wulfheard fought against thirty-three ships' crews at Southampton and he made great slaughter there and won a victory. And Wulfheard died that same year. And in the same year, Ealdorman Æthelhelm with the Dorset levies fought against the Danish host at Portland, and for a long time put the host to flight; but the Danes had possession of the place of battle and killed the ealdorman.

851. In this year Ealdorman Ceorl with the Devonshire levies fought against the heathens at Wicga's Hill and great slaughter was made there, and he won the victory. And that same year King Athelstan and Ealdorman Ealhhere annihilated a great army at Sandwich in Kent and seized nine ships and scattered the rest. And for the first time the heathens pitched a winter camp [in England]. And then in the following year [852], three hundred and fifty ships came to the mouth of the River Thames and attacked Canterbury and London, and the heathens put to flight King Beorhtwulf of Mercia and his army. Then they went south, crossing the Thames into Surrey, and King Æthelwulf and his son Æthelbald and the West Saxon army fought against them at *Acleah*, and there the greatest slaughter was made of the

---

[1] The ealdorman is a leading man of high birth found throughout the Anglo-Saxon kingdoms, and the English equivalent of the continental "count."

heathen army of which we have heard until the present day, and the West Saxons won the battle.

860. In this year King Æthelbald died and his body lies at Sherborne; and then his brother Æthelbert succeeded to the whole kingdom and maintained it in good peace and great tranquility. And in his days a great heathen army landed and attacked Winchester [the capital town of Wessex], and Ealdorman Osric and the Hampshire levies and Ealdorman Æthelwulf and the men of Berkshire fought against the enemy host, put them to flight and had possession of the place of slaughter. And King Æthelbert ruled for five years and his body lies at Sherborne.

865. In this year the heathen army camped on the Isle of Thanet and made peace with the men of Kent, and the Kentishmen promised them money in return for that peace. And under the shelter of that peace and promise of money, the heathen army covertly traveled at night and devastated all of eastern Kent. In this year [866], Æthelred, King Æthelbert's brother, succeeded to the West Saxon kingdom. And in that same year, a great hostile army [known as the "Great Danish Army"] came to the land of the English and set up winter quarters in East Anglia, crossing the mouth of the Humber to York in Northumbria [in 867], where there was great discord among those people. They had rejected their king, Osbert, and had accepted Ælla as king, a man without a proper claim to rule. Only late in the year, when they began to make war on the heathens, did they gather a great army and move to attack them at York. They stormed the city [on 21 or 23 March 867] and some of them got inside, but the Northumbrians were very soundly defeated—some inside and some outside—and both kings were killed and the rest of the Northumbrians made peace with the enemy host. . . .

870. In this year the heathen army rode across Mercia into East Anglia and set up winter quarters at Thetford; and that winter King Edmund[2] fought against them, but the Danes were victorious and killed the king and subdued the whole kingdom. . . .

871. In this year the enemy army came to Reading [a royal residence] in Wessex, and after three nights two jarls[3] rode up-country. Then Ealdorman Æthelwulf met them at Englefield and fought against them and won the victory. Then after four nights, King Æthelred and his brother Alfred [the Great] led a great army to Reading and fought against the enemy, and great slaughter was made on both sides, and Ealdorman Æthelwulf was killed and the Danes had possession of the place of slaughter. And after four nights King Æthelred and his brother Alfred fought at Ashdown against the whole heathen army which was in two companies; in one was Bagsecg and Halfdan [son of Ragnar, Lothbrok], and in the other the jarls. And there King Æthelred fought against the company of the heathen kings, whence King Bagsecg was slain. And Alfred, the king's brother, fought against the

---

[2] King Edmund is said to have refused to share his Christian kingdom with the heathen Vikings, and they tied him to a tree and shot him with arrows and cut off his head. His cult spread quickly, and his body was enshrined at Bury, where in 1020 a monastery was founded and dedicated to St. Edmund, King and Martyr.

[3] The jarl or chieftain was a Scandinavian warrior who had gathered a band of other warriors around himself and united his area of country.

company of the jarls, and Jarls Sidroc the Elder and Sidroc the Younger, and Jarls Osbearn, Fraena, and Harald were slain. Both companies were put to flight and many thousands were killed and fighting continued until nightfall. And two weeks later, King Æthelred and his brother Alfred fought against the enemy host at Basing, and there the Danes won a victory. And after two months, King Æthelred and his brother Alfred fought at *Meretun* against the enemy who, again, were in two companies; and the [English] levies put both to flight and until late in the day were victorious. There was much bloodshed on both sides; but afterwards the Danes held the place of slaughter. And Bishop Heahmund was killed there along with many other good men. And after this fight, a great summer host[4] came. And then, after Easter [15 April], King Æthelred died, having ruled for five years; and his body lies at Wimborne.

Then his brother Alfred, son of Æthelwulf, succeeded to the West Saxon kingdom. And one month later, King Alfred, with a small force, fought against the whole heathen army at Wilton, and for a long while during the day fought off the host; but then the Danes had possession of the battlefield. And during this year, nine pitched battles were fought against the enemy army in this kingdom south of the Thames besides the many small encounters that King Alfred, the king's brother, and a single ealdorman and king's thegns[5] rode on which were not counted. And during this year, nine jarls and one king were killed; and in this year the West Saxons made peace with the Viking host.

874.   In this year the heathens went from Lindsey to Repton [in Northumbria] and constructed a winter camp there, and they drove King Burgred [of Mercia] across the sea twenty-two years after he succeeded to the kingdom; and they conquered the whole kingdom. And the king traveled to Rome and settled there, and his body lies in the church of Saint Mary in the English school.[6] And in the same year, the heathens gave the kingdom of Mercia to a foolish king's thegn, and he swore oaths and gave hostages to them so that at all times the kingdom would be held ready for them whenever they needed it, and he would hold himself in readiness and, with his followers, would serve the needs of the enemy army in all things.

876.   In this year the Viking host stole away inland into Wareham and eluded the West Saxon levies, and the king concluded a peace with the heathen army, and they swore oaths to him on the sacred ring[7] which before they would not do for any nation, that they would immediately depart from the kingdom. And the enemy

---

[4] A Scandinavian army that did not remain in England over the winter and came primarily for plunder and raiding.

[5] Free warriors of the king to whom he often granted land and other privileges. A thegn is the English equivalent of the continental knight.

[6] The English "school"—not really a school at all but a quarter of the city—was located on the Vatican Hill and was frequented by churchmen, nuns and monks, pilgrims, and others who had business in Rome.

[7] The sacred ring was worn by the chief at assemblies and otherwise kept in the inner sanctuary of the heathen temple.

army stole away from the West Saxon levies by night under shelter of this pact and, provided with horses, the enemy got to Exeter. And in this year Halfdan distributed the land of the Northumbrians [among his followers] and they engaged in ploughing and tilling for themselves.

878. In this year the heathen army stole away inland to Chippenham in the middle of winter over Twelfth Night and attacked and occupied the land of the West Saxons and drove a great part of the people overseas and, with the exception of King Alfred, conquered the greater part of those people who remained. And with a small company the king went with extreme difficulty through the woods [of Selwood] and into defensible positions in the swamps [of Somerset]. And during this same winter a brother of Ivar [the Boneless] and Halfdan was in the kingdom of Wessex, in Devonshire, with twenty-three ships and was slain there and eight hundred men with him and forty men of his retinue. And the Easter after this [23 March], King Alfred with a small force built a stronghold at Athelney and with the men of that part of Somerset nearest to it continued fighting against the heathens. Then in the seventh week after Easter he rode to Egbert's stone to the east of Selwood and there met all the men of Somerset, Wiltshire and that part of Hampshire which was on this side of the sea [west of Southampton Water]; and they gladly received him. After one night he journeyed from that camp to Iley Oak and after another to Edington, and there fought against the whole heathen army, and put it to flight and pursued it up to the stronghold [at Chippenham] and laid seige there for fourteen nights. And then the host gave him preliminary hostages and great oaths that they would leave his kingdom and vowed as well that their king would receive baptism; and they fulfilled that promise in this way. After three weeks the king, Guthrum, one of thirty very honorable men in the host, came to him at Allen, which is near Athelney. King Alfred stood sponsor for him there and [some time afterwards] the loosening of the baptismal fillet[8] was performed at Wedmore, where for twelve days Guthrum stayed with the king, who honored him and his companions with gifts.

---

[8] White baptismal robes and a white band of cloth bound around the head and anointed with the chrism were worn for eight days after the baptism ceremony.

READING 5

Foundation Charter for the Abbey of Cluny, 909

Duke William of Aquitaine (909-918), when he founded the abbey of Cluny in 909 (or possibly 910), granted it far greater privileges and liberties than were customary at the time, thereby providing the precondition for Cluny's subsequent role as a generator of ecclesiastical reform across Western Christendom.

It is clear to all men of sane mind that the providence of God so decrees for any rich man that he may be able to deserve everlasting rewards by means of the goods he transitorily possesses, if he uses them well. . . .

And I, William, count [of Auvergne] and duke [of Aquitaine] by the gift of God, carefully pondering this, and desiring to provide for my own salvation while it is permissible for me, have considered it proper, nay, most necessary, that from the goods which have been temporarily conferred upon me, I am to give a small portion for the gain of my soul. . . . And in order to make this deed not a temporary but lasting one, I am to support at my own expense a congregation of monks, trusting and hoping that even though I myself am unable to despise all things, nevertheless, by taking charge of despisers of the world whom I deem to be righteous, "I may receive the reward of the righteous" [Matthew X, 41].

Therefore, . . . I hand over from my own domains to the holy apostles, Peter and Paul, the following goods legally held by me: the vill of Cluny with the court and demesne manor, and the chapel in honor of Saint Mary, mother of God, and of Saint Peter, prince of the apostles, together with all the goods pertaining to it, namely, the vills, the chapels, the serfs of both sexes, the vines, the fields, the meadows, the waters and their courses, the mills, the entrances and exits, what is cultivated and what is not, all in their entirety. . . . [I give all this] with this understanding, that a regular monastery be constructed in Cluny in honor of the holy apostles Peter and Paul, and that there the monks shall congregate and live according to the rule of the blessed Benedict. . . .

And let the monks, as well as all the aforesaid possessions, be under the power and authority of the Abbot Bernon [d. 926], who shall regularly preside over them, as long as he lives, according to his knowledge and ability. But after his death, the same monks are to have power and permission to elect as abbot and rector any one of their order whom they will choose, in keeping with the will of God and the rule promulgated by Saint Benedict, so that they may not be impeded from making a

From *The Tenth Century*, ed. R.S. Lopez, New York, Holt, Rinehart & Winston, 1959, pp. 14-15; by permission.

canonical election by our opposition or that of any other power. Every five years, then, the aforesaid monks are to pay ten shillings to the church of the apostles for their lights. . . . We further will that every day they perform works of mercy toward the poor, the needy, the stranger and the pilgrim. . . .

The same monks there congregated are to be subject neither to our sway nor to that of our relatives, nor to the splendor of the royal greatness, nor to that of any earthly power. And I warn and beseech, through God and all His saints, and by the terrible Day of Judgment, that no one of the secular princes, no count whatever, no bishop at all, nor the pontiff of the aforesaid Roman See, is to invade the property of these servants of God, or alienate it, or impair it, or give it as a benefice to any one, or appoint any prelate over them against their will. . . . And I beseech you, Oh Peter and Paul, holy apostles and glorious princes of the earth, and you, Pontiff of the pontiffs of the apostolic see, that . . . you remove from the community of the holy church of God and of life eternal the robbers and invaders and alienators of these goods. . . .

READING 6

Widukind of Corvey's Account of the Battle of the Lechfeld, 955

Widukind (fl. 10th C.), a monk of the Saxon abbey of Corvey, was well trained in the Roman classics. He began writing his "Deeds of the Saxons" during the reign of Otto I "the Great" (936-973), the second of the Saxon kings of Germany and, after 962, "emperor of the Romans." Widukind was thus contemporary or nearly contemporary with the events he described. His outlook was shaped by his own kinship to the Saxon royal family and by the fact that his abbey was a royal foundation. He dedicated his history to Otto I's daughter with the express purpose of intensifying her admiration for the exploits of her family. Otto emerges in the pages of Widukind as an heroic warrior in the ancient tradition of imperial Rome. The excerpt translated here, an account of Otto's decisive victory over the Hungarians, is inflated in tone but trustworthy in detail.

Having returned to Saxony around the first of July Otto met Hungarian legates who were apparently visiting him on account of ancient fealty and favor. In fact,

From *The Rise of the First Reich*, ed. Boyd H. Hill, Jr.; New York, John Wiley & Sons, Inc., 1969, pp. 15-18. Reprinted by permission.

however, it seemed to some that they had come in order to ascertain the outcome of the civil war [in Bavaria].

They stayed with him for some days, and he dismissed them in peace after having parceled out some small gifts. Subsequently he heard from messengers sent by his brother [Henry], the duke of the Bavarians: "The Hungarians have spread out and invaded your territory; they are determined to go to war with you." When the king heard this, he advanced to meet the enemy undaunted by the previous conflict. Only a very few of the Saxons were with him because he had been pressing for a war against the Slavs. When the camp had been set up within the city of Augsburg, an army of Franks and Bavarians came to his aid. Duke Conrad [the Red, former duke of Lotharingia] also hurried to the camp with a strong force of cavalry; his arrival encouraged the soldiers, who now did not wish to delay the battle. Conrad was dear to his companions both at home and in the field, for he was by nature bold of mind and what is rare in the brave, he was also a man of good judgment. Whenever he ran against the enemy as a horseman or a foot-soldier, he was an irresistible warrior.

Scouting forces of both sides ascertained that the two armies were not far distant from each other. Otto's forces were ordered to fast and to be ready for war on the next day [10 August 955]. At the first rays of dawn the troops received and accepted the protection of their commander and then promised him their service. And after they had sworn an oath to one another, they raised their standards and proceeded from camp, about eight legions in all.[1]

The army was led through rugged terrain so that the enemy would not have an opportunity to shoot arrows at them. The Bavarians formed the first, second and third legions, which Duke Henry's subordinates were in charge of, for the dying Henry [d.1 November 955] was absent as a result of the last campaign. The Franks constituted the fourth legion, under the command of Duke Conrad.

In the fifth and largest legion, called the "royal," was the prince himself in the midst of a thousand hand-picked youthful soldiers, and before him the victorious Archangel [Michael], thickly surrounded by troops. The Swabians made up the sixth and seventh legions; they were commanded by Burchard, whom the king's brother's daughter had married.[2] In the eighth were the Bohemians, a thousand strong, whose expertise was supply. They were in last place, presumably the safest.

But events turned out otherwise than expected, for the Hungarians did not delay at all but crossed the river Lech and surrounded the army while harassing the last legion with arrows. With a loud shout they attacked, killed or captured most of the eighth legion, and having taken possession of the baggage, they compelled the other soldiers of that legion to flee.

---

[1] A legion consisted of at least 1000 men. Widukind is here deliberately employing an archaic, Roman term.

[2] Burchard III, Duke of Swabia (954-73), married Hedwig, daughter of Henry, Duke of Bavaria (947-55), who was a brother of King Otto I.

Similarly they attacked the seventh and sixth legions and put many of them to flight. When the king discovered that the battle was still ahead of him and that the rear columns were already in danger, he sent Duke Conrad back with the fourth legion, who pulled out the captives, cast out the booty, and drove the plundering columns of the enemy forward. The enemy were surrounded on all sides, and Duke Conrad returned to the king with the standards of victory. It is somewhat strange that veteran soldiers who were accustomed to the glory of victory had delayed fighting, whereas Duke Conrad held a triumph with troops who were new and virtually ignorant of waging war. . . .

When the king saw that the whole burden of the fight was now in front he spoke in order to encourage his comrades. "It is up to us in this emergency, as you yourselves see, my soldiers, not to tolerate the enemy at a distance but meet them face to face. For up to now I have made glorious use of your energetic hands and unconquerable weapons everywhere outside my own soil and *imperium*. Shall I now turn my back on my land and realm? We are surpassed, I know, by numbers, but not by courage or arms. For we know that for the most part they are devoid of all armor, and what is a greater solace to us, they are deprived of the help of God. Their audacity is like a wall of defense, but we have the hope of divine protection. Now it would shame almost all the rulers of Europe to give in to the enemy. If the end lies near, my soldiers, it is better that we die gloriously in battle than be beaten by the enemy and enslaved or strung up like animals. I would say more, my soldiers, if I could augment your courage or boldness by words. Now let's open this conference with swords rather than with tongues."

And when he had finished speaking, he seized his shield and the Holy Lance,[3] and being the first to turn his horse to the enemy he was a most valiant warrior and excellent commander. At first the bolder of the enemy resisted, but then as they saw their companions being routed, and stunned at being surrounded by us, they were ultimately killed.

Some of those remaining whose horses were tired out entered nearby villages, and being surrounded by soldiers were burned up along with the buildings. Others swam the nearby river, and when they could not get a foothold on the farther bank, they were swallowed up by the river and perished. On that day the [Hungarian] camp was invaded and all the captives were set free. On the second and third day the remaining Hungarians from the neighboring cities were virtually annihilated so that hardly any of them got away; but the victory over such a cruel tribe was not of course won without bloodshed to our side.

Duke Conrad was fighting hard, and on fire with purpose and with the heat of the sun, which was oppressive that day, he loosened the bonds of his cuirass to take a breath of air and was killed by an arrow in the throat. On the king's command his body was picked up and honorably transported to Worms. This man,

---

[3] The Holy Lance, which supposedly contained in its shaft one of the nails of the Cross of Christ, became a symbol of rule among the Germans even as late as World War II.

famous for greatness of mind and body, was interred there with the weeping and wailing of all Franks.

Three leaders of the Hungarians were captured, and being presented to Duke Henry they died as they deserved by hanging.

The king having been made glorious by his army was hailed as father of his country and *Imperator*[4] in a celebrated triumph. Then he decreed that God and His Holy Mother be honored and praised in every church. Amidst dancing and joy he returned victorious to Saxony and was lovingly received by his people, for such a great royal victory had not been celebrated in the 200 years before the reign of Otto.

READING 7

Liudprand of Cremona's Description of the Imperial Coronation of Otto I

The title of "emperor," conferred on Charlemagne, passed to weaker and weaker descendants until it was extinguished in the early tenth century. It was revived in a new and dramatic form by Otto I (936-973) of Germany. The description by Liudprand of Cremona (c. 920-72), one of Otto's ministers, describes the circumstances that led the German king to take the imperial crown.

Berengar and Adalbert [kings of Italy from 950 to 961] were reigning, or rather raging, in Italy, where they exercised the worst of tyrannies, when John [XII, 955-964], supreme pontiff and universal pope, whose church had suffered from the savage cruelty of the aforesaid Berengar and Adalbert, sent envoys from the holy church of Rome to Otto, at that time pious king and now our august emperor, humbly begging him for the love of God and the holy apostles Peter and Paul, to rescue him and the holy church entrusted to him from their jaws, and restore it to its former prosperity and freedom.

While the Roman envoys were laying these complaints, Walpert, the venerable archbishop of Milan, having escaped half-dead from the mad rage of Berengar and Adalbert, sought the powerful protection of Otto, declaring that he could no longer bear or submit to their cruelty. . . .

From Boyd Hill, *The Rise of the First Reich*, John Wiley, Inc., New York, 1969, pp. 19-22.

[4] "Imperator" means both victorious field commander and emperor, and in this case the former is meant.

The most pious king was moved by their tearful complaints and considered not himself but the cause of Jesus Christ. Therefore, although it was contrary to custom, he appointed his young son Otto king, and leaving him in Saxony, collected his forces and marched in haste to Italy [an event that occurred in August 961]. There he quickly drove Berenger and Adalbert from the realm at once, the more quickly inasmuch as it is certain that the holy apostles Peter and Paul were fighting under his flag. The good king brought together what was scattered and mended what had been broken, restoring to each man his due possessions. Then he advanced to Rome to do the same again.

There he was welcomed with marvelous ceremony and unexampled pomp, and was anointed emperor by John the supreme bishop and universal pope [an event that occurred on 2 February 962]. Furthermore, Pope John and all the princes of the city swore solemnly on the most precious body of St. Peter that they would never give help to Berengar and Adalbert. Thereupon Otto returned to Pavia with all speed. [Otto then received reports that Pope John was living a life of sin and luxury and was trying to get Adalbert as patron and protector.]

When the envoys on their return gave this report to the emperor, he said, "He is only a boy, and will soon change if good men set him an example. I hope that honorable reproof and generous persuasion will quickly cure him of these vices. The first thing required by circumstances is that we dislodge Berengar from his position at Montefeltro. Then let us address some words of fatherly admonition to the lord Pope. His sense of shame, if not his own wishes, will soon effect a change in him for the better. Perchance if he is forced into good ways, he will be ashamed to get out of them again."

READING 8
An Account of the Lombard Kingdom in the Late Tenth Century

In this passage an anonymous Pavian writer of the early eleventh century looks back at the flourishing state of the Lombard kingdom and its capital at Pavia several decades earlier, not long after Otto I had absorbed the kingdom into his empire. Otto and his succes-

From the *Instituta regalia et ministeria camere regnum Longobardum*, in *The Tenth Century*, ed. R. S. Lopez; New York, Holt, Rinehart & Winston, 1959, pp. 15-17. By permission.

sors were usually content to rule northern Italy gently and from a distance, but by contributing to its political stability they encouraged the growing vitality of its commerce. Like Einhard and many other medieval writers, our anonymous author seems to have modeled his description on another source, the nearly contemporary *Book of the Prefect* relating to Constantinople. Nevertheless, the account of Lombard Italy abounds in factual information that can almost certainly be trusted.

Merchants entering the kingdom used to pay the 10 per cent tax *[decima]* on all merchandise at the customs houses and at the beginning of the roads subject to the king[1]. . . . All persons coming from beyond the mountains into Lombardy are obligated to pay the *decima* on horses, male and female slaves, woolen, linen, and hemp cloth, tin, and swords. On all merchandise they are obligated to give the *decima* to the delegate of the treasurer. But everything that pilgrims bound for Rome take with them for personal expenses is to be passed without payment of the *decima*. . . .

And the nation of the Angles and Saxons, who came and used to come with their merchandise and wares, when they saw their trunks and sacks being emptied at the gates, grew angry and started rows with the employees of the treasury. Abusive words were exchanged and, moreover, very often the parties inflicted wounds upon one another. But in order to cut short such great evils and to remove all danger, the king of the Angles and Saxons and the king of the Lombards agreed together as follows: The nation of the Angles and Saxons is no longer to be subject to the *decima*. And in return for this the king of the Angles and Saxons and their nation are expected and obligated to send to the king's palace in Pavia and to the king's treasury, every third year, fifty pounds of refined silver, two large and handsome greyhounds, hairy or furred, in chains, with collars covered with gilded plates sealed or enameled with the arms of the king, two excellent embossed shields, two excellent lances, and two excellent swords wrought and tested. And to the master of the treasury they are obligated to give two large coats of miniver[2] and two pounds of refined silver. And they are to receive a passport from the master of the treasury, that they may not suffer any annoyance as they come and return home.

And the duke of the Venetians, together with his Venetians, is obligated to give every year in the king's palace in Pavia fifty pounds of Venetian deniers. These deniers are of one ounce each, equally good as the Pavian deniers in regard to weight and silver content. And to the master of the treasury the duke is obligated to give one excellent silk cloak on account of the rights belonging to the king of the

---

[1] At this period, the king of Italy and the German emperor were the same person.

[2] Miniver was a white fur used mainly for robes of state.

Lombards.   And that nation [of the Venetians] does not plow, sow, or gather vintage. This tribute is called pact, and by it the nation of the Venetians are allowed to buy grain and wine in every marketplace and to make their purchases in Pavia, and they are not to suffer any annoyance.

Many wealthy Venetian merchants used to come to Pavia with their merchandise, and they paid to the monastery of Saint Martin, which is called Outgate, the fortieth shilling on all merchandise. When the prominent Venetians come to Pavia, each of them is obligated to give to the master of the treasury every year one pound of pepper, one pound of cinnamon, one pound of galangal, and one pound of ginger; and to the wife of the master of the treasury, an ivory comb and a mirror and a set of accessories, or twenty shillings of good Pavian deniers.

Likewise the men of Salerno, Gaeta, and Amalfi used to come to Pavia with abundant merchandise. And they used to give to the treasury in the king's palace the fortieth shilling, and to the wife of the treasurer they gave individually spices and accessories just as did the Venetians.

And the great and honorable and very wealthy merchants of Pavia have always received from the hand of the emperor the most honorable credentials, so that they suffer no harm or annoyance in any way, wherever they may be, whether in a market or traveling by water or by land.   And whoever acts contrary to this is obligated to pay a thousand gold *mancusi* into the king's treasury.

And the mystery [guild] of the mint of Pavia is obligated to have nine noble and wealthy masters above all the other moneyers, who are to supervise and to direct all other moneyers jointly with the master of the treasury, so that no deniers be ever struck that be inferior to those they always have struck in regard to weight and silver content, to wit, ten of twelve. And these nine masters are obligated to pay for the rent of the mint twelve pounds of Pavian deniers into the king's treasury every year and four pounds of the same to the count palatine of Pavia. If a mint master discover a forger, they are to act in this way: jointly with the count of Pavia and the master of the treasury, they are under obligation to have the right hand of the forger cut off and to turn over his entire property to the king's treasury. . . .

And there are all the gold washers who send their accounts to the treasury in Pavia, and must never sell gold to anyone else but the sworn moneyers, and are obligated to deliver it to them and to the treasurer. And the latter are obligated to buy all that gold obtained from the rivers. . . .

And there are in Pavia fishermen, who are obligated to have a master from the best members of the whole mystery. And they are obligated to keep sixty boats, and to give for every boat two deniers on the first day of each month. And these two monthly deniers they are obligated to give to their master . . . and to make sure that whenever the king is in Pavia, fish is purchased with those deniers or their own fish is brought to him in the most honorable manner. And they are obligated to give fish every Friday to the master of the treasury.

There also are in Pavia twelve tanners preparing leather, with twelve junior members. And they are obligated to prepare every year twelve excellent oxskins and to give them to the royal treasury, in order that no other man be allowed to prepare leather. And let whoever acts contrary to this pay a hundred Pavian shillings into the royal treasury. And whenever a tanner first enters the mystery to become one of these senior tanners, he is obligated to give four pounds, one half to royal treasury and the other half to the other tanners.

There also are other mysteries. All shipmen and boatmen are obligated to furnish two good men as masters under the authority of the treasurer in Pavia. Whenever the king is in Pavia, these men are obligated to go with the ships. And these two masters are obligated to outfit two large vessels, one for the king and one for the queen, and to build a house with planks, and to cover it well. As for the pilots, let them have one vessel, so that the others may be safe on the water; and they are entitled, together with their juniors, to receive every day their expenses from the king's court.

And there was in Pavia the mystery of the soapmakers, who used to make soap and to give every year on the steelyard a hundred pounds of soap to the royal treasury and ten pounds to the treasurer, in order that no one else be entitled to make soap in Pavia. . . .

And concerning all these mysteries you should know this: that no man is entitled to perform their functions unless he is a member. And should another man perform them, he is obligated to pay the *bannum* [fine] into the king's treasury and to swear that he will no longer do so. Nor ought any merchant to conclude his business in any market, unless he is a Pavian merchant. And let any one acting contrary to this pay the *bannum*. . . .

READING 9

From the "Greenland Saga"
Concerning the Discovery of North America

The Icelandic sagas mark the pinnacle of medieval Norse litera-
ture. The "Greenland Saga," like others of its kind, is based on
actual historical events. But as poetic celebrations of heroic
deeds, transmitted orally for several generations before being
transcribed, the sagas tend to coat historical facts with a crust of
legend. The voyage described here took place around A.D. 1000;
the saga was probably first committed to writing in the later 1100s.

From the *Graenlendiga Saga*, in *The Vinland Sagas: The Norse Discovery of America*, ed. and tr. Magnus Magnusson and Hermann Palsson; London, Penguin Classics, 1965, pp. 54-58. Copyright Magnus Magnusson and Hermann Palsson, 1965. Reprinted by permission of Penguin Books, Ltd.

Our oldest surviving text, in the *Flateyjarbok* of the later 1300s, is based on earlier texts that have since perished.

Some time later, Bjarni Herjolfsson sailed from Greenland to Norway and visited Earl Eirik,[1] who received him well. Bjarni told the earl about his voyage and the lands he had sighted. People thought he had shown great lack of curiosity, since he could tell them nothing about these countries, and he was criticized for this. Bjarni was made a retainer at the earl's court, and went back to Greenland the following summer.

There was now great talk of discovering new countries. Leif, the son of Eirik the Red of Brattahlid, went to see Bjarni Herjolfsson and bought his ship from him, and engaged a crew of thirty-five.

Leif asked his father Eirik to lead this expedition too, but Eirik was rather reluctant: he said he was getting old, and could endure hardships less easily than he used to. Leif replied that Eirik would still command more luck than any of his kinsmen. And in the end, Eirik let Leif have his way.

As soon as they were ready, Eirik rode off to the ship which was only a short distance away. But the horse he was riding stumbled and he was thrown, injuring his leg. "I am not meant to discover more countries than this one we now live in," said Eirik. "This is as far as we go together."

Eirik returned to Brattahlid, but Leif went aboard the ship with his crew of thirty-five. Among them was a Southerner called Tyrkir.[2]

They made their ship ready and put out to sea. The first landfall they made was the country that Bjarni had sighted last. They sailed right up to the shore and cast anchor, then lowered a boat and landed. There was no grass to be seen, and the hinterland was covered with great glaciers, and between glaciers and shore the land was like one great slab of rock. It seemed to them a worthless country.

Then Leif said, "Now we have done better than Bjarni where this country is concerned—we at least have set foot on it. I shall give this country a name and call it *Helluland*."[3]

They returned to their ship and put to sea, and sighted a second land. Once again they sailed right up to it and cast anchor, lowered a boat and went ashore. This country was flat and wooded, with white sandy beaches wherever they went; and the land sloped gently down to the sea. Leif said, "This country shall be named after its natural resources: it shall be called *Markland*."[4]

---

[1]Earl Eirik Hakonarson ruled over Norway from 1000 to 1014.

[2]"Southerner" refers to someone from central or southern Europe; Tyrkir appears to have been a German.

[3]Bjarni Herjolfsson's last landfall on his way back to Greenland from his accidental sighting of America, a glaciated rock-bound country, and Leif's first land fall on his way to find Bjarni's countries. *Helluland* can only be the southeast coast of Baffin Island or some northerly part of the coast of Labrador.

[4]*Markland* was a heavily wooded country between *Helluland* and *Vinland*, named by Leif on his voyage and probably the southeast coast of Labrador or perhaps Newfoundland.

They hurried back to their ship as quickly as possible and sailed away to sea in a north-east wind for two days until they sighted land again. They sailed towards it and came to an island which lay to the north of it.

They went ashore and looked about them. The weather was fine. There was dew on the grass, and the first thing they did was to get some of it on their hands and put it to their lips, and to them it seemed the sweetest thing they had ever tasted. Then they went back to their ship and sailed into the sound that lay between the island and the headland jutting out to the north.

They steered a westerly course round the headland. There were extensive shallows there and at low tide their ship was left high and dry, with the sea almost out of sight. But they were so impatient to land that they could not bear to wait for the rising tide to float the ship; they ran ashore to a place where a river flowed out of a lake. As soon as the tide had refloated the ship they took a boat and rowed out to it and brought it up the river into the lake, where they anchored it. They carried their hammocks ashore and put up booths. Then they decided to winter there, and built some large houses.

There was no lack of salmon in the river or the lake, bigger salmon than they had ever seen. The country seemed to them so kind that no winter fodder would be needed for livestock: there was never any frost all winter and the grass hardly withered at all.

In this country, night and day were of more even length then in either Greenland or Iceland: on the shortest day of the year, the sun was already up by 9 a.m., and did not set until after 3 p.m.[5]

When they had finished building their houses, Leif said to his companions, "Now I want to divide our company into two parties and have the country explored; half of the company are to remain here at the houses while the other half go exploring—but they must not go so far that they cannot return the same evening, and they are not to become separated."

They carried out these instructions for a time. Leif himself took turns at going out with the exploring party and staying behind at the base.

Leif was tall and strong and very impressive in appearance. He was a shrewd man and always moderate in his behavior.

One evening news came that someone was missing: it was Tyrkir the Southerner. Leif was very displeased at this, for Tyrkir had been with the family for a long time, and when Leif was a child had been devoted to him. Leif rebuked his men severely, and got ready to make a search with twelve men.

They had gone only a short distance from the houses when Tyrkir came walking towards them, and they gave him a warm welcome. Leif quickly realized that Tyrkir was in excellent humor.

Tyrkir had a prominent forehead and shifty eyes, and not much more of a face besides; he was short and puny-looking but very clever with his hands.

---

[5]This statement indicates that the location of *Vinland* must have been south of latitude fifty and north of latitude forty—anywhere between the Gulf of St. Lawrence and New Jersey.

Leif said to him, "Why are you so late, foster-father? How did you get separated from your companions?"

At first Tyrkir spoke for a long time in German, rolling his eyes in all directions and pulling faces, and no one could understand what he was saying. After a while he spoke in Icelandic. "I did not go much farther than you," he said. "I have some news. I found vines and grapes."[6]

"Is that true, foster-father?" asked Leif.

"Of course it is true," he replied. "Where I was born there were plenty of vines and grapes.

They slept for the rest of the night, and next morning Leif said to his men, "Now we have two tasks on our hands. On alternate days we must gather grapes and cut vines, and then fell trees, to make a cargo for my ship."

This was done. It is said that the tow-boat was filled with grapes. They took on a full cargo of timber; and in the spring they made ready to leave and sailed away. Leif named the country after its natural qualities and called it *Vinland.*[7]

---

[6]Many later explorers of the New England region commented on the wild grapes they found growing there. Grapes have been known to grow wild on the east coast as far north as Passamaquoddy Bay.

[7]Literally, "Wine-land." With the compound *Vin-land,* compare the Icelandic term *vinber,* "grapes" (literally "wine-berries"). In order to explain away the absence of grapes in certain parts of North America which have been suggested as the site of *Vinland,* some scholars have argued that the first element in the name is not *vin* ("wine") but *vin,* meaning "fertile land," or "oasis."

TWO

THE HIGH MIDDLE AGES

The period from about 1050 to 1300 has been called the High Middle Ages because it represented, in important respects, the zenith of medieval culture. Europe transformed itself during these years from an embattled, agrarian culture to an expanding and increasingly urbanized civilization. The papacy reached the height of its power in the course of its protracted struggle with the Holy Roman Empire. The English and French monarchies evolved toward early-modern states, with bureaucracies, official archives, a growing sense of national identity, and, in England, the beginnings of Parliament. This was the age of Europe's first universities, where students flocked to study the liberal arts and sometimes advanced into graduate-level studies in philosophy and theology, medicine and law.

Historians have traditionally regarded this period as an age of faith, pointing to the building of the great cathedrals, the power of the papacy, and the proliferation of new religious orders—Cistercians, Dominicans, Franciscans, and many more. But the splendor of this religious culture was made possible by a great commercial revival. The overall balance of trade shifted in Europe's favor, and cities rose and flourished in its river valleys—the Rhine, Rhone, Loire, Seine, Po, Arno, Thames, and countless others. Warriors and crusaders expanded Europe's territorial frontiers in all directions, reconquering most of Spain from the Muslims, establishing new principalities on the eastern shores of the Mediterranean, pushing northeastward along the Baltic coast, and carving out a prosperous new kingdom in southern Italy and Sicily at the expense of Byzantium and Islam.

Some of these territories were eventually lost, and in subsequent centuries Europe would be threatened once again by the advance of hostile armies. But despite that, the changes that Western Christendom experienced during the High Middle Ages proved to be decisive. It had become a civilization of cities and commerce, of sophisticated states and flourishing universities—and so it would remain.

CHAPTER 5

NEW FRONTIERS:
CITIES AND CRUSADES

Emerging from a world of peasants, clerics, and warriors, the townspeople of the High Middle Ages were obliged to secure from their lords or princes the privileges essential to their new vocation (document 1). These privileges, won by negotiation or rebellion (document 2), mark the birth of a new class, the burghers or *Bourgeousie* whose wealth and power would grow across the centuries. The towns achieved a corporate status—the right to operate their own courts, collect their own taxes, and pay their lords' dues in a lump sum. Within the towns, smaller corporate bodies, the guilds, bound their members to regulations governing production, quality, and prices of the goods they manufactured (document 3).

The towns were centers not only of commerce and manufacturing but of intellectual and cultural change as well. Urban wealth funded the building of cathedrals, parish churches, and hospitals, and the launching of crusades. The conquests of warriors and crusaders, in turn, opened new markets and drew new cities into Europe's expanding commercial network. The relationship between urban wealth and crusading zeal was nowhere more evident than in the First Crusade, manned by north-European knights (document 4).

The same spirituality that launched the crusades around the turn of the twelfth century also launched the Cistercian Order, whose most celebrated member, St. Bernard of Clairvaux, wrote the Rule for the Crusading Order of Knights Templars and respected them unreservedly (document 5). The Templars, through their banks, eventually offered badly-needed capital to Europe's emerging towns.

READING 1

The Customs of Newcastle-upon-Tyne

This document typifies a great many royal charters granting privileges to towns, but it is not itself a charter. It is a list, compiled during the reign of Henry II (1154-89), of the customs that the Newcastle townspeople (burgesses) enjoyed under Henry II's grandfather, Henry I (1100-35). If Henry I conceded these privileges to Newcastle in a charter, it has been lost.

These are the laws and customs which the burgesses of Newcastle-upon-Tyne had in the time of Henry, king of England, and which they still have by right:

The burgesses may distrain foreigners [i.e., seize their goods in pledge for debts or damages] within their market and without, and within their houses and without, and within their borough and without, and they may do this without the permission of the reeve (royal official), unless the [royal] courts are being held within the borough, or unless they are in the field on army service [for the king], or are doing castle-guard. But a burgess may not distrain on another burgess without the permission of the reeve.

If a burgess shall lend anything in the borough to someone dwelling outside, the debtor shall pay back the debt if he admit it, or otherwise do right in the court of the borough.

Pleas which arise in the borough shall there be held and concluded except those which belong to the king's crown.

If a burgess shall be sued in respect of any plaint he shall not plead outside the borough except for defect of court; nor need he answer, except at a stated time and place, unless he has already made a foolish answer, or unless the case concerns matters pertaining to the crown.

If a ship comes to the Tyne and wishes to unload, it shall be permitted to the burgesses to purchase what they please. And if a dispute arises between a burgess and a merchant, it shall be settled before the third tide.

Whatever merchandise a ship brings by sea must be brought to the land; except salt and herring which must be sold on board ship.

If anyone has held land in burgage for a year and a day justly and without challenge, he need not answer any claimant, unless the claimant is outside the kingdom of England, or unless he be a boy not having the power of pleading.

If a burgess have a son in his house and at his table, his son shall have the same liberty as his father.

From *English Historical Documents, Volume II, 1042-1189*, ed. D.C. Douglas and G.W. Greenaway; Oxford, Oxford University Press, 1953, pp. 970-971. Reprinted by permission.

If a villein come to reside in the borough, and shall remain as a burgess in the borough for a year and a day, he shall thereafter always remain there, unless there was a previous agreement between him and his lord for him to remain there for a certain time.

If a burgess sues anyone concerning anything, he cannot force the burgess to trial by battle, but the burgess must defend himself by his oath, except in a charge of treason when the burgess must defend himself by battle. Nor shall a burgess offer battle against a villein unless he has first quitted his burgage.

No merchant except a burgess can buy wool or hides or other merchandise outside the town, nor shall he buy them within the town except from burgesses.

If a burgess incurs forfeiture he shall give 6 oras to the reeve.

In the borough there is no "merchant" nor "heriot" nor "bloodwite" nor "stengesdint."[1]

Any burgess may have his own oven and handmill if he wishes, saving always the rights of the king's oven.

If a woman incur a forfeiture concerning bread or ale, none shall concern himself with it except the reeve. If she offend twice she shall be punished by the forfeiture. If she offend thrice justice shall take its course.

No one except a burgess may buy cloth for dyeing or make or cut it.

A burgess can give or sell his land as he wishes, and go where he will, freely and quietly unless his claim to the land is challenged.

READING 2
The Revolt of the Laon Commune

Guibert, abbot of Nogent (*d. c.* 1125), describes here in vivid, first-hand, and highly opinionated terms a bloody revolt by the commune of the northern-French hilltop town of Laon against its bishop. The revolt occurred in 1112, and Guibert recorded it in his autobiographical memoirs in about 1115. City development posed a problem in medieval society, for a city was ordinarily the property of some local lord. In cathedral towns like Laon, the city usually "belonged" to the bishop, who had the right to select town officers and to judge urban disputes. But burgesses often had interests quite different from those of the landed aristocracy. When townspeople

From *Self and Society in Medieval France: The Memoirs of Abbot Guibert of Nogent (1064?-c.1125)*, ed. and tr. John F. Benton, based on the tr. of C.C. Swinton Bland; New York, Harper & Row, 1970, pp. 167, 174-176.

[1] These are specific fines which relate to marriage, inheritance, crimes of assault with and without bloodshed.

joined together to form their own, self-governing corporation, it was called a "commune." This obviously posed a threat to the dominion of the lord, who often tried to suppress the commune. The following is a description of a blood-chilling fight for a commune in the French cathedral city of Laon. Note that the author was a churchman: his bias in this case is clear.

Now, "commune" is a new and evil name for an arrangement for them all to pay the customary head tax, which they owe their lords as a servile due, in a lump sum once a year, and if anyone commits a crime, he shall pay a fine set by law, and all other financial exactions which are customarily imposed on serfs are completely abolished. Seizing on this opportunity for commuting their dues, the people gathered huge sums of money to fill the gaping purse of so many greedy men. Pleased with the shower of income poured upon them, those men established their good faith by proffering oaths that they would keep their word in this matter.

After this sworn association of mutual aid among the clergy, nobles, and people had been established, the bishop returned with much wealth from England. Angered at those responsible for this innovation, for a long time he kept away from the city. . . .

The next day—that is, on Thursday—when the bishop and Archdeacon Gautier were engaged after the noon offices in collecting money, suddenly there arose throughout the city the tumult of men shouting, "Commune!" Then through the nave of the cathedral of Notre-Dame, and through the very door by which Gérard's killers had come and gone, a great crowd of burghers attacked the episcopal palace, armed with rapiers, double-edged swords, bows, and axes, and carrying clubs and lances. As soon as this sudden attack was discovered, the nobles rallied from all sides to the bishop, having sworn to give him aid against such an assault if it should occur. In this rally Guimar the castellan, an older nobleman of handsome presence and guiltless character, armed only with a shield and spear, ran through the church. Just as he entered the bishop's hall, he was the first to fall, struck on the back of the head with a sword by a man named Raimbert, who had been his close friend. Immediately afterward that Renier of whom I spoke before as married to my cousin, rushing to enter the palace, was struck from behind with a spear when he tried to duck under it while poised on the porch of the bishop's chapel. Struck to the ground there, he was soon consumed by the fire of the palace from his groin downward. Adon the *vidame*, sharp in small matters and even keener in important ones, separated from the rest and able to do little by himself among so many, encountered the full force of the attack as he was striving to reach the bishop's palace.[1] With his spear and sword he made such a stand that in a moment he struck

---

[1] A *vidame* (*vicedominus*) was a lay lord who was responsible for protecting and administering ecclesiastical property. At Laon, Gérard of Quierzy had been *avoué* of Saint-Jean of Laon and was succeeded as castellan of that abbey by Roger of Montaigu. Adon the *vidame* seems to have been an episcopal officer. Another important noble of Laon who fought for the bishop was Guimar the castellan.

down three of those who rushed at him. Then he mounted the dining table in the hall, where he was wounded in the knees and other parts of the body. At last, falling on his knees and striking at his assailants all round him, he kept them off for a long time, until someone pierced his exhausted body with a javelin. After a little he was burned to ashes by the fire in that house.

While the insolent mob was attacking the bishop and howling before the walls of his palace, the bishop and the people who were aiding him fought them off as best they could by hurling stones and shooting arrows. Now, as at all times, he showed great spirit as a fighter; but because he had wrongly and in vain taken up that other sword, he perished by the sword. Unable to resist the reckless assaults of the people, he put on the clothes of one of his servants and fled into the warehouse of the church, where he hid himself in a container. When the cover had been fastened on by a faithful follower, he thought himself safely hidden. As those looking for him ran hither and thither, they did not call out for the bishop but for a felon. They seized one of his pages, but he remained faithful and they could get nothing out of him. Laying hands on another, they learned from the traitor's nod where to look for him. Entering the warehouse and searching everywhere, at last they found him in the following manner.

There was a most pestilent man named Thiégaud, a serf of the abbey of Saint-Vincent. For a long time he was a servant and *prévôt* of Enguerrand of Coucy, who set him over the collection of tolls paid for crossing the bridge at a place called Sort. Sometimes he watched until there were only a few travelers passing and robbed them of all their property; then, so that they could make no complaint against him, he weighted them down and tossed them into the river. How often he had done this, God only knows. Although the number of his thefts and robberies was more than anyone could count, the unrestrained wickedness of his heart was displayed in his hideous face. When he ran afoul of Enguerrand, he committed himself completely to the commune at Laon. He who had before not spared monks or clerks or pilgrims, or, in fact, women, was finally to be the slayer of the bishop. As the leader and instigator of this abominable attack, he searched diligently for the bishop, whom he hated more bitterly than did the rest.

As they sought for him in every vessel, Thiégaud halted in front of the cask where the man was hiding, and after breaking in the head he asked again and again who was there. Hardly able to move his frozen lips under the blows, the bishop said, "A prisoner." Now, as a joke, the bishop used to call this man Isengrin, because he had the look of a wolf and that is what some people commonly call wolves. So the scoundrel said to the bishop, "Is this my Lord Isengrin stored away here?" Sinner though he was and yet the Lord's anointed, he was dragged out of the cask by the hair, beaten with many blows, and brought out in the open air in the narrow lane of the cloister before the house of the chaplain Godfrey. As he implored them piteously, ready to swear that he would cease to be their bishop, that he would give them unlimited riches, that he would leave the country, with hardened hearts they jeered at him. Then a man named Bernard of Bruyères raised his sword and brutally dashed out that sinner's brains from his holy head. Slipping between the hands of those who held him, before he died he was struck by someone else with a blow running under his eye sockets and across the middle of his nose. Brought to his end there, his legs were hacked off and many other wounds inflicted. Seeing the ring on the finger of the former bishop and not being able to draw it off easily, Thiégaud cut off the dead man's finger with his sword and took the ring. Stripped naked he was thrown into a corner in front of his chaplain's house. My God, who shall recount the mocking words that were thrown at him by passers-by as he lay there, and with what clods and stones and dirt his corpse was pelted?

READING 3

Guild Regulations
for the Shearers of Arras

These regulations, issued in 1236 for the cloth cutters in the Flemish textile center of Arras, could be applied with only minor modifications to countless guilds throughout Europe. Notice that the guild is both a commercial organization and a religious and social brotherhood.

This is the first ordinance of the shearers, who were founded in the name of the Fraternity of God and St. Julien, with the agreement and consent of those who were at the time mayor and aldermen.

1. Whoever would engage in the trade of a shearer shall be in the Confraternity of St. Julien, and shall pay all the dues, and observe the decrees made by the brethren.

2. That is to say: first, that whoever is a master shearer shall pay 14 solidi to the Fraternity. And there may not be more than one master shearer working in a house. And he shall be a master shearer all the year, and have arms for the need of the town.

3. And a journeyman shall pay 5 solidi to the Fraternity.

4. And whoever wishes to learn the trade shall be the son of a burgess or he shall live in the town for a year and a day; and he shall serve three years to learn this trade.

5. And he shall give to his master 3 *muids¹* for his bed and board; and he ought to bring the first *muid* to his master at the beginning of his apprenticeship, and another *muid* a year from that day, and a third *muid* at the beginning of the third year.

From *A Source Book for Medieval Economic History*, ed. Roy C. Cave and Herbert H. Coulson; New York, Bilbo & Tannen, Inc., 1965; pp. 250-252. Reprinted by permission.

¹Payment expressed in terms of a liquid measure ("One muid equals approximately 52 liters"—Cave and Coulson).

6. And no one may be a master of this trade of shearer if he has not lived a year and a day in the town, in order that it may be known whether or not he comes from a good place. . .

8. And if masters, or journeymen, or apprentices, stay in the town to do their work they owe 40 solidi, if they have done this without the permission of the aldermen of Arras.

9. And whoever does work on Saturday afternoon, or on the Eve of the Feast of Our Lady, or after Vespers on the Eve of the Feast of St. Julien, and completes the day by working, shall pay, if he be a master, 12 denarii, and if he be a journeyman, 6 denarii. And whoever works in the four days of Christmas, or in the eight days of Easter, or in the eight days of Pentecost, owes 5 solidi. . . .

11. And an apprentice owes to the Fraternity for his apprenticeship 5 solidi.

12. And whoever puts the cloth of another in pledge shall pay 10 solidi to the Fraternity, and he shall not work at the trade for a year and a day.

13. And whoever does work in defiance of the mayor and aldermen shall pay 5 solidi.

14. And if a master flee outside the town with another's cloth and a journeyman aids him to flee, if he does not tell the mayor and aldermen, the master shall pay 20 solidi to the Fraternity and the journeyman 10 solidi: and they shall not work at the trade for a year and a day. . . .

16. And those who are fed at the expense of the city shall be put to work first. And he who slights them for strangers owes 5 solidi: but if the stranger be put to work he cannot be removed as long as the master wishes to keep him. . . . And when a master does not work hard he pays 5 solidi, and a journeyman 2 solidi. . . .

18. And after the half year the mayor and aldermen shall fix such wages as he ought to have.

19. And whatever journeyman shall carry off from his master, or from his fellow man, or from a burgess of the town, anything for which complaint is made, shall pay 5 solidi.

20. And whoever maligns the mayor and aldermen, that is while on the business of the Fraternity, shall pay 5 solidi. . . .

22. And no one who is not a shearer may be a master, in order that the work may be done in the best way, and no draper may cut cloth in his house, if it be not his own work, except he be a shearer, because drapers cannot be masters.

23. And if a draper or a merchant has work to do in his house, he may take such workmen as he wishes into his house, so long as the work be done in his house. And he who infringes this shall give 5 solidi to the Fraternity. . . .

25. And each master ought to have his arms when he is summoned. And if he has not he should pay 20 solidi. . . .

26-30. (Other army regulations)

31. And whatever brother has finished cloth in his house and does not inform the mayor and aldermen, and it be found in his house, whatever he may say, shall forfeit 10 solidi to the Fraternity.

32. And if a master does not give a journeyman such wage as is his due, then he shall pay 5 solidi.

33. And he who overlooks the forfeits of this Fraternity, if he does not wish to pay them when the mayor and aldermen summon him either for the army or the district, then he owes 10 solidi, and he shall not work at the trade until he has paid. Every forfeit of 5 solidi, and the fines which the mayor and aldermen command, shall be written down. All the fines of the Fraternity ought to go for the purchase of arms and for the needs of the Fraternity.

34. And whatever brother of this Fraternity shall betray his confrere for others shall not work at the trade for a year and a day.

35. And whatever brother of this Fraternity perjures himself shall not work at the trade for forty days. And if he does so he shall pay 10 solidi if he be a master, but if he be a journeyman let him pay 5 solidi.

36. And should a master of this Fraternity die and leave a male heir he may learn the trade anywhere where there is no apprentice.

37. And no apprentice shall cut to the selvage for half a year, and this is to obtain good work. And no master or journeyman may cut by himself because no one can measure cloth well alone. And whoever infringes this rule shall pay 5 solidi to the Fraternity for each offense.

38. Any brother whatsoever who lays hands on, or does wrong to, the mayor and aldermen of this Fraternity, as long as they work for the city and the Fraternity, shall not work at his trade in the city for a year and a day. And if he should do so, let him be banished from the town for a year and a day, saving the appeal to Monseigneur the King and his Castellan.

39. And the brethren of this Fraternity, and the mayor and aldermen shall not forbid any brother to give law and do right and justice to all when it is demanded of them, or when someone claims from them. And he who infringes this shall not have the help of the aldermen at all.

READING 4

The First Crusade

All are agreed that Pope Urban II (1088–1099) delivered a tremendously persuasive and effective speech to the clergy and laity who attended the Council of Clermont (central France) in November 1095, thereby launching the First Crusade. But the several descriptions of the speech disagree. Robert the Monk's eyewitness account, presented here, is likely to be as accurate as any and is surely the most stirring.

The second passage demonstrates the crusaders' actions when they succeeded in taking Jerusalem in 1099. While their deeds seem repugnant to a modern audience, they were an expression of genuine piety at the time, complicating the task of judging the motives for the crusade.

A. POPE URBAN II'S SPEECH AT THE COUNCIL OF CLERMONT, NOVEMBER 27, 1095, BY ROBERT THE MONK.

Oh, race of Franks, race from across the mountains, race chosen and beloved by God—as shines forth in very many of your works—set apart from all nations by the situation of your country, as well as by your catholic faith and the honor of the holy Church! To you our discourse is addressed and for you our exhortation is intended. We wish you to know what a grievous cause has led us to your country, what peril threatening you and all the faithful has brought us.

From the confines of Jerusalem and the city of Constantinople a horrible tale has gone forth and very frequently has been brought to our ears, namely, that a race from the kingdom of the Persians, an accursed race, a race utterly alienated from God, a generation forsooth which has not directed its heart and has not entrusted its spirit to God, has invaded the lands of those Christians and has depopulated them by the sword, pillage and fire; it has led away a part of the captives into its own country, and a part it has destroyed by cruel tortures; it has either entirely destroyed the churches of God or appropriated them for the rites of its own religion. They destroy the altars, after having defiled them with their uncleanness. They circumcise the Christians, and the blood of the circumcision they either spread upon the altars or pour into the vases of the baptismal font. When they wish to torture people by a base death, they perforate their navels, and dragging forth the extremity of the intestines, bind it to a stake; then with flogging they lead the victim around until the viscera having gushed forth the victim falls prostrate upon the ground. Others they bind to a post and pierce with arrows. Others they compel to extend their necks and then, attacking them with naked swords, attempt to cut through the neck with a single blow. What shall I say of the abominable rape of the women? To speak of it is worse than to be silent. The kingdom of the Greeks is now dismembered by them and deprived of territory so vast in extent that it can not be traversed in a march of two months. On whom therefore is the labor of avenging these wrongs and of recovering this territory incumbent, if not upon you? You, upon whom

From Dana C. Munro, *Urban and the Crusaders,* University of Pennsylvania, Translations and Reprints from the Original Sources of European History, Volume I, no. 2; Philadelphia, 1895, pp. 5-8.

above other nations God has conferred remarkable glory in arms, great courage, bodily activity, and strength to humble the hairy scalp of those who resist you.

Let the deeds of your ancestors move you and incite your minds to many achievements; the glory and greatness of king Charles the Great, and of his son Louis, and of your other kings, who have destroyed the kingdoms of the pagans, and have extended in these lands the territory of the holy church. Let the holy sepulchre of the Lord our Saviour, which is possessed by unclean nations, especially incite you, and the holy places which are now treated with ignominy and irreverently polluted with their filthiness. Oh, most valiant soldiers and descendants of invincible ancestors, be not degenerate, but recall the valor of your progenitors.

But if you are hindered by love of children, parents and wives, remember what the Lord says in the Gospel, "He that loveth father or mother more than me, is not worthy of me." "Every one that hath forsaken houses, or brethren, or sisters, or father, or mother, or wife, or children, or lands for my name's sake shall receive an hundred-fold and shall inherit everlasting life." Let none of your possessions detain you, no solicitude for your family affairs, since this land which you inhabit, shut in on all sides by the seas and surrounded by the mountain peaks, is too narrow for your large population; nor does it abound in wealth; and it furnishes scarcely food enough for its cultivators. Hence it is that you murder and devour one another, that you wage war, and that frequently you perish by mutual wounds. Let therefore hatred depart from among you, let your quarrels end, let wars cease, and let all dissensions and controversies slumber. Enter upon the road to the Holy Sepulchre; wrest that land from the wicked race, and subject it to yourselves. That land which as the Scripture says "floweth with milk and honey," was given by God into the possession of the children of Israel.

Jerusalem is the navel of the world; the land is fruitful above others, like another paradise of delights. This the Redeemer of the human race has made illustrious by His advent, has beautified by residence, has consecrated by suffering, has redeemed by death, has glorified by burial. This royal city, therefore, situated at the center of the world, is now held captive by His enemies, and is in subjection to those who do not know God, to the worship of the heathens. She seeks therefore and desires to be liberated, and does not cease to implore you to come to her aid. From you especially she asks succor, because, as we have already said, God has conferred upon you above all nations great glory in arms. Accordingly undertake this journey for the remission of your sins, with the assurance of the imperishable glory of the kingdom of heaven.

When Pope Urban had said these and very many similar things in his urbane discourse, he so influenced to one purpose the desires of all who were present, that they cried out, "It is the will of God! It is the will of God!" When the venerable Roman pontiff heard that, with eyes uplifted to heaven he gave thanks to God and, with his hand commanding silence, said:

Most beloved brethren, to-day is manifest in you what the Lord says in the Gospel, "Where two or three are gathered together in my name there am I in the midst of them." Unless the Lord God had been present in your spirits, all of you would not have uttered the same cry. For, although the cry issued from numerous mouths, yet the origin of the cry was one. Therefore I say to you that God, who implanted this in your breasts, has drawn it forth from you. Let this then be your war-cry in combats, because this word is given to you by God. When an armed attack is made upon the enemy, let this one cry be raised by all the soldiers of God: It is the will of God! It is the will of God!

And we do not command or advise that the old or feeble, or those unfit for bearing arms, undertake this journey; nor ought women to set out at all, without their husbands or brothers or legal guardians. For such are more of a hindrance than aid, more of a burden than advantage. Let the rich aid the needy; and according to their wealth, let them take with them experienced soldiers. The priests and clerks of any order are not to go without the consent of their bishop; for this journey would profit them nothing if they went without permission of these. Also, it is not fitting that laymen should enter upon the pilgrimage without the blessing of their priests.

Whoever, therefore, shall determine upon the holy pilgrimage and shall make his vow to God to that effect and shall offer himself to Him as a living sacrifice, holy, acceptable unto God, shall wear the sign of the cross of the Lord on his forehead or on his breast. When, truly, having fulfilled his vow he wishes to return let him place the cross on his back between his shoulders. Such, indeed, by the two-fold action will fulfill the precept of the Lord, as He commands in the Gospel, "He that taketh not his cross and followeth after me, is not worthy of me."

B.   THE CRUSADERS TAKE JERUSALEM, 1099

On the following day, at the blast of the trumpets, they undertook the same work more vigorously, so that by hammering in one place with the battering-rams, they breached the wall. The Saracens had suspended two beams before the battlement and secured them by ropes as a protection against the stones hurled at them by their assailants. But what they did for their advantage later turned to their detriment, with God's providence. For when the tower was moved to the wall, the ropes, by which the aforesaid beams were suspended, were cut by falchions, and the Franks constructed a bridge for themselves out of the same timber, which they cleverly extended from the tower to the wall.

Already one stone tower on the wall, at which those working our machines had thrown flaming firebrands, was afire. The fire, little by little replenished by the

From the Chronicle of Fulcher of Chartres, tr., Martha E. McGinty as found in *The First Crusade*, ed. Edward Peters; Philadelphia, University of Pennsylvania Press, 1971, pp. 76-79.

wooden material in the tower, produced so much smoke and flame that not one of the citizens on guard could remain near it.

Then the Franks entered the city magnificently at the noonday hour on Friday,[1] the day of the week when Christ redeemed the whole world on the cross. With trumpets sounding and with everything in an uproar, exclaiming: "Help, God!" they vigorously pushed into the city, and straightway raised the banner on the top of the wall. All the heathen, completely terrified, changed their boldness to swift flight through the narrow streets of the quarters. The more quickly they fled, the more quickly were they put to flight.

Count Raymond and his men, who were bravely assailing the city in another section, did not perceive this until they saw the Saracens jumping from the top of the wall. Seeing this, they joyfully ran to the city as quickly as they could, and helped the others pursue and kill the wicked enemy.

Then some, both Arabs and Ethiopians, fled into the Tower of David; others shut themselves in the Temple of the Lord and of Solomon, where in the halls a very great attack was made on them. Nowhere was there a place where the Saracens could escape the swordsmen.

On the top of Solomon's Temple, to which they had climbed in fleeing, many were shot to death with arrows and cast down headlong from the roof. Within this Temple about ten thousand[2] were beheaded. If you had been there, your feet would have been stained up to the ankles with the blood of the slain. What more shall I tell? Not one of them was allowed to live. They did not spare the women and children.

The Spoils which the Christians Took

After they had discovered the cleverness of the Saracens, it was an extraordinary thing to see our squires and poorer people split the bellies of those dead Saracens, so that they might pick out besants[3] from their intestines, which they had swallowed down their horrible gullets while alive. After several days, they made a great heap of their bodies and burned them to ashes, and in these ashes they found the gold more easily.

Tancred rushed into the Temple of the Lord, and seized much of the gold and silver and precious stones. But he restored it, and returned everything or something of equal value to its holy place. I say "holy," although nothing divine was practised there at the time when the Saracens exercised their form of idolatry in religious ritual and never allowed a single Christian to enter.

> With drawn swords, our people ran through the city;
> Nor did they spare anyone, not even those pleading for mercy.
> The crowd was struck to the ground, just as rotten fruit
> Falls from shaken branches, and acorns from a wind-blown oak.

---

[1] July 15, 1099.

[2] Not all accounts agree with this high number.

[3] Besants: gold coins, so called because they were originally Byzantine. Saracen besants were dinars of the same value as the Byzantine coins.

The Sojourn of the Christians in the City

After this great massacre, they entered the homes of the citizens, seizing whatever they found in them. It was done systematically, so that whoever had entered the home first, whether he was rich or poor, was not to be harmed by anyone else in any way. He was to have and to hold the house or palace and whatever he had found in it entirely as his own. Since they mutually agreed to maintain this rule, many poor men became rich.

Then, going to the Sepulchre of the Lord and His glorious Temple, the clerics and also the laity, singing a new song unto the Lord in a high-sounding voice of exultation, and making offerings and most humble supplications, joyously visited the Holy Place as they had so long desired to do.

Oh, time so longed for! Oh, time remembered among all others! Oh, deed to be preferred before all deeds! Truly longed for, since it had always been desired by all worshippers of the Catholic faith with an inward yearning of the soul. This was the place, where the Creator of all creatures, God made man, in His manifold mercy for the human race, brought the gift of spiritual rebirth. Here He was born, died, and rose. Cleansed from the contagion of the heathen inhabiting it at one time or another, so long contaminated by their superstition, it was restored to its former rank by those believing and trusting in Him.

And truly memorable and rightly remembered, because those things which the Lord God our Jesus Christ, as a man abiding among men on earth, practised and taught have often been recalled and repeated in doctrines. And, likewise, what the Lord wished to be fulfilled, I believe, by this people so dear, both His disciple and servant and predestined for this task, will resound and continue in a memorial of all the languages of the universe to the end of the ages.

READING 5

Bernard of Clairvaux
on the Knights Templars

St. Bernard of Clairvaux (1090-1153) was the foremost figure among the first genration of Cistercian monks. He was an ardent and outspoken advocate of the Second Crusade, and a contributor to the writing of the Rule of the Knights Templars—an order of crusaders who took monastic vows. In these and other ways, Bernard demonstrated his devotion to the Crusading movement at its most zealous. St. Bernard led the order of Clairvaux, the great reforming monastic

From *The Records of Medieval Europe*, ed. Carolly Erickson; New York, Anchor Books, 1971, pp. 184-86.

order of the twelfth century. Bernard sought to assert the place of
traditional Christian values in the rapidly-changing world of the
twelfth century. In this passage, he offers his vision of the Knights
Templars, an order of warrior-monks whose self-appointed task was
to defend Jerusalem.

A new kind of knighthood is now heard of in the land; it has arisen in that region
once visited by the Rising Star from on high, and from whence he drove out the
princes of darkness with the strength of his hand—where even now with the hands
of his worthies he is crushing their minions, sons of disloyalty, and driving them
out, and is accomplishing the redemption of his people, raising again the trumpet of
our salvation in the house of his son David. . . .

He is a fearless knight, in truth, and secure on all sides, who, as he has girded his
body with iron, so has girded his soul with the shield of faith. Surely, fortified with
both these weapons, he fears neither demon nor man. Nor does he who desires to
die fear death. For what should he fear in living or in dying, for whom to live is
Christ, to die is gain?[1] To be sure, he stands faithfully and willingly for Christ; but
he desires even more to be dissolved and be with Christ, for this is better. . . .

Of Worldly Knighthood

What end and reward therefore does it have, this worldly—I do not say
knighthood [*militia*] but roguery [*malitia*]—if as a murderer a man sins mortally
and when killed, perishes eternally? . . . You [worldly knights] cover your
horses with silks; you have I know not what little cloths hanging from your
cuirasses; you paint your lances, shields and saddles; you encrust your reins and
spurs with gold, silver and gems; and in this splendor, with shameful fury,
impudently oblivious, you race on to your death. Are these the trappings of a
military man, or are they rather womanly ornaments? . . .

Of the New Knighthood

The knight of Christ, I say, is safe in slaying, safer if he is slain. He is
accountable to himself when he is slain, to Christ when he slays. "For he
beareth not the sword in vain: for he is the minister of God, a revenger to
execute wrath upon him that doeth evil, to praise him that doeth good."[2] For
when he kills a malefactor, he does not commit homicide but, I might say,
malicide, and is clearly reputed to be the vindicator of Christ, bringing punishment to evildoers, and praise in truth to good men. Moreover, when he is
himself killed, it is known that he does not perish, but triumphs. The death he
inflicts is Christ's gain; the death he dies, his own. The Christian is glorified; in
the death of a Christian, the liberality of the King is shown, when the knight is
led to his reward. . . .

[1]Philippians 1, 21.
[2]Romans 13, 4.

CHAPTER 6

MEDIEVAL SOCIETY

With this chapter we boldly violate the chronological limits of *Part Two, "The High Middle Ages,"* and extend the scope of our sources both backward and forward to explore various aspects of social history (very broadly interpreted) across the entire Middle Ages.

In the first selection (document 1), Sidonius Apollinaris (c.432-c.485)—an important late Roman writer—provides insights into the relationships between patron and clients in his times. The patron-client relationship was a characteristic personal bond among freemen of the late Roman Empire and early Middle Ages, and Sidonius was one of the greatest patrons of late-fifth-century Gaul.

Document 2, from the Saga of Gunnlaug, gives a vivid depiction of the role of feuds in Viking society. The blood feud was, indeed, a characteristic social ingredient of early medieval Western Europe as a whole. In order to control feuding to at least some degree, communities resorted to the judicial ordeal, rooted in Germanic custom but now transformed into a Christian contest. The ordeal was a means of referring a dispute to the judgment of God. The procedure varied in form depending on place and circumstances. A favorite form of ordeal among the medieval north European nobility was the "judicial duel" or "trial by combat" in which two knights—the plaintiff and the accused, or their representatives ("champions")—fought it out, believing that God would grant the victory to the righteous party. The judicial duel is well illustrated by the trial of Ganelon, from the celebrated heroic poem, the *Song of Roland* (document 3).

One of the greatest poets of the late twelfth century, Marie de France, was a master of the Romance genre that flourished in her time. Her tale of *The*

Nightingale (document 4) exemplifies both the simple, artless beauty of the Romance style and the theme of adultery, suitably repented or punished, which occurs in many other contemporary romances as well. Although the setting of our next selection, "St. Theodora" (document 5), is late-fifth-century Byzantium, it is actually excerpted from a late-thirteenth-century collection of saints' lives known as *The Golden Legend*. It therefore typifies high-medieval rather than Byzantine attitudes and modes of expression.

Our remaining selections include passages showing how parental plans for an arranged marriage might be foiled by the refusal of consent by one of the proposed marriage partners (document 6); how a wife's property might be siphoned off by a needy and oppressive husband, to the consternation of the wife's kinfolk (document 7); how the papacy protected Jews—to an extent—from local and grassroots persecution (document 8); and how the extreme social and economic strains of the fourteenth century could erupt into violence and bloodshed on the part of lower classes (document 9).

READING 1

Two Letters of Sidonius Apollinaris

Sidonius Apollinaris was a rich landholder who later in life
became bishop of Clermont-Ferrand in south-central Gaul. He
was also a writer, poet, and a prolific correspondent, many of
whose letters have survived. They provide us with illuminating
and often vivid depictions of life in late-fifth-century Gaul.
Sidonius describes it as, on the whole, a good life despite the fact
that the Western Roman Empire was disintegrating around him.
  As a person of power and wealth, Sidonius was the patron of
many clients (freemen dependent on a superior). The two letters
excerpted here both show Sidonius protecting his clients. But the
tone of the two letters is very different because he is writing to
different sorts of people. In the first he is addressing an inferior, in
the second, a superior.

Letter to Pudens:

  The son of your nurse has run off with the daughter of mine—a scandalous
thing, which would have estranged you and me had I not known that you knew
nothing of the deed being done. But after some words disclaiming complicity you
think fit to beg that this flagrant offence go unpunished. I consent on one
condition—that you release the ravisher from his hereditary position of *inquilinus*,[1]
becoming his patron instead of his master. The woman is already free. The only
thing that will cause her to be regarded as taken in lawful marriage, not made over
as a plaything, will be that our culprit, on whose behalf you plead, should promptly
be made a client instead of a tribute-payer, and so begin to have the standing of a
plebian[2] rather than of a *colonus*. For nothing short of this arrangement or amends
can in any degree set right this insult to me: and I am content to make this
concession to your prayers and to our friendship—that, if the conferring of
freedom releases the husband, no punishment shall fetter the ravisher. Farewell.

Letter to Censorius, bishop of Auxerre:

  The bearer of this letter holds the honourable office of deacon. He with his
family, seeking an escape from the whirlwind of Gothic depredation, was carried
into your territory by the very impetus of his flight, so to speak. There on some

From Sidonius Apollinaris, *Poems and Letters, vol. ii,* tr. W. B. Anderson; Cambridge,
Harvard University Press, 1936, pp. 239, 241, 275.

[1]A colonus or bound laborer.
[2]This is a polite, antiquarian affectation. By this time "plebian" meant common free person, and
denoted no special status.

farm land, belonging to a church over which your holiness is set, this starving newcomer made a small sowing of seed on some half-tilled soil; and he earnestly pleads to be allowed to garner the whole crop. If you cherish him with the kindness due to "them who are of the household of the faith," I mean by waiving the rent due from the land, then he, a stranger whose outlook is as limited as his means, will consider that little acquisition as good as the profits of farming his native soil. Should you, as is your custom, let him off the statutory payment due for his exceedingly small bit of land, he will regard himself as liberally equipped with travelling expenses and will return with words of gratitude on his lips. If by his hand you make me the happy recipient of a characteristically gracious message your letter will be regarded here by the brethren one and all as a blessing dropped straight from heaven. Deign to hold me in remembrance, my lord bishop.

READING 2
Gunnlaug's Feud

This account, from the Icelandic *Saga of Gunnlaug*, depicts the feud between Gunnlaug and Hrafn and its bloody outcome. Feuds were all too common in Viking society; they remind us of the important fact that the Vikings were not a monolithic force that devoted all their energies to preying on Christendom. On the contrary, like their Christian contemporaries, they fought and preyed on each other as well, and their communities were therefore wracked by internal strife. The passage also contains a good example of the trait of deceptiveness that was an important element in the Viking ethos.

Gunnlaug told the Earl Thorkel he would no longer endure the contempt and scorn of his retainers for his quarrel with Hrafn. He requested the earl to find him a guide, so the earl gave Gunnlaug leave to depart and found him two guides for the journey.

Gunnlaug now traveled with a party of six from Hladir in to Lifangr, and on one and the same day Hrafn left there with four men in the morning, and Gunnlaug rode in the evening. From there Gunnlaug went on to Veradal, and evening after evening he arrived where Hrafn had been staying the night before. Gunnlaug made no stay but pressed straight on through the night, and in the morning at sunrise they saw each other.

From *Erik the Red and Other Icelandic Sagas*, tr. Gwyn Jones; New York, Oxford University Press, 1980, pp. 211-214.

"It is good," said Gunnlaug, when they stood face to face, "that we have found each other at last."

Hrafn said he had no quarrel with that. "And now," he continued, "choose which you like, whether we all fight, or just you and I; but let both sides have an equal number of men."

Gunnlaug said it was all one to him, whichever they did. However, Grim and Olaf, Hrafn's cousins, made it plain they would not stand by while just the two of them fought; and Gunnlaug's kinsman Thorkel the Black said the same. "Then you two," said Gunnlaug to the earl's guides, "must sit on one side and help neither party, but live to tell the tale of our encounter." And so they did.

They clashed together and fought bravely, all of them. Grim and Olaf together attacked Gunnlaug alone, and their exchanges ended in his killing them both, with no wound to himself.

Meanwhile Hrafn and Gunnlaug's kinsman Thorkel the Black were fighting together, and Thorkel fell before Hrafn and lost his life.

So, in the end, all their comrades fell. Then Hrafn and Gunnlaug clashed together with heavy strokes and headlong assaults one upon the other, fighting without pause or remorse. Gunnlaug wielded the sword Æthelred's gift: it was the best of weapons, and at last he landed a great blow on Hrafn with this sword and cut his leg from under him. Yet none the more did Hrafn fall to the ground, but fell back on a tree-stump and steadied his own stump back upon it.

"You are past fighting now," said Gunnlaug. "I will fight no longer with a maimed man."

"True," replied Hrafn, "I have had the worse of the draw. Yet I could give a good account of myself still if I might have something to drink."

"No foul play then," said Gunnlaug, "if I bring you water in my helmet."

"No foul play," promised Hrafn.

So Gunnlaug went to a brook, scooped up water in his helmet, and carried it back to Hrafn. Hrafn reached out for it with his left hand, but cut at Gunnlaug's head with the sword in his right, giving him a dreadful wound.

"That was foul play from you to me," said Gunnlaug, "and little like a man, when I was trusting you."

"True," replied Hrafn, "but this drove me to it, that I grudge you the embraces of Helga the Fair."

And now once more they fought furiously together, and it ended at last when Gunnlaug overcame Hrafn, and Hrafn lost his life there.

Then the earl's guides came forward and bandaged Gunnlaug's head-wound, while he sat there chanting this verse:

> Fearless he heard our spear-din,
> Hrafn, that oak rough-rinded,
> Swordhacked and hewn attacked us,
> His storm-rent bough unbending.
> Here was a gale in Hordland!

Roared spears and swords round Gunnlaug;
Daunting their flight this morning
On Dinganes, ring-bearer."

Next they saw to the dead men, and finally they got Gunnlaug on to his horse and brought him the whole way down to Lifangr. He lay there for three nights and received all his rites from a priest, and then he died, and was buried there at the church. Everyone thought it the greatest loss, this, in respect of Gunnlaug and Hrafn too, and all the more so because of the circumstances attendant on their deaths.

READING 3

The Trial of Ganelon,
from *The Song of Roland*

This passage, from the most celebrated epic poem of the High Middle Ages, dates from the late eleventh or early twelfth century. But in its account of the wars and court of Charlemagne some 300 years earlier, *The Song of Roland* probably draws on oral tradition. This excerpt provides a vivid account of the ordeal, a procedure for determining guilt or innocence that was originally Germanic but became Christianized and thereby received authentication through the participation of churchmen and through Christian ritual.

The ordeal, which was believed to reveal God's judgment, took several forms depending on time, place, and local custom. Accused people might be required to plunge their hands into boiling water or carry a piece of red hot iron a certain distance. If their hands healed they were declared innocent; if not, they were guilty. Similarly, they might be plunged into a pond—if they sank they were innocent, but if they floated they were guilty (the pure water would not accept "a guilty person").

Among the north European nobility a favored form of the ordeal was the one depicted here, "trial by combat": the accuser and accused—or their stand-ins—fight with lances and swords, often to the death. This passage, in which the issue is the ultimate crime of treason against one's lord, provides not only a vivid account of the judicial combat but also of its Christian context (and of the hazards of losing one's case).

From *The Song of Roland*, tr. Frederick Bliss Luquiens; New York, Collier Books, 1952, pp. 92-100.

And when the King returned from Ronceval,
In iron chains lay Ganelon. Him they brought
To the great square, and tied him to a post
With leathern thongs, and beat him fearfully
With staves and knotted ropes—and he deserved
No else. But judgment yet awaited him.

And Charles, so it is written in the Book
Of Frankish Kings, summoned from many lands
His men, and gathered them in his own church.
It was a day of festival, some say
Of blessèd Saint Sylvester, and there and then
Was Ganelon judged before the throne of Charles.

"My lords," said Charles the King, "what punishment
Is meet for Ganelon, who in Paynim Spain
Gave death to twenty thousand men of mine
On Ronceval's red field? And he betrayed
For gold my nephew, whom no mortal man
Shall see again, and Oliver his friend,
The brave and courteous, and the twelve great Peers
Of France." And Ganelon answered, saying: "Ay,
But Roland sent me wilfully to death
In Saragossa. Him I slew, as me
He would have slain. But treason was it not."
And the Franks said: "Sit we in judgment now." . . .

And Ganelon, hearing, straightway turned him where
His thirty kinsmen stood, and in their midst
He whom they all acknowledged as their lord,
Pinabel, Castellan of Sorence, renowned
For his fair speech, yet more for fighting well
Upon the field of battle. To him spake
Ganelon, saying: "Friend, I trust in you.
Save me this day from calumny and death."
And he: "Fear not. If any mortal man
Adjudge thee to be hanged, shall this my sword
Give him the lie, when or wherever the King
Shall bid us fight til death." And Ganelon then,
Glad with new courage, knelt before his friend.

So to their council turned the chosen Franks
And all the judges, some from Normandy
And bright Auvergne, and some from Saxon lands
And far Bavaria—ay, and many others.
But all because of Pinabel were afraid,
Timidly saying each to other: "Come,

Let be this thing. Implore we the great King
To pardon Ganelon, who shall swear an oath
To serve him from this day in love and faith.
Roland is dead—nor silver nor red gold
Can bring him back. And surely he is mad
Who champions dead men." Thus the cowards spake.

And so they came to the great King of France,
And knelt before his throne, and him implored
To pardon whom he hated, if he swore
To serve him from that day in love and faith.
"Let him not die. It is too late. His death
Will not bring back the dead . . ."

And the King's face was darkened, when he saw
That all were faithless. Crying out as one
Pierced to the heart, he cursed them all. And lo,
There leapt before his throne a valiant knight,
Count Thierry, younger brother of Duke Geoffrey,
Black-haired, and bronzed by Spanish suns, in build
Slender and supple, nor tall nor overshort.
And thus he spake to the great King: "O Charles,
Despair not thus, for there is one at least
To serve you, one who has not will alone
But lawful right to serve you, for I spring
From noble stock. Whatever wrong was done
By Roland, he fought for you, and that alone
Gave him the right to live. He who betrayed
The King's best soldier, betrayed the King as well.
And I adjudge him to be hanged, and thrown
His worthless corpse to dogs and ravening beasts
Of prey. Let him die a traitor's death! God's wounds!
If there be any who shall say me nay,
With this my girded sword shall I not fail
To uphold my judgment" And the listening Franks
Applauded, crying: "You have spoken well."

Pinabel stood before the King—a knight
Swifter of foot than any steed of war,
And tall and strong and brave, and whom he smote
Tarried not long among his fellow men.
And to the King he said: "Sire, it is yours
To be obeyed. Command there be an end
Of idle clamor. Here I give the lie
To this Count Thierry, and will fight with him."
Into the King's right hand he put his glove
Of tawny deerskin, who made answer, "Ay,

But you must give good hostages," and straight
His kinsmen, thirty of them, pledged themselves.
And likewise did the King give hostages,
And bade his soldier guard them, till the fight
Was ended, and God had shown the truth to all.

And when Count Thierry likewise laid his glove
In the King's hand, they brought to a wide field
Benches of wood, where sat them down the twain,
Until the chosen judges, at their head
Ogier of Denmark, bade them gird themselves.
And then the brave knight called for steeds and arms.

But ere they joined in mortal strife, confessed
Their carnal sins, and holy priests absolved
And signed them with the cross, and mass was sung,
And blessèd bread and wine were tasted—ay,
The twain made gifts to the great church of Aix.[1]
And then they stood before the King, and fixed
Their spurs upon their feet, and blithely donned
Their coats of mail, burnished and strong and light,
And girt their swords, and hung their quartered sheilds
about their shoulders and took their spears, and mounted.
And all the Franks were sad, remembering
Their captain, Roland, fearing for his fame,
For God alone knows what the end shall be.

Below the town a green field lay, and there
They fought together. First, they loosed their reins,
Drove deep their spurs, and rode each upon other,
And shattered each the other's shield, and rent
His linkèd hauberk, and cut his saddle girth.
The leathern saddles turned, and threw the riders
Headlong—and all who saw cried out in fear.

Both knights were thrown to the earth, but in a flash
Sprang to their feet, and let their chargers be,
And rushed each on the other with drawn swords,
And each the other's helmet smote, with blows
That well-nigh shattered them. And all the Franks
Cried out in fear; and the King knelt, and prayed. . . .

And then with all his strength did Pinabel
Heave his great sword, and smote the other's helm,
And from the fire thereof the grass was kindled.

[1]Charlemagne's palace Church at Aix-la-Chapelle (or Aachen).

Down crashed the trenchant blade, cleaving the helm
Asunder. The sharp steel drew crimson blood
From Thierry's cheek, and ever tearing down
Rent the bright hauberk on his breast. But God,
In His great mercy, kept the knight from death.

But when Count Thierry felt the biting steel
Upon his face, and saw his own red blood
On the green grass about him, sudden rage
Gave him new strength, and with a fearful cry
He swung his heavy sword on high and down
Upon his rival's helmet. The keen blade
Cut through, and found the flesh and bone beneath—
No mortal man could feel that blow, and live.
And so the fight was ended, and the Franks
Cried with one voice: "It is the will of God!
Thus has He shown the right. Let Ganelon
Be hanged, and with him all his hostages."

Then to the victor came the King, with arms
Outstretched, and followed by his best loved knights,
. . .And the King embraced
His champion, with the hem of his great cloak
Wiping the crimson blood from the deep gash
Upon his cheek. Then gently they disarmed him,
And on a mule of Araby he rode
Back to the city, honored by them all.
But when they came to Aix, and in the square
Set foot to earth, the traitor Ganelon
Was brought to judgment, and his hostages.

And Charles gathered his counsellors, and said:
"What shall I do with those who pledged their lives
For love of Ganelon, those who cast their lot
With Pinabel?" And they, by Frankish law,
Adjudged them all to death. And Charles the King
Bade hang them all on one accursèd tree,
And swore by his white beard, if one escaped,
The executioner should pay for him
With his own life. Whereto the hangman answered
With a grim laugh, and "Never fear, my lord,"
And bade a hundred of his men drag off
The thirty hostages. And so they died,
Paying the price of treachery, for it brings
Black death to others, not to self alone.

But ere the judges turned them home—for some
Had come to Aix from Brittany, and some

From Normandy, or far Bavaria—ay,
From many a distant country—they adjudged
A fearful death to Ganelon, for they bade
That he be strongly fettered hand and foot
To four swift steeds, and then a furious mob
Drove them with sharpened sticks through a wide field
His mortal frame was rent apart, his limbs
Torn from his wretched body, and his blood
Crimsoned the grass. So perished Ganelon—ay,
If any man betray a fellow man,
It is not right that he should boast thereof.

READING 4

Marie de France, *The Nightingale*

This touching story by the renowned poet Marie de France is a brief but characteristic example of the late-twelfth and thirteenth-century Romance tradition. The style is unaffected and almost childlike—sweet but never saccharine. Its theme, common to Romances (as to contemporary lyric poetry), is adulterous yet unconsummated love between a bachelor knight and a married lady (i.e., the wife of a lord).

I am going to tell you a story that the Bretons made into a lay. In their country it is called "The Laustic," which is "rossignol" in French, and "nightingale" in plain English.

In the country of Saint Malo there was a famous city where two knights lived, each in a strong house. The city won great renown from the worth of these barons. One of them had married a woman who was courteous, well dressed and wise. She took great care of herself according to the custom of the time. The other knight was a bachelor, well known among his peers for his prowess and great valor, and for his welcoming nature. He spent freely, went often to tournaments, and gave generously of what he owned. He loved his neighbor's wife; and so earnestly did he plead his suit, and so great was his worth, that she loved him above all others, as much as for the good that she heard of him as for his nearness to her. They loved each other wisely and well, keeping their love a secret, and taking care not to be discovered or surprised or even suspected. This was easy to do because their dwellings were so close together, with no barrier to divide them but a high wall of

From *Medieval Age*, ed. A. Flores; New York, Dell, 1963, pp. 330-33, tr. Muriel Kittel.

brown stone. When the lady stood at the window of the room where she lay, she could talk to her lover on the other side of the wall and he could talk to her, and they could exchange tokens by throwing or casting them over the wall. They lived happily with nothing to trouble them, except that they could not come together when they wished, for the lady was strictly guarded when he was in the country. But they found recompense for that in being able to talk to each other either at night or by day. No one could prevent them from going to their windows and seeing each other from there.

They loved one another for a long time, until it came to be summer, when hedges and field grow green again and the meadows are filled with flowers. Above the flowers the little birds sing with great sweetness, and it is not surprising that he who feels the desire of love should give himself up to it. To tell you the truth about the knight, he gave himself up to it with all his heart, and so on her side did the lady, with both looks and words. Often on nights when the moon shone and her lord slept, she would get up and, wrapping herself in her cloak, she would go to the window and stand there for her lover's sake. For she knew that he would be doing the same and watching most of the night. They took pleasure in looking at one another, since this was all they could have. She rose and stood there so many times that her lord became angry, and asked why she rose, and where she went.

"Sir," the lady answered, "no one can have joy in this world who does not hear the nightingale sing. This is why you see me here. His song in the night is so sweet that I feel it gives me great pleasure. It gives me such delight, and I long for it so much, that I cannot close my eyes."

When her lord heard her reply, he laughed with rage and malice. His only thought was to capture the nightingale. There was not a servant in the house who did not make a snare or net or trap and set it in the orchard. There was not a hazel bush or chestnut tree where they did not place a snare of lime, so that they trapped the bird and caught it. When they had taken the nightingale, they brought it still living to their master. He was overjoyed when he held it in his hands, and going to his lady's chamber, said: "Madame, where are you? Come here and speak to me. I have snared the nightingale that kept you awake so long. Now you can sleep in peace; he will never wake you again."

When the lady heard this, she was filled with anger and sorrow, and asked her lord for the bird; but in his spite he killed it. He broke its neck with his own hands, and then did a dreadful thing: he threw the body at the lady so that it stained her bodice with blood just above her breast. Immediately afterward he left the room.

The lady took the little body, wept softly, and cursed all those who had betrayed the nightingale by making traps and nets, for they had robbed her of a great joy.

"Woe is me, poor wretch," she cried. "Nevermore can I rise in the night to stand at the window, where I used to see my lover. He will think me false, so I must make a plan. I shall send him the nightingale and tell him what has happened."

She wrapped the little bird in a piece of samite, embroidered with gold, wherein was written the whole story. She called one of her servants and charged him to carry it to her lover. The servant went to the knight, saluted him on his lady's behalf, told him all the message and gave him the nightingale. When all was told and shown, the knight, who had listened attentively, was saddened by the event, but he was neither base nor dilatory. He had a casket made, not of iron nor of steel, but all of fine gold, set with rare and costly gems, and fastened with a tightly fitting lid. In this box he place the nightingale, had it sealed, and carried it with him always.

This adventure was told: it could not remain hidden. The Bretons made a lay about it, which they called "The Laustic."

READING 5

St. Theodora, from *The Golden Legend*

The story of St. Theodora, despite its early Byzantine setting, is excerpted from the thirteenth-century Italian work *The Golden Legend*, a collection of saints' lives by Jacopo da Voragine. Jacopo, a Dominican friar who later became bishop of Genoa, enlivened his stories with wondrous episodes and captivating adventures. As a result, his *Golden Legend*, intended as devotional reading, became one of the best-sellers of its own and subsequent generations.

Theodora, a woman of noble rank, lived in Alexandria, in the time of the Emperor Zeno, and had for husband a rich and God-fearing man. The Devil however, being jealous of her holiness, aroused another rich man to lust after her; and he sent many messengers to her with presents, to persuade her to yield to him. But she repulsed the messengers and spurned the presents. So much did the man molest her, however, that she had no rest, and began to pine away. At length the man sent a sorceress to her, who urged her mightily to have compassion on him and to give her consent to him. She replied that never would she commit so grave a sin before the eyes of God, Who sees all; but to this the witch answered: "Whatsoever is done by day, God knows and sees, but the things that are done when day is ended and the sun is sinking, God sees not." Deceived by the sorceress' words, Theodora said that the man should come to her in the evening, and that she would do his will.

When these tidings were brought to the man, he exulted exceedingly; and coming to her at the appointed hour, he lay with her and then went away. Then Theodora, returning to herself, shed bitter tears, and struck herself in the face,

From Jacob of Voraigne, *The Golden Legend*, tr. Granger Ryan and Helmut Ripperger; New York, Longmans, Green & Co., 1941, pp. 539-543.

saying: "Alas, woe is me, for I have lost my soul and destroyed the beauty of my honor!" At his return, her husband found her desolate and mourning, and not knowing the reason thereof, sought to console her; but she would not be comforted.

The next morning, therefore, she went to a convent of nuns, and asked the abbess whether God could know a certain grave sin which she had committed at evenfall. "Nothing can be hidden from God," said the abbess, "and God knows and sees all that is done, no matter what the hour." Weeping sorrowfully, Theodora answered: "Give me the book of the holy Gospel, that I may know my lot." And when she opened the book, she read: "What I have written, I have written." Then she returned to her home; and some days later, when her husband was absent, she cut off her hair, put on the vesture of a man, and hastened to a monastery of monks, about eight miles distant from the city. There she begged to be received among the monks, and her request was granted; and when they asked her name, she said that she was called Theodore. In the monastery she fulfilled all her duties with humility, and her service was pleasing to all.

After several years had passed, the abbot summoned Brother Theodore, and commanded him to yoke the oxen and to bring a tun of oil from the city. Meanwhile her husband spent himself in tears, fearing that she had departed with another man. Then an angel of the Lord said to him: "Arise in the morning, and stand in the street called the Martyrdom of Peter the Apostle, and the one who will come toward thee will be thy wife." This he did, and Theodora came that way with her camels, and saw and recognized her husband, and said within herself: "Alas, alas, my good husband, how much do I toil to expiate the sin that I committed against thee!" But when she came near to him, she merely greeted him, saying: "A blessing upon thee, my lord!" Her husband, however, knew her not, and waited for her all that day and night. Then he cried out that he had been deceived, but a voice said to him: "The one who greeted thee yestermorning was thy wife."

So great was the blessed Theodora's sanctity that she wrought many miracles. Thus she rescued a man who had been torn by a wild beast, and by her prayers restored him to life and then she pursued the beast and cursed him, and the animal fell dead at once. The Devil, being unable to bear her holiness, appeared to her and said: "Most degraded and adulterous of women, thou has abandoned thy husband to come here and to heap contempt upon me but by my dread powers I shall stir up strife against thee, and if I fail to make thee deny thy Crucified, say that I exist not!" At this she made the sign of the cross, and instantly the Devil vanished.

Then, one day, as she was returning from the city with her camels, and took shelter in a certain house, a girl came to her and said: "Lie with me!" Theodora repulsed her, and she went to another and lay with him; and when she became big with child, she was asked of whom she had conceived, and said: "That monk Theodore slept with me!" When the child was born, they carried it to the abbot of the monastery. The abbot sternly rebuked Theodore, and, when the latter pleaded for pardon, laid the child upon his shoulders and drove him out of the monastery.

Thereafter Theodora remained for seven years outside of the monastery, and nurtured the child with the milk of the flocks. Envying her great patience, the Devil appeared to her in the semblance of her husband, and said to her: "What dost thou here, my lady? Behold, I languish with yearning for thee, and have no consolation. Come then, my light, for even if thou hast consorted with another man, I forgive thee!" But she, thinking that it was her husband, said to him: "No more shall I dwell with thee, for the son of John the knight has lain with me, and I wish to do penance for the wrong I have done thee!" Then she prayed, and he vanished at once, and she knew it had been the Devil. Another time the demons appeared to her in the form of savage beasts, and a man drove them on and said: "Devour that whore!" But at her prayer they vanished; and in like manner she conquered the Devil many other times.

When the seven years had passed, the abbot, giving consideration to Theodora's patience, reconciled her, and received her back into the monastery with the child. After two years, during which she lived a praiseworthy life, she took the boy into her cell, and closed the door; whereupon the abbot posted monks to hear what she would say to him. Then she embraced and kissed the child, and said: "Sweet my son, the end of my life approaches, and I leave thee to God, Who shall be thy Father and thy Helper. Sweetest son, persevere in fasting and prayer, and serve thy brethren devoutly!" With these words she breathed forth her spirit, and fell asleep happily in the Lord, about the year 470. And the boy, seeing her dead, wept with abandon.

That very night, the following vision was shown to the abbot. He saw a great wedding feast prepared, whither came the orders of the angels and the prophets and the martyrs and all the saints. In their midst was a woman alone, surrounded with ineffable glory; and she came to the wedding, and sat upon the couch, and all stood nigh and called upon her. And a voice proclaimed: "Behold the monk Theodore, who was falsely accused of begetting a child! . . . She was chastised because she had defiled her husband's bed!" Awakening, the abbot hastened to her cell with the brethren, and found her dead; and going in, they uncovered her, and discovered that she was a woman. Then the abbot called the father of the girl who had defamed her, and said to him: "Thy daughter's husband is dead!" And he drew back the coverings, and showed him that she was a woman. And a great fear came upon all who heard this. Then an angel of the Lord said to the abbot: "Arise speedily, mount thy horse, and go into the city; and if anyone come toward thee, lead him hither!" And as he rode into the city, a man came turning toward him. When the abbot asked him whither he was going, he answered; "My wife is dead, and I go to see her!" The abbot therefore took Theodora's husband upon his horse, and when they came to Theodora, they both wept exceedingly. Then they buried her with many praises. Then the husband took his wife's cell, and abode therein for two years, until he fell asleep in the Lord. As for the child, he followed in the footsteps of his foster-mother, and shone with the probity of his life; wherefore, when the abbot died, the monks, with one voice, elected him their abbot.

La Tour-Landry: A Marriage Proposal

According to medieval canon law—the law of the Church—no marriage ceremony could take place without the consent of both the bride and the groom. Virtually all marriages in the higher reaches of society were products of negotiations between the bride's and groom's parents, with the goal of enhancing the wealth or prestige (or both) of the families involved. But some marriages, although ideal with regard to family strategies, might be objectionable to one or the other of the intended marriage partners. If either chose not to enter the marriage, and if they had the fortitude to upset their parents' plan, they enjoyed the full backing of canon law. Such was the case in the present excerpt, taken from *The Book of the Knight* (1371) by Geoffrey de La Tour-Landry. It may well be significant that La Tour-Landry wrote this book for the instruction of his daughters.

It happened that my friends urged me to be married into a noble place, and my father brought me to see her that I should have, and there we had great cheer, and my father set me to talking to her, that I might have greater knowledge of her manners, and so we fell to talking of prisoners. "Damsel," I said, "it would be better to fall to be your prisoner than to marry another, for I trust your prison should not be so hard to me as it would be were I taken by Englishmen." And she answered, "I have seen some not long since that I wish had been my prisoner." "Would you," I asked, "put them in some evil prison?" "No," said she, "I would keep them as I would my own body." I said, "Happy is he that might come into so noble a prison." What shall I say? She loved me enough, and had a quick eye, and there were many words. And so at last she became quite familiar with me, for she asked me two or three times not to wait long before coming to see her again. And at this I marveled, seeing that I was never acquainted with her, nor had I spoken with her before that time; and she knew well that folk were about to marry us together.

When we were parted my father asked me, "How do you like her? Tell me your opinion." And I said she was both good and fair, but she should be to me no nearer than she was. And I told my father how it seemed to me, about her estate and language; and so I said I would not have her, for she was so pert and light of manners that she caused me to be displeased with her, for which I have thanked God many times since.

From *Chaucer's World*, ed. Edith Rickert, New York Columbia University Press, 1948, pp. 52-53.

READING 7

Giovanni Morelli, *Memoir*

These words of warning, dating from 1403, disclose clearly that
wives normally had certain property under their own control. A
husband could not legally touch this property except, as in the
present instance, by browbeating and intimidating his wife.
Notice the irritation of the wife's relatives, who themselves would
have retained some interest in the property had she not consigned
it to her husband.

My sister Sandra's financial undoing came about through the fault of her
husband, Jacopo, because of the bad state of his business affairs, but also through
her own fault and foolishness in being too obedient to her husband. Seeing him in
need, she went too far and pledged several farms that were in her name, without
saying a word of this to us, her brothers, or to any other friend or relative. This too
was Jacopo's fault. Knowing how obedient and sweet she was, he did not warn her
but like a culprit would take her by surprise, arriving with a notary and witnesses,
looking very upset, and urging her to the transaction. Through fear and obedience
and because she was ashamed to deny her husband in the presence of others, she did
as she was told, although she suspected she was making a mistake. The outcome
is that she has been living in our house for some time now as a young widow with
a twelve-year-son and no dowry, and if God does not send us some remedy she is
likely to be here a good deal longer.

I decided to write this down for the benefit of whoever reads it as a warning that
no one, man or woman, should ever divest rights or property either from fear, or
flattery, or some other motive.

From Julia O'Faolain and Lauro Martines, *Not in God's Image*; New York, Harper & Row,
1973, pp. 169-170.

READING 8

Papal Protection of the Jews:
A Bull of Gregory X, 1272

In this papal letter addressed to all Christians, Gregory X (1271-1276) repeats the legislation of previous popes and then (as indicated in the letter) adds some important provisions of his own. Papal policy toward the Jews tended to shield them from local and regional anti-Semitic violence. Most Jewish leaders in Western Christendom, having few options, placed themselves and their people under direct papal protection (as against the authority of kings and local magnates). At the same time, the Jews promised full compliance with papal demands and exactions, which could at times be heavy.

Gregory, bishop, servant of the servants of God, extends greetings and the apostolic benediction to the beloved sons in Christ, the faithful Christians, to those here now and to those in the future. Even as it is not allowed to the Jews in their assemblies presumptuously to undertake for themselves more than that which is permitted them by law, even so they ought not to suffer any disadvantage in those [privileges] which have been granted them. Although they prefer to persist in their stubbornness rather than to recognize the words of their prophets and the mysteries of the Scriptures, and thus to arrive at a knowledge of Christian faith and salvation; nevertheless, inasmuch as they have made an appeal for our protection and help, we therefore admit their petition and offer them the shield of our protection through the clemency of Christian piety. In so doing we follow in the footsteps of our predecessors of blessed memory, the popes of Rome—Calixtus, Eugene, Alexander, Clement, Celestine, Innocent, and Honorius.

We decree moreover that no Christian shall compel them or any one of their group to come to baptism unwillingly. But if any one of them shall take refuge of his own accord with Christians, because of conviction, then, after his intention will have been manifest, he shall be made a Christian without any intrigue. For, indeed, that person who is known to have come to Christian baptism not freely, but unwillingly, is not believed to possess the Christian faith.

Moreover no Christian shall presume to seize, imprison, wound, torture, mutilate, kill, or inflict violence on them; furthermore no one shall presume, except by judicial action of the authorities of the country, to change the good customs in the land where they live for the purpose of taking their money or goods from them or from others.

In addition, no one shall disturb them in any way during the celebration of their festivals, whether by day or by night, with clubs or stones or anything else. Also no

From *The Jew in the Medieval World*, R.J. Marcus, ed.; Cincinnati, Sinai Press, 1938, pp. 152-154.

one shall exact any compulsory service of them unless it be that which they have been accustomed to render in previous times. [Up to this point Gregory X has merely repeated the bull of his predecessors.]

Inasmuch as the Jews are not able to bear witness against the Christians, we decree furthermore that the testimony of Christians against Jews shall not be valid unless there is among these Christians some Jew who is there for the purpose of offering testimony.

Since it happens occasionally that some Christians lose their Christian children, the Jews are accused by their enemies of secretly carrying off and killing these same Christian children and of making sacrifices of the heart and blood of these very children. It happens, too, that the parents of these children, or some other Christian enemies of these Jews, secretly hide these very children in order that they may be able to injure these Jews, and in order that they may be able to extort from them a certain amount of money by redeeming them from their straits. [Following the lead of Innocent IV, 1247, Gregory attacks the ritual murder charge at length.]

And most falsely do these Christians claim that the Jews have secretly and furtively carried away these children and killed them, and that the Jews offer sacrifice from the heart and the blood of these children, since their law in this matter precisely and expressly forbids Jews to sacrifice, eat, or drink the blood, or to eat the flesh of animals having claws. This has been demonstrated many times at our court by Jews converted to the Christian faith: nevertheless very many Jews are often seized and detained unjustly because of this.

We decree, therefore, that Christians need not be obeyed against Jews in a case or situation of this type, and we order that Jews seized under such a silly pretext be freed from imprisonment, and that they shall not be arrested henceforth on such a miserable pretext, unless—which we do not believe—they be caught in the commission of the crime. We decree that no Christian shall stir up anything new against them, but that they should be maintained in that status and position in which they were in the time of our predecessors, from antiquity till now.

We decree, in order to stop the wickedness and avarice of bad men, that no one shall dare to devastate or to destroy a cemetery of the Jews or to dig up human bodies for the sake of getting money. [The Jews had to pay a ransom before the bodies of their dead were restored to them.] Moreover, if any one, after having known the content of this decree, should—which we hope will not happen—attempt audaciously to act contrary to it, then let him suffer punishment in his rank and position, or let him be punished by the penalty of excommunication, unless he makes amends for his boldness by proper recompense. Moreover, we wish that only those Jews who have not attempted to contrive anything toward the destruction of the Christian faith be fortified by the support of such protection . . . .

Given at Orvieto by the hand of the Magister John Lectator, vice-chancellor of the Holy Roman Church, on the 7th of October, in the first indiction [cycle of fifteen years], in the year 1272 of the divine incarnation, in the first year of the pontificate of our master, the Pope Gregory X.

READING 9

An Account of the
English Peasants' Revolt, 1381

This detailed description is drawn from the *Anonimalle Chronicle,* written in French by an unknown monk of St. Mary's, York. It is the most authoritative surviving history of the revolt and may well have drawn some of its information from a lost London chronicle. The writer was a contemporary, and, notwithstanding his obvious hostility toward the rebels, his account is generally trustworthy. A careful examination of the rebels' goals will suggest the reasons for his hostility.

The author uses the term "commons" (lowercase) to mean "common folk," not members of Parliament.

In the year 1381, because the subsidies[1] were lightly granted at the parliament and because various lords and commons were advised that the subsidies were not duly or loyally levied, but commonly extracted from the poor and not from the rich, the king's council ordained certain commissions to make inquiry into each township how they were levied. One of these commissions was sent to Essex to a certain Thomas Brampton,[2] who was regarded as a king or great magnate in that area because of the great estate that he kept. He had summoned before him a hundred of the neighboring townships, and wished to have from them a new subsidy. Then the men came together to the number of a hundred or more; on this Thomas ordered them put into prison; and the commons rose against him and would not be arrested, but tried to kill Thomas. And because of these doings Sir Robert Belknap, chief justice of the Common Pleas of our lord the king, was sent to the shire with a commission of inquiry and indictments against various persons. Therefore the commons rose against him and came before him and told him that he was a traitor to the king and the realm. [The peasants killed certain royal officials] as an example to others; for it was their purpose to slay all lawyers and all jurors and all the servants of the king they could find.

[The revolt spread in central and eastern England. Large masses of peasants and poor laborers converged on London, hoping for aid from the king.]

From *The Great Revolt 1381,* C.W.C. Oman, Oxford, The Clarendon Press, 1906, pp. 186-205. Revised by J.W. Leedom.

[1]A newly enacted, unprecedented poll tax—i.e., a tax on all individuals. The idea was dropped after the revolt of 1381; its revival, in 1990, contributed to the fall of Prime Minister Margaret Thatcher.

[2]A royal tax collector.

At the same time the commons of Kent razed various places and tenements of the people who would not rise with them. They laid siege with energy to Rochester Castle, and the constable defended himself vigorously for half a day, but at last, for fear that he had of the multitude of men deaf to reason, he delivered up the castle to them. And there they made their chief a certain Wat Tyler of Maidstone to maintain them and be their counsellor. And on the next Monday they came to Canterbury [on 10 June], and 4,000 of them entered into the church of St. Thomas and, kneeling down, they cried with one voice on the monks to elect a monk to be archbishop of Canterbury, "for he who is now archbishop is a traitor, and will be beheaded for his iniquity." And when they had done this, the commons went into the town to their fellows, and they summoned the mayor and the bailiffs to swear to be faithful and loyal to King Richard and to the true commons of England. And afterwards they took 500 men of the town with them to London.

At this time the commons had as their counsellor a chaplain of evil disposition named Sir John Ball, who advised them to get rid of all the lords, and of the archbishops and bishops, and abbots, and priors, and most of the monks and canons, saying that their possessions should be distributed among the laity, for which statements he was esteemed among the commons as a prophet, and labored with them to strengthen them in their malice—and a fit reward he got, when he was hanged, drawn, and quartered, and beheaded as a traitor.

At this time the king was in a turret of the great Tower of London, and could see the manor of the Savoy[3] and the Hospital of Clerkenwell, and the house of Simon Hosteler near Newgate, all on fire at once. And next day, Friday, the commons of the countryside and the commons of London assembled in fearful strength, to the number of 100,000 or more. And some came to Tower Hill, and when the king knew that they were there, he sent them orders by messenger to join their friends at Mile End, saying that he would come to them very soon.

And at this time the king proclaimed to them that he would confirm and grant it that they should be free, and generally should have their will, and that they might go through all the realm and catch all the traitors and bring them to him in safety, and then he would deal with them as the law demanded. Under color of this grant Wat Tyler and some of the commons took their way to the tower, to seize the archbishop. There they cut off the heads of Master Simon Sudbury, the archbishop of Canterbury,[4] and of Sir Robert Hales, Prior of the Hospital of St. John's, treasurer of England, and of Sir William Appleton, a great lawyer and surgeon.

At this moment the mayor of London came up, and the king bade him go to the commons and make their chieftain come to him. And when he was summoned, he came to the king with great confidence, mounted on a little horse so the commons could see him. And he dismounted, holding in his hand a dagger which he had taken from another man, and when he had dismounted he half bent his knee, and

[3]The London residence of the Duke of Lancaster, John of Gaunt; the present location of one of London's finest and most expensive hotels, the "Savoy."

[4]Archbishop Simon Sudbury was also the king's chancellor.

then took the king by the hand, saying to him, "Brother, be of good comfort and joyful, for you shall have, in the fortnight to come, praise from the commons even more than you have yet had, and we shall be good companions." And the king said, "Why will you not go back to your own country?" But the other answered with a great oath that neither he nor his fellows would depart until they had got their charter such as they wished to have it. And he [Wat Tyler] asked that from henceforth there should be no outlawry, and that no lord should have lordship save civilly, and that there should be equality among all people save only the king, and that the goods of the holy Church should not remain in the hands of the religious people, nor of parsons and vicars; but that the clergy already in possession should have a sufficient sustenance, and the rest of the goods should be divided among the people of the parish. And he demanded that there should be no more villeins in England, and no serfdom or villeinage, but that all men should be free and of one condition. To this the king gave an easy answer, and said that he should have all that he could fairly grant, reserving for himself only the regality of his crown; and then he bade him to go back to his home, without making further delay.

At this time a certain valet from Kent, who was in the king's retinue, asked that the said Wat might be pointed out to him; and when he saw him, he said aloud that he knew him for the greatest thief and robber in all Kent. And for these words Wat tried to strike him with his dagger; but because he strove to do so, the mayor of London, William Walworth, reasoned with the said Wat for his own violent behavior and spite, done in the king's presence, and arrested him. And at this Wat stabbed the mayor with his dagger in the stomach with great wrath; but, as it pleased God, the mayor was wearing armor and took no harm, but like a hardy and vigorous man drew his cutlass, and struck back at the said Wat and gave him a deep cut on the neck, and then a great cut on the head. And during this scuffle one of the king's household drew his sword, and ran Wat two or three times through the body, mortally wounding him.

And when the commons saw their chieftain, Wat Tyler, was dead in such a manner, they fell to the ground there among the wheat, like beaten men, imploring the king for mercy for their misdeeds. And the king granted them mercy, and most of them took to flight.

And afterwards the king sent out his messengers into diverse parts, to capture the malefactors and put them to death. And many were taken and hanged at London, and they set up many gallows around the city of London, and in other cities and boroughs of the south country. At last, as it pleased God, the king, seeing that too many of his liege subjects would be undone, and too much blood spilled, took pity in his heart, and granted them all pardon, on condition that they should never rise again, under pain of losing life or limb, and that each of them should buy his charter of pardon, and pay the king as fee for his seal [on the charter] twenty shillings, to make him rich. And so finished this wicked war.

CHAPTER 7

NEW PATHS TO GOD: MONKS AND PHILOSOPHERS

The Cistercians, whose greatest representative in the twelfth century, St. Bernard abbot of Clairvaux (document 1), we encountered in the previous chapter ⌈consti-tuted a drastically reformed version of Benedictine monasticism.⌉ Francis of Assisi (*c*. 1182-1226), perhaps the most beloved saint of the High Middle Ages, broke with the cloistered tradition of Benedictine monasticism altogether, and his order refused gifts of manors. St. Francis himself was an unassuming, impetuous person. The Franciscan rule of 1223 (document 2) reflects an effort by the papacy to provide the order with a logical organizational structure alien to Francis himself but perhaps necessary for the survival of his order. Francis was a town dweller, and he and his followers placed strong emphasis on preaching and serving in towns. The intense urban piety that inspired them also gave rise to the first major heretical movements since late antiquity. The Albigensians and Waldensians, although condemned by the papacy, flourished in the towns of southern Europe (documents 3 and 4). Against them and others, the cause of Catholic orthodoxy was upheld and strongly asserted at the Fourth Lateran Council (1215), convened and chaired by the ablest pope of the High Middle Ages, Innocent III (document 5).

The second half of this chapter is devoted to the major philosophers and philosophical issues of the High Middle Ages. St. Anselm (d. 1109), the most important speculative philosopher of his generation, was a monk of deep piety, penetrating intellect, and political acumen whose "ontological proof" of God (document 6), although rejected by some high-medieval theologians (including Thomas Aquinas), was used by Descartes, who plagiarized only from the best. Anselm's argument seems at first sight a bit silly, but it is not easily dismissed. Our excerpt from the writing of Peter Abelard (d. 1142) exemplifies the twelfth-century shift from monastic schools to urban schools. Abelard's *Sic et non* (document 7) bears witness to the new spirit of intellectual debate in the urban schools, although Abelard carried the idea of debate farther than most. Hollister's *Medieval Europe* presents one of the five celebrated arguments of St. Thomas Aquinas (d. 1274) for the existence of God; all five are presented here (document 8). St. Thomas Aquinas has traditionally been regarded as the spokesman of thirteenth-century Catholic theology, but he was opposed by theologians in his own day and several of his opinions were condemned among the philosophical positions rejected by Etienne Tempier, bishop of Paris, in 1277, three years after Aquinas's death (document 9).

The final passage, William of Ockham (d. 1349) on "universals"—one of the central themes of high medieval philosophy—breaks the chronological boundaries set forth in the text but is valuable in showing the chill that fourteenth-century skepticism, as exemplified in Ockham, cast on the heady optimism of thirteenth-century scholasticism (document 10).

READING 1

A Description of Clairvaux

Clairvaux, one of the earliest Cistercian daughter houses, had the celebrated St. Bernard (1090-1153) as its first abbot. This contemporary description portrays one of the characteristic and most important of the early twelfth-century Cistercian monasteries.

At the first glance as you entered Clairvaux by descending the hill you could see that it was a temple of God; and the still, silent valley bespoke, in the modest simplicity of its buildings, the unfeigned humility of Christ's poor. Moreover, in this valley full of men, where no one was permitted to be idle, where one and all were occupied with their allotted tasks, a silence deep as that of night prevailed. The sounds of labor, or the chants of the brethren in the choral service, were the only exceptions. The orderliness of this silence, and the report that went forth concerning it, struck such a reverence even into secular persons that they dreaded breaking it,—I will not say by idle or wicked conversation, but even by proper remarks. The solitude, also, of the place—between dense forests in a narrow gorge of neighboring hills—in a certain sense recalled the cave of our father St. Benedict,[1] so that while they strove to imitate his life, they also had some similarity to him in their habitation and loneliness. . . .

Although the monastery is situated in a valley, it has its foundations on the holy hills, whose gates the Lord loveth more than all the dwellings of Jacob. Glorious things are spoken of it, because the glorious and wonderful God therein worketh great marvels. There the insane recover their reason, and although their outward man is worn away, inwardly they are born again. There the proud are humbled, the rich are made poor, and the poor have the Gospel preached to them, and the darkness of sinners is changed into light. A large multitude of blessed poor from the ends of the earth have there assembled, yet have they one heart and one mind; justly, therefore, do all who dwell there rejoice with no empty joy. They have the certain hope of perennial joy, of their ascension heavenward already commenced. In Clairvaux, they have found Jacob's ladder, with angels upon it some descending, who so provide for their bodies that they faint not on the way; others ascending, who so rule their souls that their bodies hereafter may be glorified with them.

For my part, the more attentively I watch them day by day, the more do I believe that they are perfect followers of Christ in all things. When they pray and speak to

From *A Source Book of Mediaeval History*, ed. Frederic Austin Ogg; New York, American Book Company, 1907, pp. 258-60.

[1]The famous founder of the monastery of Monte Cassino and the compiler of the Benedictine Rule.

God in spirit and in truth, by their friendly and quiet speech to Him, as well as by their humbleness of demeanor, they are plainly seen to be God's companions and friends. When, on the other hand, they openly praise God with psalms, how pure and fervent are their minds, is shown by their posture of body in holy fear and reverence, while by their careful pronunciation and modulation of the psalms, is shown how sweet to their lips are the words of God—sweeter than honey to their mouths. As I watch them, therefore, singing without fatigue from before midnight to the dawn of day, with only a brief interval, they appear a little less than the angels, but much more than men. . . .

As regards their manual labor, so patiently and placidly, with such quiet countenances, in such sweet and holy order, do they perform all things, that although they exercise themselves at many works, they never seem moved or burdened in anything, whatever the labor may be. Whence it is manifest that that Holy Spirit worketh in them who disposeth of all things with sweetness, in whom they are refreshed, so that they rest even in their toil. Many of them, I hear, are bishops and earls, and many illustrious through their birth or knowledge; but now, by God's grace, all distinction of persons being dead among them, the greater any one thought himself in the world, the more in this flock does he regard himself as less than the least. I see them in the garden with hoes, in the meadows with forks or rakes, in the fields with scythes, in the forest with axes. To judge from their outward appearance, their tools, their bad and disordered clothes, they appear a race of fools, without speech or sense. But a true thought in my mind tells me that their life in Christ is hidden in the heavens. Among them I see Godfrey of Peronne, Raynald of Picardy, William of St. Omer, Walter of Lisle, all of whom I knew formerly in the old man, whereof I now see no trace, by God's favor. I knew them proud and puffed up; I see them walking humbly under the merciful hand of God.

READING 2

The Rule of St. Francis, 1223

St. Francis (1181-1226), son of a cloth merchant of the Italian hillside town of Assisi, founded a religious order that differed significantly from traditional Benedictine monasticism. His followers, the Friars Minor (Lesser Brothers) were bound to both individual and corporate poverty. Instead of being cloistered in a monastery, they worked and preached in the outside world,

From *A Source Book for Mediaeval History*, ed. O.J. Thatcher and E.H. McNeal; New York, 1905, pp. 498-504.

particularly in cities. In 1210 Francis won the provisional approval of Pope Innocent III for his brief, simple Rule consisting of
carefully chosen quotations from the Bible. The Franciscan Order
grew so swiftly during the following decade that the original Rule
of 1210 no longer sufficed. The more elaborate Rule of 1223,
issued in Francis's name, was prepared by others under the
authorization of Innocent's successor, Pope Honorius III. It
preserves Francis's basic ideals but frames them in a much more
coherent organizational structure with appropriate jurisdictional
safeguards. The document should be read with an effort to
untangle the original ideals form the later structure.

1. This is the rule and life of the Minor Brothers, namely, to observe the holy
gospel of our Lord Jesus Christ by living in obedience, in poverty, and in chastity.
Brother Francis promises obedience and reverence to Pope Honorius and to his
successors who shall be canonically elected, and to the Roman Church. The other
brothers are bound to obey brother Francis, and his successors.

2. If any, wishing to adopt this life, come to our brothers [to ask admission],
they shall be sent to the provincial ministers, who alone have the right to receive
others into the order. The provincial ministers shall carefully examine them in the
catholic faith and the sacraments of the church. And if they believe all these and
faithfully confess them and promise to observe them to the end of life, and if they
have no wives, or if they have wives, and the wives have either already entered a
monastery, or have received permission to do so, and they have already taken the
vow of chastity with the permission of the bishop of the diocese [in which they
live], and their wives are of such an age that no suspicion can rise against them, let
the provincial ministers repeat to them the word of the holy gospel, to go and sell
all their goods and give to the poor [Matt. 19:21]. But if they are not able to do so,
their good will is sufficient for them. And the brothers and provincial ministers
shall not be solicitous about the temporal possessions of those who wish to enter
the order; but let them do with their possessions whatever the Lord may put into
their minds to do. Nevertheless, if they ask the advice of the brothers, the
provincial ministers may send them to God-fearing men, at whose advice they may
give their possessions to the poor. The ministers shall give them the dress of a
novice, namely: two robes without a hood, a girdle, trousers, a hood with a cape
reaching to the girdle. But the ministers may add to these if they think it necessary.
After the year of probation is ended they shall be received into obedience [that is,
into the order], by promising to observe this rule and life forever. And according
to the command of the pope they shall never be permitted to leave the order and
give up this life and form of religion. For according to the holy gospel no one who
puts his hand to the plough and looks back is fit for the kingdom of God [Luke

9:62]. And after they have promised obedience, those who wish may have one robe with a hood and one without a hood. Those who must may wear shoes, and all the brothers shall wear common clothes, and they shall have God's blessing if they patch them with coarse cloth and pieces of other kinds of cloth. But I warn and exhort them not to despise nor judge other men who wear fine and gay clothing, and have delicious foods and drinks. But rather let each one judge and despise himself.

3. The clerical brothers shall perform the divine office according to the rite of the holy Roman church, except the psalter, from which they may have breviaries. The lay brothers shall say 24 Paternosters at matins, 5 at lauds, 7 each at primes, terces, sexts, and nones, 12 at vespers, 7 at completorium, and prayers for the dead. And they shall fast from All Saints' day [November 1] to Christmas. They may observe or not, as they choose, the holy Lent which begins at epiphany [January 6] and lasts for 40 days, and which our Lord consecrated by his holy fasts. Those who keep it shall be blessed of the Lord, but those who do not wish to keep it are not bound to do so. But they shall all observe the other Lent [that is, from Ash Wednesday to Easter]. The rest of the time the brothers are bound to fast only on Fridays. But in times of manifest necessity they shall not fast. But I counsel, warn, and exhort my brothers in the Lord Jesus Christ that when they go out into the world they shall not be quarrelsome or contentious, nor judge others. But they shall be gentle, peaceable, and kind, mild and humble, and virtuous in speech, as is becoming to all. They shall not ride on horseback unless compelled by manifest necessity or infirmity to do so. When they enter a house they shall say, "Peace be to this house." According to the holy gospel, they may eat of whatever food is set before them.

4. I strictly forbid all the brothers to accept money or property either in person or through another. Nevertheless, for the needs of the sick, and for clothing the other brothers, the ministers and guardians may, as they see that necessity requires, provide through spiritual friends, according to the locality, season, and the degree of cold which may be expected in the region where they live. But, as has been said, they shall never receive money or property.

5. Those brothers to whom the Lord has given the ability to work shall work faithfully and devotedly, so that idleness, which is the enemy of the soul, may be excluded and not extinguish the spirit of prayer and devotion to which all temporal things should be subservient. As the price of their labors they may receive things that are necessary for themselves and the brothers, but not money or property. And they shall humbly receive what is given them, as is becoming to the servants of God and to those who practise the most holy poverty.

6. The brothers shall have nothing of their own, neither house, nor land, nor anything, but as pilgrims and strangers in this world, serving the Lord in poverty and humility, let them confidently go asking alms. Nor let them be ashamed of this, for the Lord made himself poor for us in this world. This is that highest pitch of poverty which has made you, my dearest brothers, heirs and kings of the kingdom of heaven, which has made you poor in goods, and exalted you in virtues. Let this

be your portion, which leads into the land of the living. Cling wholly to this, my most beloved brothers, and you shall wish to have in this world nothing else than the name of the Lord Jesus Christ. And wherever they are, if they find brothers, let them show themselves to be of the same household, and each one may securely make known to the other his need. For if a mother loves and nourishes her child, how much more diligently should one nourish and love one's spiritual brother? And if any of them fall ill, the other brothers should serve them as they would wish to be served.

7. If any brother is tempted by the devil and commits a mortal sin, he should go as quickly as possible to the provincial minister, as the brothers have determined that recourse shall be had to the provincial ministers for such sins. If the provincial minister is a priest, he shall mercifully prescribe the penance for him. If he is not a priest, he shall, as may seem best to him, have some priest of the order prescribe the penance. And they shall guard against being angry or irritated about it, because anger and irritation hinder love in themselves and in others.

8. All the brothers must have one of their number as their general minister and servant of the whole brotherhood, and they must obey him. At his death the provincial ministers and guardians shall elect his successor at the chapter held at Pentecost, at which time all the provincial ministers must always come together at whatever place the general minister may order. And this chapter must be held once every three years, or more or less frequently, as the general minister may think best. And if at any time it shall be clear to the provincial ministers and guardians that the general minister is not able to perform the duties of his office and does not serve the best interests of the brothers, the aforesaid brothers, to whom the right of election is given, must, in the name of the Lord, elect another as general minister. After the chapter at Pentecost, the provincial ministers and guardians may, each in his own province, if it seems best to them, once in the same year convoke the brothers to a provincial chapter.

9. If a bishop forbids the brothers to preach in his diocese, they shall obey him. And no brother shall preach to the people unless the general minister of the brotherhood has examined and approved him and given him the right to preach. I also warn the brothers that in their sermons their words shall be chaste and well chosen for the profit and edification of the people. They shall speak to them of vices and virtues, punishment and glory, with brevity of speech, because the Lord made the word shortened over the earth [Rom. 9:28].

10. The ministers and servants shall visit and admonish their brothers and humbly and lovingly correct them. They shall not put any command upon them that would be against their soul and this rule. And the brothers who are subject must remember that for God's sake they have given up their own wills. Wherefore I command them to obey their ministers in all the things which they have promised the Lord to observe and which shall not be contrary to their souls and this rule. And whenever brothers know and recognize that they cannot observe this rule, let them go to their ministers, and the ministers shall lovingly and kindly receive them and

treat them in such a way that the brothers may speak to them freely and treat them as lords speak to, and treat, their servants. For the ministers ought to be the servants of all the brothers. I warn and exhort the brothers in the Lord Jesus Christ to guard against all arrogance, pride, envy, avarice, care, and solicitude for this world, detraction, and murmuring. And those who cannot read need not be anxious to learn. But above all things let them desire to have the spirit of the Lord and his holy works, to pray always to God with a pure heart, and to have humility, and patience in persecution and in infirmity, and to love those who persecute us and reproach us and blame us. For the Lord says, "Love your enemies and pray for those who persecute and speak evil of you" [cf. Matt. 5:44]. "Blessed are they who suffer persecution for righteousness' sake, for theirs is the kingdom of heaven" [Matt. 5:10]. He that endureth to the end shall be saved [Matt. 10:22].

11. I strictly forbid all the brothers to have any association or conversation with women that may cause suspicion. And let them not enter nunneries, except those which the pope has given them special permission to enter. Let them not be intimate friends of men or women, lest on this account scandal arise among the brothers or about brothers.

12. If any of the brothers shall be divinely inspired to go among Saracens and other infidels they must get the permission to go from their provincial minister, who shall give his consent only to those who he sees are suitable to be sent. In addition, I command the ministers to ask the pope to assign them a cardinal of the holy Roman church, who shall be the guide, protector, and corrector of the holy church, and steadfast in the catholic faith, they may observe poverty, humility, and the holy gospel of our Lord Jesus Christ, as we have firmly promised to do. Let no man dare act contrary to this confirmation.

READING 3
An Account of the Albigensian Heresy

This account, written between 1208 and 1213, antedates the Fourth Lateran Council (Reading 5) by only a few years and helps explain the council's severely anti-Albigensian stance. Although it is more nearly a diatribe than an objective work of investigative reporting, it does make clear that, by Catholic standards, the Albigensian (or Cathar) beliefs were quite exotic. Blending Christian ideas with the religious dualism of ancient Persia, the

From *Heresies of the High Middle Ages*, ed. Walter L. Wakefield and Austin P. Evans; New York, Columbia University Press, 1969, pp. 231-235. Reprinted by permission.

Albigensians appear to have been not only anti-Catholic but anti-Semitic as well.

The question remains, to what extent can a document of this sort be trusted? Could one trust an analysis of the United States government in an Iraqi government newspaper? Or a discussion of Catholic doctrine written by an Albigensian? The answer is not simple. Perhaps one might expect such hostile testimony to be more or less accurate in its general outline but selective or deceptive in detail. To what degree does the following document provide a believable picture?

The group of heretics inhabiting our region, that is to say, the dioceses of Narbonne, Béziers, Carcassonne, Toulouse, Albi, Rodez, Cahors, Agen, and Perigueux [all in southern France], believe and have the effrontery to say that there are two gods, that is, a good God and a strange god, using the text of Jeremiah: "As you have forsaken me," He said, "and served a strange god in your own land, so you shall serve strangers in a land not your own." The present world and all that is visible therein, they declare, were created and made by the malign god, for they show by whatever arguments they can command that these are evil. Of the world they say that it is "wholly seated in wickedness," and that "a good tree cannot bring forth evil fruit, neither can an evil tree bring forth good fruit." They hold that all good things come from the good God and from the evil one all evil things. The Mosaic law, they say, was imparted by the evil god, for they cite from the words of the Apostle, "The Law is one of sin and death" and "worketh wrath." They declare that when Christ gave the bread to His disciples, He told them, "Take ye and eat," and, touching Himself with His hand, said, "This is my body"; wherefore they do not believe that anyone consecrates the Host. They speak slightingly of marriage of the flesh because Christ said, "Whoever shall look on a woman," and so on. They reject baptism of children performed with actual water because children do not have faith, for which they cite the Gospel, "He that believeth not shall be condemned." They do not believe in the resurrection of the bodies of this world, for Paul said, "Flesh and blood cannot possess the kingdom of God." Whatever is ritually observed in the Church Universal they call vain and absurd, for they hold that doctrine to be a thing of men and without basis, whereby one worships God in vain.

In their secret meetings their elders recount that the wicked god first fashioned his creatures and at the beginning of his act of creation, made four beings, two male and two female, a lion and a bee-eater, an eagle and a spirit. The good God took from him the spirit and the eagle and with them He produced the things which He made. After a long time, the malign god, enraged by his spoliation, sent a certain son of his, whom they call Melchizedek, Seir, or Lucifer, with a great and splendid host of men and women to the court of the good God, to find whether guile might not avenge his father for his own. And on beholding him distinguished in beauty and intelligence, the good God appointed him prince, priest, and steward over His own people, and through him gave a testament to the people of Israel. In the absence of the Lord, he beguiled the people into disbelief of the truth, promising them that much more, better, and delightful things than those which they had in their own land would be given them in his. They yielded to his blandishments, spurning their God and the testament given them. He bore away some of them and scattered them throughout his realms. The more noble, a designation which these people took to themselves, he sent into this world, which they call the last lake, the farthest earth, and the deepest hell. He sent the souls, so they say, leaving the bodies prostrate in the desert, abandoned by the spirits, for as John says in the Apocalypse, "The great dragon, that old serpent, devil and Satan, struck with his tail the third part of the stars and dashed them to earth." Such, they say, are "the sheep which are lost of the house of Israel," to whom Christ was sent, as He himself says in the Gospel: "The Son of man is come to seek and to save that which was lost"; and also, "The Son of man came not to destroy souls but to save." That Seir, as they assert, was the father of the lawgiver, for which they cite in the Law: "The Lord came from Sinai, and from Seir he was born to us"; and in Ezechiel, "Son of man, set thy face against Mount Seir, and prophesy concerning it, and say to it: Behold, Mount Seir, and I will make thee desolate and waste. I will destroy thy cities and thou shalt be desolate; and thou shalt know that I am the Lord, because thou hast been an everlasting enemy and hast shut up the children of Israel in the hands of the sword." Also, they say that the malign god exists without beginning or end, and rules as many and as extensive lands, heavens, people and creatures as the good God. The present world, they say, will never pass away or be depopulated. They have the daring to assert that the Blessed Mary, mother of Christ, was not of this world. For they say in their secret meetings that Christ, in whom they hope for salvation, was not in this world except in a spiritual sense within the body of Paul, citing Paul himself: "Do you seek a proof of Christ that speaketh in me?" For they say that Paul, "sold under sin," brought the Scriptures into this world and was held prisoner, that he might reveal the ministry of Christ.

For they believe that Christ was born in the "land of the living," of Joseph and Mary, whom they say were Adam and Eve; there He suffered and rose again; thence He ascended to His Father; there He did and said all that was recorded of Him in the New Testament. With this testament, and with His disciples, His father and mother, He passed through seven realms, and thence freed His people. In that land of the living, they believe, there are cities and outside them castles, villages and woodlands, meadows, pastures, sweet water and salt, beasts of the forest and domestic animals, dogs and birds for the hunt, gold and silver, utensils of various kinds, and furniture. They also say that everyone shall have his wife there and sometimes a mistress. They shall eat and drink, play and sleep, and do all things just as they do in the world of the present. And all will be, as they say, well pleasing to God when "the saints shall rejoice in glory; they shall be joyful in their beds," and when they shall have "two-edged swords in their hands to execute vengeance upon the nations," and when the children of Zion shall praise His name in choir and with the timbrel, for "this glory will be to all his saints." For God himself, they say, has two wives, Collam and Colibam, and from them He engendered sons and daughters, as do humans. On the basis of this belief, some of them hold there is no sin in man and woman kissing and embracing each other, or even lying together for intercourse, nor can one sin in doing so for payment.

They also believe that when the soul leaves the human body, it passes to another body, either of a human or of a beast, unless the person shall have died while under their instruction. If, however, he shall have died while continuing steadfast among them, they say that the soul goes to a new earth, prepared by God for all the souls that are to be saved, where it finds clothing, that is, the body prepared for it by its own father and mother. There all await the general resurrection which they shall experience, so they say, in the land of the living, with all their inheritance which they shall recover by force of arms. For they say that until then they shall possess that land of the malign spirit and shall make use of the clothing of the sheep, and shall eat the good things of the earth, and shall not depart thence until all Israel is saved. Also they teach in their secret meetings that Mary Magdalen was the wife of Christ. She was the Samaritan woman to whom He said, "Call thy husband." She was the woman taken in adultery, whom Christ set free lest the Jews stone her, and she was with Him in three places, in the temple, at the well, and in the garden. After the Resurrection, He appeared first to her. They say that John the Baptist is one of the chief malign spirits.

READING 4
An Account of the Waldensian Heresy

The same questions should be asked of this source as of the previous one. The author, Rainier Sacconi, was an inquisitor, and his testimony can therefore be expected to be both well informed and unsympathetic. Compare the canon of the Fourth Lateran Council (Reading 5) relating to the priest's role in the consecration of the eucharist.

The doctrines described here were first promulgated in the later twelfth century by a townsman of Lyons (southern France) named Valdes or "Waldo." He and his followers are customarily called

From *The Birth of Popular Heresy*, ed. and tr. R. I. Moore (Documents of Medieval History Series); London, Edward Arnold Ltd., 1975, pp. 144-145. Reprinted by permission.

"Waldensians" by modern historians but were known at the time as the "Poor Men of Lyons." Which of the two doctrines, Waldensian or Albigensian, came closest to anticipating modern Protestant beliefs?

We have said enough of the heresy of the Cathars. Now let us turn to that of the *Leonistae*, or Poor Men of Lyons. They are divided into two parts, the Poor Men from North of the Alps [*Pauperes Ultramontani*] and the Poor Men of Lombardy, the latter being descended from the former.

The first, the Poor Men from across the Alps, say that the New Testament prohibits all swearing as mortal sin. They also reject secular justice, on the ground that kings, princes and potentates ought not to punish evil-doers. They say that an ordinary layman may consecrate the body of the Lord, and I believe that they apply this to women as well for they have never denied it to me. They allege that the Roman Church is not the Church of Jesus Christ.

The Poor Men of Lombardy agree with the others about swearing and secular justice. On the eucharist they are even worse, holding that it may be consecrated by any man who is not in mortal sin. They say that the Roman Church is a church of evil, the beast and harlot which are found in the Book of Revelations, and that it is no sin to eat meat during Lent or on Friday against the precept of the Church, if it is done without offence to others.

They also say that the Church of Christ remained in bishops and other prelates until St. Sylvester, and failed in him, until they themselves restored it, though they do say there have always been some who have feared God and been saved. They believe that children can be saved without baptism.

This work was faithfully compiled by Brother Rainier in A.D. 1250. Deo Gratias.

READING 5

A Canon from the Fourth Lateran Council, 1215

In 1215 Pope Innocent III presided over a universal council of the Church at his Lateran basilica in Rome. More than 1200 prelates attended, including the Patriarchs of Jerusalem and recently conquered Constantinople, along with envoys from all the kingdoms and major principalities of Christendom. The canons

From *Disciplinary Decrees of the General Councils*, ed. and tr., H. J. Schroeder; St. Louis, B. Herder Book Co., 1937, pp. 242-244.

(decrees) of the Fourth Lateran Council reflect the efforts of the high-medieval papacy to reform, systematize, and standardize religious practice throughout Europe. Among other things, clerical dress was standardized; bishops were ordered to preach regularly and to maintain schools; priests were forbidden to participate in judicial ordeals and to charge fees for performing sacraments; lay people were commanded to do penance and receive the eucharist at least once a year.

The excerpt below illustrates the Church's concern over the spread of the Albigensian and Waldensian heresies, with their denial of papal authority and of the priesthood's exclusive power to perform the sacrament of the eucharist. Notice the emphasis on combating heresy by force, through the Albigensian Crusade (then in full gallop) and accompanying judicial proceedings. The Church's response to heresy bears some similarity to the response of modern states to treason.

CANON 3

We excommunicate and anathematize every heresy that raises itself against the holy, orthodox and Catholic faith which we have above explained; condemning all heretics under whatever name they may be known, for while they have different faces, they are nevertheless bound to each other by their tails, since in all of them vanity is a common element. Those condemned, being handed over to the secular rulers or their bailiffs, let them be abandoned, to be punished with due justice, clerics being first degraded from their orders. As to the property of the condemned, if they are laymen, let it be confiscated; if clerics, let it be applied to the churches from which they received revenues. But those who are only suspected, due consideration being given to the nature of the suspicion and the character of the person, unless they prove their innocence by a proper defense, let them be anathematized and avoided by all until they have made suitable satisfaction; but if they have been under excommunication for one year, then let them be condemned as heretics. Secular authorities, whatever office they may hold, shall be admonished and induced and if necessary compelled by ecclesiastical censure, that as they wish to be esteemed and numbered among the faithful, so for the defense of the faith they ought publicly to take an oath that they will strive in good faith and to the best of their ability to exterminate in the territories subject to their jurisdiction all heretics pointed out by the Church; so that whenever anyone shall have assumed authority, whether spiritual or temporal, let him be bound to confirm this decree by oath. But if a temporal ruler, after having been requested and admonished by the Church, should neglect to cleanse his territory of this heretical foulness, let him be excommunicated by the metropolitan and the other bishops of the province. If he refuses to make satisfaction within a year, let the matter be made known to the supreme pontiff, that he may declare the ruler's vassals absolved from their allegiance and may offer the territory to be ruled by Catholics, who on the extermination of the heretics may possess it without hindrance and preserve it in the purity of faith; the right, however, of the chief ruler is to be respected so long as he offers no obstacle in this matter and permits freedom of action. The same law is to be observed in regard to those who have no chief rulers (that is, are independent). Catholics who have girded themselves with the cross for the extermination of the heretics shall enjoy the indulgences and privileges granted to those who go in defense of the Holy Land.

We decree that those who give credence to the teachings of the heretics, as well as those who receive, defend, and patronize them, are excommunicated; and we firmly declare that after any one of them has been branded with excommunication, if he has deliberately failed to make satisfaction within a year, let him incur *ipso jure* the stigma of infamy and let him not be admitted to public offices or deliberations, and let him not take part in the election of others to such offices or use his right to give testimony in a court of law. Let him also be intestable, that he may not have the free exercise of making a will, and let him be deprived of the right of inheritance. Let no one be urged to give an account to him in any matter, but let him be urged to give an account to others. If perchance he be a judge, let his decisions have no force, nor let any case be brought to his attention. If he be an advocate, let his assistance by no means be sought. If a notary, let the instruments drawn up by him be considered worthless, for, the author being condemned, let them enjoy a similar fate. In all similar cases we command that the same be observed. If, however, he be a cleric, let him be deposed from every office and benefice, that the greater the fault the graver may be the punishment inflicted.

If any refuse to avoid such after they have been ostracized by the Church, let them be excommunicated till they have made suitable satisfaction. Clerics shall not give the sacraments of the Church to such pestilential people, nor shall they presume to give them Christian burial, or to receive their alms or offerings; otherwise they shall be deprived of their office, to which they may not be restored without a special indult of the Apostolic See. Similarly, all regulars, on whom also this punishment may be imposed, let their privileges be nullified in that diocese in which they have presumed to perpetrate such excesses.

But since some, under "the appearance of godliness, but denying the power thereof," as the Apostle says (II Tim, 3:5), arrogate to themselves the authority to preach, as the same Apostle says: "How shall they preach unless they be sent?" (Rom. 10:15), all those prohibited or not sent, who, without the authority of the Apostolic See or of the Catholic bishop of the locality, shall presume to usurp the office of preaching either publicly or privately, shall be excommunicated and unless they amend, and the sooner the better, they shall be visited with a further suitable penalty. We add, moreover, that every archbishop or bishop should himself or through his archdeacon or some other suitable persons, twice or at least once a year make the rounds of his diocese in which report has it that heretics dwell, and there compel three or more men of good character or, if it should be deemed advisable, the entire neighborhood, to swear that if anyone know of the presence there of heretics or others holding secret assemblies, or differing from the common way of the faithful in faith and morals, they will make them known to the bishop. The latter shall then call together before him those accused, who, if they do not purge themselves of the matter of which they are accused, or if after the rejection of their error they lapse into their former wickedness, shall be canonically punished. But if any of them by damnable obstinacy should disapprove of the oath and should perchance be unwilling to swear, from this very fact let them be regarded as heretics.

We wish, therefore, and in virtue of obedience strictly command, that to carry out these instructions effectively the bishops exercise through their dioceses a scrupulous vigilance if they wish to escape canonical punishment. If from sufficient evidence it is apparent that a bishop is negligent or remiss in cleansing his diocese of the ferment of heretical wickedness, let him be deposed from the episcopal office and let another, who will and can confound heretical depravity, be substituted.

READING 6

From St. Anselm's *Proslogion*

A native of northwestern Italy, St. Anselm (d. 1109) migrated to Normandy to become a monk, and later abbot, of the monastery of Bec. In 1093 he became archbishop of Canterbury and was twice exiled as a result of conflicts with the Anglo-Norman monarchy over ecclesiastical liberties.

Anselm was a devotee of St. Augustine (d. 430), who was himself influenced by Plato's doctrine of the superiority of meditation to observation. Notice that Anselm's ontological argument is more nearly a meditation that a formal proof, and that it depends on pure reason rather than on the workings of the physical world. One must bear in mind that Anselm is addressing monks rather than students or skeptics. He is writing to believers, with the aim

From *The Basic Writings of St. Anselm*, tr, S.N. Deane; La Salle, Ill., The Open Court Publishing Co., 1903, pp. 1-11.

of helping them to understand more fully the faith to which they
have already committed their lives.

    After I had published, at the solicitous entreaties of certain brethren, a brief
work (the *Monologion*) as an example of meditation on the grounds of faith, in the
person of one who investigates, in a course of silent reasoning with himself,
matters of which he is ignorant; considering that this book was knit together by the
linking of many arguments, I began to ask myself whether there might be found a
single argument which would require no other for its proof than itself alone; and
alone would suffice to demonstrate that God truly exists, and that there is a supreme
good requiring nothing else, which all other things require for their existence and
well-being; and whatever we believe regarding the divine Being.
    Although I often and earnestly directed my thought to this end, and at some
times that which I sought seemed to be just within my reach, while again it wholly
evaded my mental vision, at last in despair I was about to cease, as if from the
search for a thing which could not be found. But when I wished to exclude this
thought altogether, lest, by busying my mind to no purpose, it should keep me from
other thoughts, in which I might be successful; then more and more, though I was
unwilling and shunned it, it began to force itself upon me, with a kind of
importunity. So, one day, when I was exceedingly wearied with resisting its
importunity, in the very conflict of my thoughts, the proof of which I had despaired
offered itself, so that I eagerly embraced the thoughts which I was strenuously
repelling.
    Thinking, therefore, that what I rejoiced to have found, would, if put in writing,
be welcome to some readers, of this very matter, and of some others, I have written
the following treatise, in the person of one who strives to lift his mind to the
contemplation of God, and seeks to understand what he believes. In my judgment,
neither this work nor the other, which I mentioned above, deserved to be called a
book, or to bear the name of an author; and yet I thought they ought not to be sent
forth without some title by which they might, in some sort, invite one into whose
hands they fell to their perusal. I accordingly gave each a title, that the first might
be known as, An Example of Meditation on the Grounds of Faith, and its sequel as,
Faith Seeking Understanding.
    Be it mine to look up to thy light, even from afar, even from the depths. Teach
me to seek thee, and reveal thyself to me when I seek thee, for I cannot seek thee,
except thou teach me, nor find thee, except thou reveal thyself. Let me seek thee in
longing, let me long for thee in seeking; let me find thee in love, and love thee in
finding. Lord, I acknowledge and I thank thee that thou hast created me in this
thine image, in order that I may be mindful of thee, may I conceive of thee, and love
thee; but that image has been so consumed and wasted away by vices, and obscured
by the smoke of wrong-doing, that it cannot achieve that for which it was made,
except thou renew it, and create it anew. I do not endeavor, O Lord, to penetrate thy

sublimity, for in no wise do I compare my understanding with that; but I long to understand in some degree thy truth, which my heart believes and loves. For I do not seek to understand that I may believe, but I believe in order to understand. For this also I believe,—that unless I believed, I should not understand.

And so, Lord, do thou, who dost give understanding to faith, give me, so far as thou knowest it to be profitable, to understand that thou art as we believe; and that thou art that which we believe. And, indeed, we believe that thou art a being than which nothing greater can be conceived. Or is there no such nature, since the fool hath said in his heart, there is no God (Psalms xiv. I)? But, at any rate, this very fool, when he hears of this being of which I speak—a being than which nothing greater can be conceived—understands what he hears, and what he understands is in his understanding; although he does not understand it to exist.

For, it is one thing for an object to be in the understanding, and another to understand that the object exists. When a painter first conceives of what he will afterwards perform, he has it in his understanding, but he does not yet understand it to be, because he has not yet performed it. But after he has made the painting, he both has it in his understanding, and he understands that it exists, because he has made it.

Hence, even the fool is convinced that something exists in the understanding, at least, than which nothing greater can be conceived. For, when he hears of this, he understands it. And whatever is understood, exists in the understanding. And assuredly that, than which nothing greater can be conceived, cannot exist in the understanding alone. For, suppose it exists in the understanding alone: then it can be conceived to exist in reality; which is greater.

Therefore, if that, than which nothing greater can be conceived, exists in the understanding alone, the very being, than which nothing greater can be conceived, is one, than which a greater can be conceived. But obviously this is impossible. Hence, there is no doubt that there exists a being, than which nothing greater can be conceived, and it exists both in the understanding and in reality.

And it assuredly exists so truly, that it cannot be conceived not to exist. For, it is possible to conceive of a being which cannot be conceived not to exist; and this is greater than one which can be conceived not to exist. Hence, if that, than which nothing greater can be conceived, can be conceived not to exist, it is not that, than which nothing greater can be conceived. But this is an irreconcilable contradiction. There is, then, so truly a being than which nothing greater can be conceived to exist, that it cannot even be conceived not to exist; and this being thou art, O Lord, our God.

So truly, therefore, dost thou exist, O Lord, my God, that thou canst not be conceived not to exist; and rightly. For, if a mind could conceive of a being better than thee, the creature would rise above the Creator; and this is most absurd. And, indeed, whatever else there is, except thee alone, can be conceived not to exist. To thee alone, therefore, it belongs to exist more truly than all other beings, and hence in a higher degree than all others. For, whatever else exists does not exist so truly, and hence in a less degree it belongs to it to exist. Why, then, has the fool said in his heart, there is no God (Psalms xiv. I), since it is so evident, to a rational mind, that thou dost exist in the highest degree of all? Why, except that he is dull and a fool?

But how has the fool said in his heart what he could not conceive; or how is it that he could not conceive what he said in his heart—since it is the same to say in the heart, and to conceive?

But, if really, nay, since really, he both conceived, because he said in his heart; and did not say in his heart, because he could not conceive; there is more than one way in which a thing is said in the heart or conceived. For, in one sense, an object is conceived, when the word signifying it is conceived; and in another when the very entity, which the object is, is understood.

In the former sense, then, God can be conceived not to exist; but in the latter, not at all. For no one who understands what fire and water are can conceive fire to be water, in accordance with the nature of the facts themselves, although this is possible according to the words. So, then, no one who understands what God is can conceive that God does not exist; although he says these words in his heart, either without any, or with some foreign, signification. For, God is that than which a greater cannot be conceived. And he who thoroughly understands this, assuredly understands that this being so truly exists, that not even in concept can it be non-existent. Therefore, he who understands that God so exists, cannot conceive that he does not exist.

I thank thee, gracious Lord, I thank thee; because what I formerly believed by thy bounty, I now so understand by thine illumination, that if I were unwilling to believe that thou dost exist, I should not be able to understand this to be true.

What art thou, then, Lord God, than whom nothing greater can be conceived? But what art thou, except that which, as the highest of all beings, alone exists through itself, and creates all other things from nothing? For, whatever is not this is less than a thing which can be conceived of. But this cannot be conceived of thee. What good, therefore, does the supreme God lack, through which every good is? Therefore, thou art just, truthful, blessed, and whatever it is better to be than not to be. For it is better to be just than not just; better to be blessed than not blessed.

READING 7

From Peter Abelard's *Sic et Non*

Peter Abelard's (1079-1142) *Sic et non* ("yes and no") intrigued his students and deeply annoyed many of his conservative contemporaries by pitting divergent authoritative opinions—from the Bible, Church Fathers, and Papal Councils—against one another. The reconciliation of divergent opinions was to become a basic methodology in both medieval theology and medieval law. Abelard, however, got into trouble by declining to reconcile the contradictory views that he set forth, leaving it to his students to resolve such issues as whether anything happens by chance, whether it is permissible to lie, and whether sin is pleasing to God. Abelard's use of reason to refine faith is characteristic of medieval scholasticism.

Among the many words of the holy fathers some seem not only to differ from one another but even to contradict one another. Hence it is not presumptuous to judge concerning those by whom the world itself will be judged. Bearing in mind our foolishness, we believe that our understanding is defective rather than the writings of those to whom truth himself said, "It is not you who speak but the spirit of your father who speaks in you." Why should it seem surprising if we, lacking the guidance of the holy spirit, fail to understand them?

Our achievement of understanding is impeded especially by unusual modes of expression and by the different significances that can be attached to one and the same word. We must also take special care that we are not deceived by corruptions of the text or by false attributions when sayings of the fathers are quoted that seem to differ from the truth or to be contrary to it; for many apocryphal writings are set down under names of saints to enhance their authority, and even the texts of the divine scripture are corrupted by the errors of scribes. If, in scripture, anything seems absurd, you are not permitted to say, "The author of this book did not hold the truth," but rather that the book is defective or that the interpreter erred or that you do not understand. But if anything seems contrary to truth in the works of later authors, the reader or auditor is free to judge, so that he may approve what is pleasing and reject what gives offence, unless the matter is established by certain reason or canonical authority.

In view of these considerations we have undertaken to collect various sayings of the fathers that give rise to questioning because of their apparent contradictions.

From Peter Abelard, *Sic et Non (Yes and No)* 1138; Brian Tierney, *Sources of Medieval History*, pp. 172-175.

Assiduous and frequent questioning is indeed the first key to wisdom. For by doubting we come to inquiry; and through inquiring we perceive the truth.

READING 8
St. Thomas Aquinas on the Existence of God

St. Thomas Aquinas (c. 1225-1274) was a Dominican friar who became the greatest of the scholastic philosophers. A prolific writer, his most important work was the reconciling of pagan philosophies, especially those of Averroes and Aristotle, with Christian thought. The following passage gives "the five ways of St. Thomas," five proofs for the existence of God. The arguments rest largely on observation, not on introspection as Anselm's ontological argument does (see p. 167). This passage offers a sketch of Thomas's methodical approach, as well as demonstrating his careful mix of natural reason and revealed religion.

ARTICLE 1.   IS IT SELF-EVIDENT THAT THERE IS A GOD?

I maintain then that the proposition 'God exists' is self-evident in itself, for, as we shall see later, its subject and predicate are identical, since God is his own existence. But, because what it is to be God is not evident to us, the proposition is not self-evident to us, and needs to be made evident. This is done by means of things which, though less evident in themselves, are nevertheless more evident to us, by means, namely, of God's effects.

The awareness that God exists is not implanted in us by nature in any clear or specific way. Admittedly, man is by nature aware of what by nature he desires, and he desires by nature a happiness which is to be found only in God. But this is not, simply speaking, awareness that there is a God, any more than to be aware of someone approaching is to be aware of Peter, even should it be Peter approaching: many, in fact, believe the ultimate good which will make us happy to be riches, or pleasure, or some such thing.

Someone hearing the word 'God' may very well not understand it to mean 'that than which nothing greater can be thought,' indeed, some people have believed

From Thomas Aquinas, *Summa Theologiae*, ed. Thomas Gilby, O.P.; New York, Image Books, 1969, pp. 64-70.

God to be a body. And even if the meaning of the word 'God' were generally recognized to be 'that than which nothing greater can be thought,' nothing thus defined would thereby be granted existence in the world of fact, but merely as thought about. Unless one is given that something in fact exists than which nothing greater can be thought—and this nobody denying the existence of God would grant—the conclusion that God in fact exists does not follow.

ARTICLE 2.   CAN IT BE MADE EVIDENT?

The truths about God which St. Paul says we can know by our natural powers of reasoning—that God exists, for example—are not numbered among the articles of faith, but are presupposed to them. For faith presupposes natural knowledge, just as grace presupposes nature and all perfections presuppose that which they perfect. However, there is nothing to stop a man accepting on faith some truth which he personally cannot demonstrate, even if that truth in itself is such that demonstration could make it evident.

Effects can give comprehensive knowledge of their cause only when commensurate with it: but, as we have said, any effect whatever can make it clear that a cause exists. God's effects, therefore, can serve to demonstrate that God exists, even though they cannot help us to know him comprehensively for what he is.

ARTICLE 3. IS THERE A GOD?

[Objections to the affirmative:]

1. It seems that there is no God. For if, of two mutually exclusive things, one were to exist without limit, the other would cease to exist. But by the word 'God' is implied some limitless good. If God then existed, nobody would ever encounter evil. But evil is encountered in the world. God therefore does not exist.

2. Moreover, if a few causes fully account for some effect, one does not seek more. Now it seems that everything we observe in this world can be fully accounted for by other causes, without assuming a God. Thus natural effects are explained by natural causes, and contrived effects by human reasoning and will. There is therefore no need to suppose that a God exists.

[REPLY: There are five ways in which one can prove that there is a God.]

The first and most obvious way is based on change. Some things in the world are certainly in process of change: this we plainly see. Now anything in process of change is being changed by something else. This is so because it is characteristic of things in process of change that they do not yet have the perfection toward which they move, though able to have it; whereas it is characteristic of something causing change to have that perfection already. For to cause change is to bring into being what was previously only able to be, and this can only be done by something that already is: thus fire, which is actually hot, causes wood, which is able to be hot, to be become actually hot, and in this way causes change in the wood. Now the same thing cannot at the same time be both actually X and potentially X, though it can be actually X and potentially Y: the actually hot cannot at the same time be potentially hot, though it can be potentially cold. Consequently, a thing in process of change cannot itself cause that same change; it cannot change itself. Of necessity therefore anything in process of change is being changed by something else. Moreover, this something else, if in process of change, is itself being changed by yet another thing; and this last by another. Now we must stop somewhere, otherwise there will be no first cause of the change, and, as a result, no subsequent causes. For it is only when acted upon by the first cause that the intermediate causes will produce the change: if the hand does not move the stick, the stick will not move anything else. Hence one is bound to arrive at some first cause of change not itself being changed by anything, and this is what everybody understands by God.

The second way is based on the nature of causation. In the observable world causes are found to be ordered in series; we never observe, nor ever could, something causing itself; for this would mean it preceded itself, and this is not possible. Such a series of causes must however stop somewhere; for in it an earlier member causes an intermediate and the intermediate a last (whether the intermediate be one or many). Now if you eliminate a cause you also eliminate its effects, so that you cannot have a last cause, nor an intermediate one, unless you have a first. Given therefore no stop in the series of causes, and hence no first cause, there would be no intermediate causes either, and no last effect, and this would be an open mistake. One is therefore forced to suppose some first cause, to which everyone gives the name 'God.'

The third way is based on what need not be and on what must be, and runs as follows. Some of the things we come across can be but need not be; for we find them springing up and dying away, thus sometimes in being and sometimes not. Now everything cannot be like this, for a thing that need not be, once was not; and if everything need not be, once upon a time there was nothing. But if that were true there would be nothing even now, because something that does not exist can only be brought into being by something already existing. So that if nothing was in being nothing could be brought into being, and nothing would be in being now, which contradicts observation. Not everything therefore is the sort of thing that need not be; there has got to be something that must be. Now a thing that must be, may or may not owe this necessity to something else. But just as we must stop somewhere in a series of causes, so also in the series of things which must be and owe this to other things. One is forced therefore to suppose something which must be, and owes this to no other thing than itself; indeed it itself is the cause that other things must be.

The fourth way is based on the gradation observed in things. Some things are found to be more good, more true, more noble, and so on, and other things less. But such comparative terms describe varying degrees of approximation to a superlative; for example, things are hotter and hotter the nearer they approach what is hottest. Something, therefore, is the truest and best and most noble of things, and hence the most fully in being; for Aristotle says that the truest things are the things most fully in being. Now when many things possess some property in common, the one most fully possessing it causes it in the others; here, to use Aristotle's example, the hottest of all things, causes all other things to be hot. There is something therefore which causes in all other things their being, their goodness, and whatever other perfection they have. And this we call 'God.'

The fifth way is based on the guidedness of nature. An orderedness of actions to an end is observed in all bodies obeying natural laws, even when they lack awareness. For their behavior hardly ever varies, and will practically always turn out well; which shows that they truly tend to a goal, and do not merely hit it by accident. Nothing however that lacks awareness tends to a goal, except under the direction of someone with awareness and with understanding; the arrow, for example, requires an archer. Everything in nature, therefore, is directed to its goal by someone with intelligence, and this we call 'God.'

[Replies to objections 1 and 2:]

Hence:

1. As Augustine says, since God is supremely good, he would not permit any evil at all in his works, unless he were sufficiently almighty and good to bring good even from evil. It is therefore a mark of the limitless goodness of God that he permits evils to exist, and draws from them good.

2. Natural causes act for definite purposes under the direction of some higher cause, so that their effects must also be referred to God as the first of all causes. In the same manner contrived effects must likewise be referred back to a higher cause than human reasoning and will, for these are changeable and can cease to be, and, as we have seen, all changeable things and things that can cease to be require some first cause which cannot change and of itself must be.

READING 9

Bishop Etienne Tempier's Condemnations of 1277

Among the conservative churchmen concerned about the juxtaposition of philosophical speculation and Christian belief was Etienne Tempier, bishop of Paris in Aquinas's lifetime. Although Bishop Tempier's condemnations applied primarily to other theologians, some of whose philosophical inquiries led to conclusions contrary to Christian revelation, the philosophical system of Thomas himself, despite his effort to reconcile Christianity and Greek logic, was not immune to Tempier's prohibitions. In addition to showing the conservative reaction against pure speculation, the condemnations also highlight the richness of ideas in the theology faculty.

Stephen[1] by divine permission unworthy servant of the church of Paris, sends greetings in the Son of the glorious Virgin to all those who will read this letter:

We have received frequent reports, inspired by zeal for the faith, on the part of important and serious persons to the effect that some students of the arts in Paris are exceeding the boundaries of their own faculty and are presuming to treat and discuss, as if they were debatable in the schools, certain obvious and loathsome errors. Those students are not hearkening to the admonition of Gregory, "Let him who would speak wisely exercise great care, lest by his speech he disrupt the unity of his listeners," particularly when in support of the aforesaid errors they adduce pagan writings that—shame on their ignorance—they assert to be so convincing that they do not know how to answer them. For they say that these things are true according to philosophy but not according to the Catholic faith, as if there were two contrary truths and as if the truth of Sacred Scripture were contradicted by the truth in the sayings of the accursed pagans.

Lest, therefore, this unguarded speech lead simple people into error, we, having taken counsel with the doctors of Sacred Scripture and other prudent men, strictly forbid these and like things and totally condemn them.

That there is no more excellent state than to study philosophy.

That the only wise men in the world are the philosophers.

That one should not hold anything unless it is self-evident or can be manifested from self-evident principles.

From Arthur Hyman and James J. Walsh, *Philosophy in the Middle Ages*; Indianapolis, Hackett Publishing Company, 1973, pp. 542–549.

[1]Etienne is French for Stephen.

That man should not be content with authority to have certitude about any question.

That our intellect by its own natural power can attain to a knowledge of the first cause—this does not sound well and is erroneous if what is meant is immediate knowledge.

That we can know God by his essence in this mortal life.

That nothing can be known about God except that He is, or His existence.

That what is impossible absolutely speaking cannot be brought about by God or by another agent—this is erroneous if we mean "impossible according to nature."

That God could not move the heaven in a straight line, the reason being that He would then leave a vacuum.

That God cannot produce the effect of a secondary cause without the secondary cause itself.

That the world, although it was made from nothing, was not newly made and, although it passed from nonbeing to being, the nonbeing did not precede being in duration but only in nature.

That it is impossible to refute the arguments of the Philosopher [Aristotle] concerning the eternity of the world unless we say that the will of the first being embraces incompatibles.

That nothing happens by chance, but everything comes about by necessity, and that all the things that will exist in the future will exist by necessity.

That forms are not divided except through matter.

That the soul is inseparable from the body, and that the soul is corrupted when the harmony of the body is corrupted.

That our will is subject to the power of the heavenly bodies.

That in all his actions man follows his appetite, and always the greater appetite.

That after a conclusion has been reached about something to be done, the will does not remain free, and that punishments are provided by law only for the correction of ignorance and in order that the correction may be a source of knowledge for others.

That happiness is had in this life and not in another.

That raptures and visions are caused only by nature.

That the Christian law impedes learning.

That there are fables and falsehoods in the Christian law just as in others.

That one does not know anything more by the fact that he knows theology.

That the teachings of the theologian are based on fables.

That the natural philosopher has to deny absolutely the newness of the world because he bases himself on natural causes and natural reasons, whereas the faithful can deny the eternity of the world because he bases himself on supernatural causes.

That a philosopher must not concede the resurrection to come, because it cannot be investigated by reason—this is erroneous because even a philosopher must "bring his mind into captivity to the obedience of Christ" [II Cor 10:5].

READING 10

William of Ockham on Universals

The English Franciscan philosopher William of Ockham (c. 1290-1349) was deeply skeptical of the intellectual synthesis of faith and reason forged by Thomas Aquinas and other high-medieval theologians. His skepticism extended to the issue of "universals," which had occasioned philosophical debate since the time of the ancient Greeks: Does our idea of "dog" or "cat" or "woman" or "man"—or of a triangle or a cube, or of goodness or beauty— derive from a perfect exemplar of one of these things (the ideal dog, cat, woman, man, triangle, etc.) existing in heaven—or in the mind of God? Such was Plato's belief, and he was followed by St. Augustine and by Augustine's intellectual followers in succeeding centuries. Aristotle, on the other hand, believed that universals do not exist as separate entities but only in particular, concrete manifestations of the universal idea; i.e., the human mind acquires the idea of dogness—of the ideal dog—by a process of abstraction: we observe a number of individual dogs and determine what they have in common. In short, the universal does exist, but only in the particular. This was the view of such high-medieval Aristotelians as Thomas Aquinas. Ockham argues, on the other hand, that universals do not exist at all. They are mere names. Ockham's denial of universals became known as "nominalism" from the Latin *nomina*—"names." William of Ockham, an English Franciscan, adopted the scholastic method but rejected its central premise that reason sustained faith. Instead, he argued that human reason could not extend past those things that were known through the senses. The following passage is typical of his conclusions. The main issue is the relationship between universal terms, like "man," and individual objects, like Peter and Paul. This problem had vexed philosophers for centuries: Ockham here poses the question in a new way that leads directly to his elegant solution.

I am enquiring now, whether this universal is something real from the part of the thing which is outside of the soul. All whom I meet agree by saying that the entity which is somehow universal is really in the individual, although some say that it is distinguished only formally, and some that it is not distinguished at all according to

From Anne Fremantle, *The Age of Belief*, New York, Signet Books, 1957, pp. 208-209.

the nature of the thing, but only according to reason. All these opinions coincide in that the universals are allowed to exist somehow away from the thing, so that their universality is held to be really present in the singular objects themselves. This latter opinion is simply false and absurd. Against this is my case. There is no unitary, unvaried or simple thing in a multiplicity of singular things, nor in any kind of created individuals, together and at the same time. If such a thing were allowed, it would be numerically one, therefore it would not be in singular objects nor would it be of their essence. But the singular and the universal thing are themselves two things, really distinct and equally simple, therefore if the singular thing is numerically one, the universal thing will be numerically one also.

If humanity were different from particular individuals and a part of their essence, one and the same invariable thing would be in many individuals, and so this same numerically one and invariable thing would be at different places, which is false. In the same way, that same invariable thing would, say, be condemned in Judas and saved in Christ, and hence, there would be something condemned and miserable in Christ, which is absurd.

To conclude, I say that there is no such thing as a universal, intrinsically present in the things to which it is present. No universal, except that which is such by voluntary agreement, is existent in any way outside of the soul, but everything that can be predicated of many things is by its nature in the mind either psychologically or logically.

CHAPTER 8

WORLDS IN COLLISION: PAPACY AND EMPIRE

In the mid-eleventh century, as the High Middle Ages dawned, the papacy was just beginning to emerge as an international force, whereas the kings of Germany (Holy Roman emperors) were at the height of their power. Emperor Henry III (1039-1056) appointed popes as readily as he appointed the bishops of his own German kingdom. But with Henry III's premature death, reformers at the papal court took advantage of a weak imperial regency government to assert papal independence from imperial control (document 1A). Subsequently, the fiery reformer Gregory VII (pope: 1073-1085), gripped by the ideal of a papal monarchy asserting its authority over kings, princes, and bishops, struggled fiercely against Henry III's son and successor, Henry IV (documents 1B-1E). Gregory was determined to abolish the traditional royal/imperial privilege of appointing bishops and abbots at will, and Henry IV was equally determined to preserve it. The resulting papal-imperial conflict, known as the Investiture Controversy, was finally resolved in the Concordat of Worms of 1122 (document 1F). But the power of the international papacy continued to grow.

The incident at Besançon (document 2) is an excellent illustration of the relationship between papacy (a *very* strong pope: Hadrian IV) and empire (a *very* strong emperor: Frederick Barbarossa). The following document, (document 3), by the most powerful of all medieval popes, Innocent III (1198-1216), illustrates the papal ideology at its height. It was Innocent III who placed the gifted monarch Frederick II on the imperial throne, much to the regret of subsequent popes. Salimbene's account of Frederick II's misfortunes omits the misfortune that Salimbene's account of Frederick's life has survived (document 4). Finally, the passage from Dante's *De Monarchia*—supporting the authority of the Holy Roman Empire—takes explicit exception to Pope Innocent III's "sun-moon" analogy (document 5).

READING 1

Documents of the
Investiture Controversy, 1059-1122

A. THE PAPAL ELECTION DECREE OF 1059

Despite a characteristically medieval effort to seek historical precedents for their act, Pope Nicholas II and his reform cardinals revolutionized the papal election process. Traditionally, popes had been selected either by the king/emperor or by factions among the Roman nobility. But the reformers were determined to terminate lay control of ecclesiastical appointments, and they began at the top. Henry IV was still a child in 1059, but the reformers correctly anticipated that the German Imperial court would bitterly oppose this papal declaration of independence. They address the problem in clauses 5 and 6.

In the name of the Lord God, our Saviour Jesus Christ, in the 1059th year from his incarnation, in the month of April, in the 12th indiction, in the presence of the holy gospels, the most reverend and blessed apostolic pope Nicholas presiding in the Lateran patriarchal basilica which is called the church of Constantine, . . .

Fortified by the authority of our predecessors and the other holy fathers, we decide and declare:

1. On the death of a pontiff of the universal Roman Church, first, the cardinal bishops, with the most diligent consideration, shall elect a successor; then they shall call in the other cardinal clergy [to ratify their choice], and finally the rest of the clergy and the people shall express their consent to the new election.

2. In order that the disease of venality may not have any opportunity to spread, the devout clergy shall be the leaders in electing the pontiff, and the others shall acquiesce. And surely this order of election is right and lawful, if we consider either the rules or the practice of various fathers, or if we recall that decree of our predecessor, St. Leo, for he says: "By no means can it be allowed that those should be ranked as bishops who have not been elected by the clergy, and demanded by the people, and consecrated by their fellow-bishops of the province with the consent of the metropolitan." But since the apostolic seat is above all the churches in the earth, and therefore can have no metropolitan over it, without doubt the cardinal bishops perform in it the office of the metropolitan, in that they advance the elected prelate to the apostolic dignity [that is, choose, consecrate, and enthrone him].

3. The pope shall be elected from the church in Rome, if a suitable person can be found in it, but if not, he is to be taken from another church.

From *A Source Book for Mediaeval History*, ed. O. J. Thatcher and E. H. McNeal; New York, Charles Scribner's Sons, 1905, pp. 128-131, 136-138, 151-156, 164-166.

4. In the papal election—in accordance with the right which we have already conceded to Henry and to those of his successors who may obtain the same right from the apostolic see—due honor and reverence shall be shown our beloved son, Henry, king and emperor elect [that is, the rights of Henry shall be respected].

5. But if the wickedness of depraved and iniquitous men shall so prevail that a pure, genuine, and free election cannot be held in this city, the cardinal bishops with the clergy and a few laymen shall have the right to elect the pontiff wherever they shall deem most fitting.

6. But if after an election any disturbance of war or any malicious attempt of men shall prevail so that he who is elected cannot be enthroned according to custom in the papal chair, the pope elect shall nevertheless exercise the right of ruling the holy Roman Church, and of disposing of all its revenues, as we know St. Gregory did before his consecration.

But if anyone, actuated by rebellion or presumption or any other motive, shall be elected or ordained or enthroned in a manner contrary to this our decree, promulgated by the authority of the synod, he with his counsellors, supporters, and followers shall be expelled from the holy Church of God by the authority of God and the holy apostles Peter and Paul, and shall be subjected to perpetual anathema as Antichrist and the enemy and destroyer of all Christianity; nor shall he ever be granted a further hearing in the case, but he shall be deposed without appeal from every ecclesiastical rank which he may have held formerly. Whoever shall adhere to him or shall show him any reverence as if he were pope, or shall aid him in any way, shall be subject to like sentence. Moreover, if any rash person shall oppose this our decree and shall try to confound and disturb the Roman Church by his presumption contrary to this decree, let him be cursed with perpetual anathema and excommunication, and let him be numbered with the wicked who shall not arise on the day of judgment. Let him feel upon him the weight of the wrath of God the Father, the Son, and the Holy Spirit, and let him experience in this life and the next the anger of the holy apostles, Peter and Paul, whose Church he has presumed to confound. Let his habitation be desolate and let none dwell in his tents [Ps. 69:25]. Let his children be orphans and his wife a widow. Let him be driven forth and let his sons beg and be cast out from their habitations. Let the usurer take all his substance and let others reap the fruit of his labors. Let the whole earth fight against him and let all the elements be hostile to him, and let the powers of all the saints in heaven confound him and show upon him in this life their evident vengeance. But may the grace of omnipotent God protect those who observe this decree and free them from the bonds of all their sins by the authority of the holy apostles Peter and Paul.

B. THE "DICTATUS PAPAE" OF GREGORY VII

These twenty-seven points were compiled at the papal court
around 1075 at the instigation of Pope Gregory VII. The *Dictatus*

Papae (dictates of the pope) were not made public, but were probably intended as a guide to papal lawyers. Few of the claims were new, yet together they constitute a silent manifesto for the Gregorian idea of papal monarchy. Gregory VII took these claims very seriously and made them the basis of his international policy. A careful reading will explain why Gregory's opponents included bishops as well as kings.

1. That the Roman church was established by God alone.
2. That the Roman pontiff alone is rightly called universal.
3. That he alone has the power to depose and reinstate bishops.
4. That his legate, even if he be of lower ecclesiastical rank, presides over bishops in council, and has the power to give sentence of deposition against them.
5. That the pope has the power to depose those who are absent [i.e., without giving them a hearing].
6. That, among other things, we ought not to remain in the same house with those whom he has excommunicated.
7. That he alone has the right, according to the necessity of the occasion, to make new laws, to create new bishoprics, to make a monastery of a chapter of canons, and vice versa, and either to divide a rich bishopric or to unite several poor ones.
8. That he alone may use the imperial insignia.
9. That all princes shall kiss the foot of the pope alone.
10. That his name alone is to be recited in the churches.
11. That the name applied to him belongs to him alone.
12. That he has the power to depose emperors.
13. That he has the right to transfer bishops from one see to another when it becomes necessary.
14. That he has the right to ordain as a cleric anyone from any part of the church whatsoever.
15. That anyone ordained by him may rule [as bishop] over another church, but cannot serve [as priest] in it, and that such a cleric may not receive a higher rank from any other bishop.
16. That no general synod may be called without his order.
17. That no action of a synod and no book shall be regarded as canonical without his authority.
18. That his decree can be annulled by no one, and that he can annul the decrees of anyone.
19. That he can be judged by no one.
20. That no one shall dare to condemn a person who has appealed to the apostolic seat.

21. That the important cases of any church whatsoever shall be referred to the Roman Church [that is, to the pope].

22. That the Roman Church has never erred and will never err to all eternity, according to the testimony of the holy scriptures.

23. That the Roman pontiff who has been canonically ordained is made holy by the merits of St. Peter, according to the testimony of St. Ennodius, bishop of Pavia, which is confirmed by many of the holy fathers, as is shown by the decrees of the blessed pope Symmachus.

24. That by his command or permission subjects may accuse their rulers.

25. That he can depose and reinstate bishops without the calling of a synod.

26. That no one can be regarded as catholic who does not agree with the Roman Church.

27. That he has the power to absolve subjects from their oath of fidelity to wicked rulers.

C. THE DECREE AGAINST LAY INVESTITURE

"Investiture" was the formal installation ceremony in which new prelates were given the insignia of their offices. An incoming bishop or abbot would receive a ring and a staff, symbolic of his "marriage" to the church and his role as shepherd of his flock. It had long been customary for churchmen to receive their investiture from lay lords. Bishops and abbots were normally invested by their territorial princes—counts, dukes, kings, or the Holy Roman emperor. The papal reform party condemned this practice as the key symbolic expression of lay control over ecclesiastical appointments. Lay investiture was first prohibited at the Roman Lenten Synod of 1059, which also promulgated the Papal Election Decree. For a time the investiture issue was largely ignored and forgotten. But Gregory VII issued a second investiture ban at a Roman synod in 1075, and subsequent papal synods legislated against the practice repeatedly. The following document, a product of Gregory VII's synod of 1078, is probably quite similar to the investiture decree of 1075, which no longer survives.

Since we know that investitures have been made by laymen in many places, contrary to the decrees of the holy fathers, and that very many disturbances injurious to the Christian religion have thereby arisen in the Church, we therefore decree: that no clergyman shall receive investiture of a bishopric, monastery, or church from the hand of the emperor, or the king, or any lay person, man or woman. And if anyone has ventured to receive such investiture, let him know that it is annulled by apostolic authority, and that he is subject to excommunication until he has made due reparation.

D. HENRY IV DEPOSES GREGORY VII

The Holy Roman emperors depended heavily on the support of powerful and loyal bishops. Accordingly, Gregory VII's energetic opposition to the appointment of churchmen by laymen earned him the fierce opposition of Henry IV and his hand-picked bishops. When Gregory suspended some of them, Henry responded by convening a synod at Worms in January 1076, and dispatching a letter to Gregory under his prepapal name, Hildebrand.

Henry, king not by usurpation, but by the holy ordination of God, to Hildebrand, not pope, but false monk.

This is the salutation which you deserve, for you have never held any office in the church without making it a source of confusion and a curse to Christian men instead of an honor and a blessing. To mention only the most obvious cases out of the many, you have not only dared to touch the Lord's anointed, the archbishops, bishops, and priests; but you have scorned them and abused them, as if they were ignorant servants not fit to know what their master was doing. This you have done to gain favor with the vulgar crowd. You have declared that the bishops know nothing and that you know everything; but if you have such great wisdom you have used it not to build but to destroy. Therefore we believe that St. Gregory, whose name you have presumed to take, had you in mind when he said: "The heart of the prelate is puffed up by the abundance of subjects, and he thinks himself more powerful than all others." All this we have endured because of our respect for the papal office, but you have mistaken our humility for fear, and have dared to make an attack upon the royal and imperial authority which we received from God. You have even threatened to take it away, as if we had received it from you, and as if the empire and kingdom were in your disposal and not in the disposal of God. Our Lord Jesus Christ has called us to the government of the empire, but he never called you to the rule of the Church. This is the way you have gained advancement in the Church: through craft you have obtained wealth; through wealth you have obtained favor; through favor, the power of the sword; and through the power of the sword, the papal seat, which is the seat of peace; and then from the seat of peace you have expelled peace. For you have incited subjects to rebel against their prelates by teaching them to despise the bishops, their rightful rulers. You have given to laymen the authority over priests, whereby they condemn and depose those whom the bishops have put over them to teach them. You have attacked me, who, unworthy as I am, have yet been anointed to rule among the anointed of God, and who, according to the teaching of the fathers, can be judged by no one save God alone, and can be deposed for no crime except infidelity. For the holy fathers in the time of the apostate Julian did not presume to pronounce sentence of deposition against him, but left him to be judged and condemned by God. St. Peter himself said: "Fear God, honor the king" [1 Pet. 2:17]. But you, who fear not God, have dishonored me, whom He hath established. St. Paul, who said that even an angel from heaven should be accursed who taught any other than the true doctrine, did not make an exception in your favor, to permit you to teach false doctrines. For he says: "But though we, or an angel from heaven, preach any other gospel unto you than that which we have preached unto you, let him be accursed" [Gal. 1:8]. Come down, then, from that apostolic seat which you have obtained by violence; for you have been declared accursed by St. Paul for your false doctrines and have been condemned by us and our bishops for your evil rule. Let another ascend the throne of St. Peter, one who will not use religion as a cloak of violence, but will teach the life-giving doctrine of that prince of the apostles. I, Henry, king by the grace of God, with all my bishops, say unto you; "Come down, come down, and be accursed through all the ages."

E. GREGORY VII DEPOSES HENRY IV

Gregory responded at the Roman Synod of February 1076 by exercising one of the papal prerogatives that he had claimed in the *Dictatus Papae* (clause 12). He reminded his readers, in the form of a prayer, that the papacy derives its power from the authority granted by Jesus to the Apostle Peter, the first pope and Rome's patron saint.

St. Peter, prince of the apostles, incline thine ear unto me, I beseech thee, and hear me, thy servant, whom thou hast nourished from mine infancy and has delivered from mine enemies that hate me for my fidelity to thee. Thou art my witness, as are also my mistress, the mother of God, and St. Paul thy brother, and all the other saints, that thy holy Roman Church called me to its government against my own will, and that I did not gain thy throne by violence; that I would rather have ended my days in exile than have obtained thy place by fraud or for worldly ambition. It is not by my efforts, but by thy grace, that I am set to rule over the Christian world which was specially entrusted to thee by Christ. It is by thy grace and as thy representative that God has given to me the power to bind and to loose in heaven and in earth. Confident of my integrity and authority, I now declare in the name of omnipotent God, the Father, Son, and Holy Spirit, that Henry, son of the emperor Henry, is deprived of his kingdom of Germany and Italy; I do this by thy authority and in defence of the honor of thy Church, because he has rebelled against it. He who attempts to destroy the honor of the Church should be deprived of such honor as he may have held. He has refused to obey as a Christian should, he has not returned to God from whom he had wandered, he has had dealings with excommunicated persons, he has done many iniquities, he has despised the warnings which, as thou art witness, I sent to him for his salvation, he has cut himself off from thy Church, and has attempted to rend it asunder; therefore, by thy authority, I place him under the curse. It is in thy name that I curse him, that all people may know that thou art Peter, and upon thy rock the Son of the living God has built his Church, and the gates of hell shall not prevail against it.

F. THE CONCORDAT OF WORMS, 1122

After dragging on for several decades, the Investiture Controversy was settled in 1122 by a compromise between Pope Calixtus II (1119-1124) and Emperor Henry V (1106-1125), Henry IV's son and heir. The settlement drew a distinction between a prelate's spiritual and secular authority: the former was conferred by investiture with ring and staff, the latter by receipt of the "regalia"—a scepter symbolizing territorial lordship. The Concordat of Worms was followed by a generation of peace between empire and papacy.

1. Calixtus, bishop, servant of the servants of God, to his beloved son, Henry, by the grace of God emperor of the Romans, Augustus.

We hereby grant that in Germany the elections of the bishops and abbots who hold directly from the crown shall be held in your presence, such elections to be conducted canonically and without simony or other illegality. In the case of disputed elections you shall have the right to decide between the parties, after consulting with the archbishop of the province and his fellow-bishops. You shall confer the regalia of the office upon the bishop or abbot elect by giving him the scepter, and this shall be done freely without exacting any payment from him; the bishop or abbot elect on his part shall perform all the duties that go with the holding of the regalia.

In other parts of the empire the bishops shall receive the regalia from you in the same manner within six months of their consecration, and shall in like manner perform all the duties that go with them. The undoubted rights of the Roman Church, however, are not to be regarded as prejudiced by this concession. If at any time you shall have occasion to complain of the carrying out of these provisions, I will undertake to satisfy your grievances as far as shall be consistent with my office. Finally, I hereby make a true and lasting peace with you and with all of your followers, including those who supported you in the recent controversy.

2. In the name of the holy and undivided Trinity.

For the love of God and his holy Church and of Pope Calixtus, and for the salvation of my soul, I, Henry, by the grace of God, emperor of the Romans, Augustus, hereby surrender to God and his apostles, Sts. Peter and Paul, and to the holy Catholic Church, all investiture by ring and staff. I agree that elections and consecrations shall be conducted canonically and shall be free from all interference. I surrender also the possessions and regalia of St. Peter which have been seized by me during this quarrel, or by my father in his lifetime, and which are now in my possession, and I promise to aid the Church to recover such as are held by any other persons. I restore also the possessions of all other churches and princes, clerical or secular, which have been taken away during the course of this quarrel, which I have, and promise to aid them to recover such as are held by any other persons.

Finally, I make true and lasting peace with Pope Calixtus and with the holy Roman Church and with all who are or have ever been of his party. I will aid the Roman Church whenever my help is asked, and will do justice in all matters in regard to which the Church may have occasion to make complaint.

All these things have been done with the consent and advice of the princes whose names are written below: Adelbert, archbishop of Mainz; Frederick, archbishop of Cologne, etc.

READING 2
The Incident at Besançon

Pope Hadrian IV (1154-59), born Nicholas Breakspear, was the only English pope in the history of the Catholic Church and one of the most gifted popes of the twelfth century. His letter to the great Holy Roman Emperor Fredrick II, "Barbarossa" (1157), is a deft blend of affection and disapproval.

"Bishop Hadrian, the servant of the servants of God, to his beloved son Frederick, the illustrious emperor of the Romans, greeting and apostolic benediction.

"We recollect having written, a few days since, to the Imperial Majesty, of that dreadful and accursed deed, an offense calling for atonement, committed in our time, and hitherto, we believe, never attempted in the German lands. In recalling it to Your Excellency, we cannot conceal our great amazement that even now you have permitted so pernicious a deed to go unpunished with the severity it deserves. For how our venerable brother E[skil], archbishop of Lund, while returning from the apostolic see, was taken captive in those parts by certain godless and infamous men—a thing we cannot mention without great and heartfelt sorrow—and is still held in confinement; how in taking him captive, as previously mentioned, those

From, *The Deeds of Frederick Barbarossa*, by Otto of Freising, tr. by C.C. Mierow; New York, W.W. Norton, 1966, pp. 181-184.

men of impiety, a seed of evildoers, children that are corrupters, drew their swords and violently assaulted him and his companions, and how basely and shamefully they treated them, stripping them of all they had, Your Most Serene Highness knows, and the report of so great a crime has already spread abroad to the most distant and remote regions. To avenge this deed of exceptional violence, you, as a man to whom we believe good deeds are pleasing but evil works displeasing, ought with great determination to arise and bring down heavily upon the necks of the wicked the sword which was entrusted by divine providence to you 'for the punishment of evildoers and for the praise of them that do well,'[1] and should most severely punish the presumptuous. But you are reported so to have ignored and indeed been indifferent to this deed, that there is no reason why those men should be repentant at having incurred guilt, because they have long since perceived that they have secured immunity for the sacrilege which they have committed.

"Of the reason for this indifference and negligence we are absolutely ignorant, because no scruple of conscience accuses our heart of having in aught offended the glory of Your Serenity. Rather have we always loved, with sincere affection, and treated with an attitude of due kindness, your person as that of our most dear and specially beloved son and most Christian prince, who, we doubt not, is by the grace of God grounded on the rock of the apostolic confession.

"For you should recall, O most glorious son, before the eyes of your mind, how willingly and how gladly your mother, the Holy Roman Church, received you in another year, with what affection of heart she treated you, what great dignity and honor she bestowed upon you, and with how much pleasure she conferred the emblem of the imperial crown, zealous to cherish in her most kindly bosom the height of Your Sublimity, and doing nothing at all that she knew was in the least at variance with the royal will.

"Nor do we regret that we fulfilled in all respects the ardent desires of your heart; but if Your Excellency had received still greater benefits[2] at our hand (had that been possible), in consideration of the great increase and advantage that might through you accrue to the Church of God and to us, we would have rejoiced, not without reason.

"But now, because you seem to ignore and hide so heinous a crime, which is indeed known to have committed as an affront to the Church universal and to your empire, we both suspect and fear that perhaps your thoughts were directed toward this indifference and neglect on this account: that at the suggestion of a evil man, sowing tares, you have conceived against your most gracious mother the Holy Roman Church and against ourselves—God forbid!—some displeasure or grievance.

---

[1] I Peter 2:14.

[2] *Beneficia*; the emperor and his attendants took this in its feudal sense of "benefice," thus concluding that the pope claimed overlordship of the empire, and taking great offense at this alleged claim.

"On this account, therefore, and because of all the other matters of business which we know to impend, we have thought best to dispatch at this time from our side to Your Serenity two of the best and dearest of those whom we have about us, namely, our beloved sons, Bernard, cardinal priest of St. Clement's, and Roland, cardinal priest of St. Mark's and our chancellor, men very notable for piety and wisdom and honor. We very earnestly beseech Your Excellency that you receive them with as much respect as kindness, treat them with all honor, and that whatever they themselves set forth before Your Imperial Dignity on our behalf concerning this and concerning other matters to the honor of God and of the Holy Roman Church, and pertaining also to the glory and exaltation of the empire, you accept without any hesitation as though proceeding from our mouth. Give credence to their words, as if we were uttering them." [September 20, 1157.]

When this letter had been read and carefully set forth by Chancellor Rainald in a faithful interpretation, the princes who were present were moved to great indignation, because the entire content of the letter appeared to have no little sharpness and to offer even at the very outset an occasion for future trouble. But what had particularly aroused them all was the fact that in the aforesaid letter it had been stated, among other things, that the fullness of dignity and honor had been bestowed upon the emperor by the Roman pontiff, that the emperor had received from his hand the imperial crown, and that he would not have regretted conferring even greater benefits (*beneficia*) upon him, in consideration of the great gain and advantage that might through him accrue to the Roman Church. And the hearers were led to accept the literal meaning of these words and to put credence in the aforesaid explanation because they knew that the assertion was rashly made by some Romans that hitherto our kings had possessed the imperial power over the City, and the kingdom of Italy, by gift of the popes, and that they made such representations and handed them down to posterity not only orally but also in writing and in pictures. Hence it is written concerning Emperor Lothar, over a picture of this sort in the Lateran palace:

> Coming before our gates, the king vows to safeguard the City,
> Then, liegeman to the Pope, by him he is granted the crown.

Since such a picture and such an inscription, reported to him by those faithful to the empire, had greatly displeased the prince when he had been near the City in a previous year [1155], he is said to have received from Pope Hadrian, after a friendly remonstrance, the assurance that both the inscription and the picture would be removed, lest so trifling a matter might afford the greatest men in the world an occasion for dispute and discord.

When all these matters were fully considered, and a great tumult and uproar arose from the princes of the realm at so insolent a message, it is said that one of the ambassadors, as though adding sword to flame, inquired: "From whom then does he have the empire, if not from our lord the pope?" Because of this remark, anger reached such a pitch that one of them, namely, Otto, count palatine of Bavaria (it was said), threatened the ambassador with his sword. But Frederick, using his authority to quell the tumult, commanded that the ambassadors, being granted safe-conduct, be led to their quarters and that early in the morning they should set forth on their way; he ordered also that they were not to pause in the territories of the bishops and abbots, but to return to the City by the direct road, turning neither to the right nor the left.

READING 3
Two Letters of Pope Innocent III

These two brief passages illustrate Pope Innocent III's (1198-1215) claims for the power and authority of the papacy.

A. TO ACERBUS AND THE CLERGY OF TUSCANY, 1198

Innocent III to Acerbius, prior, and to the other clergy in Tuscany.

As God, the creator of the universe, set two great lights in the firmament of heaven, the greater light to rule the day and the lesser light to rule the night [Gen 1:15, 16], so He set two great dignities in the firmament of the universal church, . . . the greater to rule the day, that is, souls, and the lesser to rule the night, that is, bodies. These dignities are the papal authority and the royal power. And just as the moon gets her light from the sun, and is inferior to the sun in quality, quantity, position, and effect, so the royal power gets the splendor of its dignity from the papal authority . . . .

B. TO THE DUKE OF BOHEMIA, 1204

Although there have been many in Bohemia who have worn a royal crown, yet they never received the papal permission to call themselves king in their documents. Nor have we hitherto been willing to call you king, because you were crowned king by Philip, duke of Suabia, who himself had not been legally c   ned, and therefore could not legally crown either you or anyone else. But sin   eved us, and deserting the duke of Suabia, have gone over to th   emperor-elect, and he regards you as king, we, at his re   ation of your obedience, are willing hereafter to call you   why this favor has been granted you, strive to shun th

From *A Source Book for Mediaeval History* by O.H. That
Charles Scribners Sons, 1905, pp. 208, 218.

show that you have deserved our favor which we have so graciously shown you, and try also to retain it. See that you are solemnly crowned by Otto as soon as possible.

READING 4

Salimbene on the Emperor Frederick II

Frederick II (1208-1250) ruled both Germany and most of Italy and was the nemesis of the thirteenth-century papacy after Innocent III. Salimbene, a Franciscan friar and an historian, was personally acquainted with Frederick II but didn't like him—as will be clear from this passage.

Frederick II, formerly emperor, although he was great and rich and a mighty emperor, had nevertheless many misfortunes. Concerning these something should be said. The first of all his misfortunes was that his first-born son Henry, who should have ruled after him, went over to the Lombards against his will, and so Frederick captured him, bound him, and put him in prison. Thus the emperor could say with Job, "They whom I loved are turned against me."

His second misfortune was that he wished to subjugate the Church, so that the pope and the cardinals and other prelates should be poor, and should go on foot. And he did not try to do this by divine zeal, but because he was not a good Catholic, and because he was very avaricious and greedy, and wanted to have the riches and treasures of the Church for himself and his sons. He wished to put down the power of the churchmen, so that they could not undertake anything against him. And he told this to certain of his secretaries, from whom, and afterwards, it became known . . . .

The third of his misfortunes was that he wanted to conquer the Lombards and could not, because when he had them on one side, he lost them on the other. . . .

His fourth misfortune was that Pope Innocent IV deposed him from the empire in the plenary council of Lyons, and made public there all his wickedness and iniquities . . .

His fifth misfortune was that while he was still living, his empire was given to another, namely, the landgrave of Thuringia [Henry Raspe]. Although death took him quite soon, yet Frederick was sorrowful when he saw that his empire had been given to another. . . .

The Portable Medieval Reader, ed. J.B. Ross and M.M. McLaughlin; New York, 1949, pp. 362-365.

His sixth misfortune was when Parma rebelled against him, and went over completely to the Church, which was the cause of all his ruin.

The seventh misfortune was when the men of Parma took his city, Vittoria, which he had built near Parma, and burned, razed, and completely destroyed it, and filled up the holes so that no vestige of it remained, according to the Apocalypse, "A city which was and is not more." Also, they put Frederick and his army shamefully to flight, and killed many of them, and led many captive to their city of Parma. . . . Also they despoiled him and took his whole treasury. . . . The cry of Frederick could be that of Job: "He hath stripped me of my glory, and taken the crown from my head." This can be taken to mean Pope Innocent IV, who deposed him from the empire, or the city of Parma, which literally stripped him and took his crown from his head. A certain man of Parma found this crown in the city of Vittoria when it was destroyed, and carried it publicly in his hand, but the men of Parma took it away from him. . . . I have seen and known this man, and I have also seen the crown, and held it in my hand; it was of great weight and of great value. The men of Parma gave him two hundred pounds imperial for it, and a little house near the church of St. Christine, which formerly was a bathing and drinking place for horses. . . .

Frederick's eighth misfortune was when his princes and barons rebelled against him, like Teobaldo Francesco, who shut himself up in Cappacio, and afterwards died wretchedly; after his eyes had been put out and he had been tortured, he was slain by Frederick. There were also Piero della Vigna and many others, whom it would take too long to name. Concerning these, Frederick could say with Job: "All my inward friends abhorred me, and they whom I loved are turned against me." The one whom he greatly loved was Piero della Vigna, whom he had raised up from nothing, so that he could say, "I have lifted you out of the dust," for Piero had been a poor man, and the emperor had made him his secretary, and had called him "logothete," wishing to honour him greatly. . . .

His ninth misfortune was when his son, King Enzio, was captured by the Bolognese, which was right and just, for he had captured at sea prelates who were going to the council of Pope Gregory IX. . . . Thus it could not be, that the emperor would not be pierced by this sword of sorrow, that is, the capture of his son by his enemies at such a time. For then all hope of his victory perished.

The tenth and last of his misfortunes was when he heard that the Marquis Uberto Pelavicini had greater lordship over the Lombards than he himself could ever have, although Uberto was on his side. He was old and thin and weak and one-eyed, because when he lay as a baby in the cradle, a cock had pecked his eye, that is, it had extracted it from his head with its beak, and eaten it.

To these ten misfortunes of the Emperor Frederick we can add two more, so that we shall have twelve: first, that he was excommunicated by Pope Gregory IX; and second, that the Church tried to take away from him the kingdom of Sicily. And he was not without blame in this, for when the Church sent him across the sea to recover the Holy Land, he made a peace with the Saracens without advantage for the Christians. Moreover, he had the name of Muhammad publicly chanted in the church of God, as we have set down in another chronicle, where we described the twelve crimes of Frederick. . . .

READING 5
From *Dante's De Monarchia*

In his treatise *De Monarchia*, the great Florentine writer Dante (1265-1321) urges a world order under the governance of the Holy Roman Empire (rather than the papacy). In this passage, Dante attacks the theory of papal supremacy and, in particular, the metaphor of the empire being symbolized by the moon, shining only by reflecting the sun-like glory of the Church (a favorite metaphor of Pope Innocents III's: see above, reading 3A). Dante's great goal is the establishment, through imperial intervention, of political order in war-torn Italy—and in faction-ridden Florence. Florence, Dante's birthplace, was strifetorn in the era following the fall of Frederick II. The German kings no longer exercised real control; the papacy was too distant and too preoccupied with Roman affairs; and Florentine civic government was split between those who longed for more autonomy and those who wanted firmer external control. These troubled circumstances led Dante, one of the most reflective men of any age, to write this political treatise.

The analogy of sun and moon is not applicable to temporal authority, as if it were reflected from the divine right of spiritual authority.

It is asserted by those against whom the remaining discussion is directed that the Empire's authority is subordinate to the Church's as a workman is under the direction of an architect. They use several different arguments, based some of them on the Holy Scripture and some on the deeds of either popes or emperors, from whose deeds they make certain theoretical inferences.

They say, in the first place, that, according to Genesis, God created two great luminaries, a greater and a lesser, one to govern the day and the other the night. This, they say, is an allegory for two types of power, spiritual and temporal. Then

From *On World-Government* or *De Monarchia* by Dante Alighieri, tr. H.W. Schneider; New York, The Liberal Arts Press, 1950, pp. 42-45.

they argue that as the lesser luminary, the moon, has no light of its own except as it receives it from the sun, so temporal power has no authority except as it is derived from spiritual.

To overthrow this and other arguments of theirs, we should note that, as the Philosopher[1] says in his treatise on *Fallacies*, the way to win an argument is to expose an error. Now since error can occur in both the matter and the form of an argument, there are two kinds of fallacies: assuming what is false or inferring incorrectly. The Philosopher objected to Parmenides and Melissus on both of these grounds, saying, "They admit falsehoods and they don't know how to make syllogisms." Here I include under "false" also improbable opinions, for in questions of probable knowledge they have the force of falsehoods. If the fallacy is formal, the critic must destroy the conclusion by showing that the syllogistic structure has been violated. But if the fallacy is material, it is either a case of assuming what is wholly false or relatively false. If an assumption is wholly false, one of the premises must be denied; if it is relatively false, a distinction must be made.

With this procedure in mind, we can better criticize this and the following arguments if we call attention to two types of fallacious appeals to a mystic interpretation: either looking for it where it does not exist, or accepting a meaning which is improper. Regarding the first type Augustine says in his *City of God:* "Not everything narrated is significant, for the insignificant must be narrated in order to bring out the significant. The ploughshare alone turns the furrow, but the other parts of the plough are also needed." Concerning the second type, too, Augustine has something to say in his *Christian Doctrine,* when he is speaking about those who seek a meaning different from the author's intention and says that they make the same mistake that a traveller makes who leaves the road but finally in his digression arrives at the same point to which the road leads; and he adds, "Such a person should be warned that his bad habit of leaving the road may lead him on to cross-roads and wrong roads." Then he gives the specific reason why this is a dangerous way of treating Holy Scripture, saying, "Faith will totter, if the authority of the divine Scriptures vacillates." For my part I would say that if such mistakes arise from ignorance, we should carefully correct and pardon them, as we would a person who is afraid of lions in the clouds; but, if they are committed purposely, such interpreters should be treated not as ignoramuses but more as we would treat a tyrant who does not use public regulations for the common welfare but tries to twist their meaning for his own purposes. O greatest of crimes, to abuse the intention of the eternal Spirit, even if it happens in dreams! For the sin is not against Moses, or David or Job, or Matthew or Paul, but against the Holy Spirit, who speaks through them. For though there may be many writers of the divine word, there is but one who dictates it, namely, God, who was pleased to reveal himself to us by using many pens.

---

[1]Dante, like Aquinas and Bishop Tempier, refers to Aristotle as "the Philosopher."

After these preliminary observations I can return to the criticism of the argument according to which the two luminaries signify two types of government, an argument which rests entirely on this analogy. There are two ways of showing that this interpretation of the passage in Genesis is inadmissable. First, since governments are not in the essence of human existence but in its circumstantial conditions of "accidents," God would have been guilty of creating backwards, if he had first created types of government and then had created man, which would be absurd to attribute to God. For he made the two luminaries on the fourth day and man on the sixth, according to the text. Besides, since governments exist to guide men toward specific goals, as we shall show, there would have been no use for them if man had remained in the state of innocence in which he was created. For devices such as governments are remedies for the infirmity of sin. Since man was not only not a sinner on the fourth day but didn't exist at all, God would not have acted in accordance with his goodness if he had devised remedies on the fourth day. For it would be a silly physician who prepared a plaster to apply to the future abscess of an unknown person. It is therefore impossible to maintain that God created governments on the fourth day, and therefore Moses must have meant something different from what they imagine.

But this falsehood can also be destroyed by using the gentler method of exposing a material fallacy, and instead of calling the opponent an out-and-out liar, we can make a distinction which he overlooked. Thus I maintain that from the fact that the moon does not shine brightly unless it receives light from the sun, it does not follow that the moon itself depends on the sun. For one must keep in mind that the being of the moon is one thing, its power another, and its functioning a third. In its being the moon is in no way dependent on the sun, and not even in its power and functioning strictly speaking, for its motion comes directly from the prime mover, some of whose rays shine on it. For it has a little light of its own, as we observe in eclipses, but in order to increase its power and efficacy it gets light from the sun, where it is plentiful. In like manner, I maintain, temporal power receives from spiritual power neither its being, nor its power or authority, nor even its functioning, strictly speaking, but what it receives is the light of grace, which God in heaven and the pope's blessing on earth cause to shine on it in order that it work more effectively.

Lastly, there is a formal fallacy in their argument, for the predicate of the conclusion is not identical with that of the major premise as it should be. Their argument runs thus: the moon receives light from the sun or spiritual power; the temporal power is the moon; therefore the temporal power receives its authority from the spiritual power. In the major premise it is light that the moon receives and in the conclusion it is authority, which are two quite different things, both as to their substance and their meaning, as I have explained.

CHAPTER 9

NEW STATES:
ENGLAND AND FRANCE

Royal authority had been growing in England since the Norman Conquest of 1066, when William the Conqueror established tight control of the realm (document 1). William I's great grandson, King Henry II (1154-1189), extended royal power significantly (document 2). But in King John's reign (1199-1216) a baronial reaction compelled the monarchy to recognize the traditional rights of the nobility and other free English people in the *Magna Carta* (the Great Charter: document 3). The conflict between royal authority and the customary rights of subjects found further expression in the legislation of King Edward I (1272-1307, document 4).

In France, our documents illustrate the gradual rise of the French Capetian monarchy from the victory of King Louis VI (1108-1136) over Thomas of Marle—a veritable Saddam Hussein of twelfth-century Picardy (document 5)—to the ordinance of Philip Augustus (1180-1223) on the governance of France during his absence on the Third Crusade (document 6), to the accounts of relics received by King Louis IX (St. Louis, 1226-1270, document 7) and the conflicts between King Philip IV, "the Fair" (1285-1314) with the papacy (document 8).

READING 1

William the Conqueror
Subdues Northern England

For about five years after his victory at the battle of Hastings in 1066, William the Conqueror and his Normans were kept busy eliminating pockets of English resistance and suppressing native rebellions such as the one described here. Edwin and Morcar, the pre-Conquest earls of Mercia and Northumbria, did not fight at Hastings and were therefore permitted for a time to keep their earldoms.

The passage shows some of the ways in which William consolidated his new regime in England. The author, Orderic Vitalis, was writing a full generation after the event. His sources, oral and written, were generally trustworthy and he used them carefully. But the account of wanton Norman wives which concludes this excerpt is probably exaggerated. Hugh of Grandmesnil did not forfeit his estates, as Orderic suggests, but became a wealthy landholder in central England and bequeathed his lands to one of his sons. Orderic's account of the Norman Conquest is relatively unbiased since he was himself half English and half French. He described himself as an "Englishman" but spent his youth and adulthood in the Norman abbey of Saint-Evroul where he died In 1142.

In that same year (1068), the distinguished youths Edwin and Morcar, the sons Earl Alfgar, rebelled, and as they were joined by many others the entire kingdom of England was in upheaval. King William, however, made peace: in return for count Edwin subduing his brother and nearly a third of England, William promised him his daughter in marriage. But later, owing to the deceitful counsel of the Normans who are a very envious and covetous people, William denied Edwin the hand of the woman for whom he had waited so long. Quite irritated, the two brothers were incited to open rebellion, and a large number of the English and the Welsh soon followed. . . .

[At about this time] Bleddyn king of the Welsh went to the aid of his uncles, bringing a multitude of natives with him. Meeting together, many of the English and Welsh nobles complained about the intolerable injuries and indignities which they had suffered at the hands of the Normans and their companions. Using

From Orderic Vitalis, *The Ecclesiastical History*, ed. A. Le Prevost; vol. 2, Paris, 1840, pp. 182-186; tr. David S. Spear.

messengers they succeeded in stirring up the insurgents throughout the island, both in secret and in public. All swore to strive against the Normans and regain their former liberties. Trouble broke out first and most viciously in the furthest regions beyond the Humber, with the rebels garrisoning themselves in the forests, marshes, estuaries, and even in some of the towns. The city of York was the most explosive, and not even the archbishop himself dared to try to quiet it. Many of the natives began to live in tents, scorning houses whose comforts they thought would make them soft. Indeed, it was for this reason that the Normans called them savages.

King William decided to examine carefully even the remote areas of the realm and to garrison the most advantageous locations against the excursions of the enemy. These fortifications, which the Normans called castles, were seldom found in England before this, and because of them the English, even though they were exceptionally warlike and fearless, found their position greatly weakened. The king built a castle at Warwick, and brought Henry the son of Roger of Beaumont to hold it. Edwin and Morcar, considering with their men the dangers of battle, then sought William's forgiveness, which they obtained so far as they were able. The king next erected a castle at Nottingham and commended it to William Peverel.

Hearing of these events the people of York were disinclined to continue their uprising, and promptly gave up the keys of the city to the king, along with some hostages. Since he was a little leary of their loyalty he built a castle right in the town itself, which he handed over to some carefully chosen knights. After this Archill, the most powerful of the Northumbrians, made peace with the king, and gave over his son to William as a hostage. The bishop of Durham also went to the king seeking peace for Malcolm king of the Scots, and brought the conditions back to Scotland. Malcolm, although he was counted on by the English contingent and was prepared to wage a vigorous campaign on their behalf, nonetheless remained quiet when he heard the peace terms which were offered him. He promptly sent his messengers back with the bishop of Durham, and swore through them that he would remain faithful to the king. Thus by preferring peace to war he was able both to further his own interest and to please many of his own people. For the Scots, although certainly hardy in battle, love leisure and quiet as well, not wishing to disturb the affairs of their neighbors, and are more inclined towards the Christian faith than the pursuit of arms. The king then withdrew, careful though to build castles at Lincoln, Huntingdon, and Cambridge, and to entrust them to his strongest men.

At this time certain Norman women, terribly inflamed by the passions of lust, sent messengers to their men demanding that they return home, adding that unless they did so quickly they would take other mates. They did not themselves dare to cross over to their husbands since they were unaccustomed to sailing, nor did they wish to seek after them in England since there the men were constantly armed and making daily expeditions in which no small amount of blood was lost on both sides. The king of course wanted to keep his knights with him under such unstable conditions, and consequently he offered them lands, revenues, and positions of great power, promising them even more when the whole kingdom should be free from the threat of the enemy. The barons and knights were at a loss, for as long as the king and their own brothers and friends remained surrounded and in danger, they realized that they would be labelled cowards or out-and-out deserters. Yet if they remained, their wives would pollute their beds with the stain of infidelity and besmirch the reputations of their offspring. Finally Hugh of Grandmesnil, who oversaw the Gewissae, that is the area around Winchester, and his brother-in-law Humphrey of Tilleul who had commanded Hastings ever since the day it was first built, along with many others, reluctantly departed while their king still labored with the enemy. They returned to their lewd wives in Normandy, but in so doing relinquished their lands, and neither they nor their heirs were able to recover them afterwards.

READING 2
Three Writs of Henry II

These three writs, inaugurated by the administration of King Henry II (1154-1189) and sold to plaintiffs by the royal government, constitute significant extensions of the king's authority over land law. In addition, by making royal justice more accessible, these legal procedures helped extend the authority of the king and his courts.

A.   ASSIZE OF MORT D'ANCESTOR

The king to the sheriff, greetings. If G. son of O. will give surety for continuing his claim, then summon by good summoners twelve men, free and legal,[1] from the district of _____, to be before me or my justices on _____, ready to acknowledge by oath if O., father of G., was seised in demesne as of fee of one virgate of land in that manor on the day that he died; if he died after my coronation; and whether the aforesaid G. is his closest heir. In the meantime they shall have the view of that land, and you shall write down their names. And summon by good summoners R., who holds that land, to be there in order to hear the determination. And you are to bring the summoners and this writ.

From Ranulf de Glanvill, *Tractatus de legibus et consuetudinibus regni Angliae,* ed. G.E. Woodbine; New Haven, 1932. tr. J.W. Leedom.

[1]Literally, "law-worthy", it's usually translated as "twelve free and lawful men," or "twelve free and legal men."

B. ASSIZE OF NOVEL DISSEISIN

The king to the sheriff, greetings. A complaint has been made by N. that R. has unlawfully and without judgment disseised him of his free tenement in _____ since my last crossing to Normandy. And so I command you that if the said N. will give you surety for continuing his claim, to restore to that holding the goods and chattels taken from it, and the said tenement with its chattels is to remain in peace until _____. In the meantime, have twelve men, free and lawful, from the district view the land, and you shall write down their names. And summon them by good summoners to be before me or my justices, ready to make recognizance concerning it. And place under bond and pledges R., or his bailiff if, he cannot be found, to be there in order to hear their determination. And you are to bring the summoners and this writ.

C. WRIT OF RIGHT

The king to Earl W., greetings. I command you without delay to give full right to N. concerning the ten carucates of land in Middleton, which he claims from you by the service of one knight's fee for all service. And unless you do this so that I hear no more complaint about default of judgment, the sheriff of Nottingham will do it.

READING 3

From *Magna Carta*, 1215

King John's difficulties reached their climax with a major baronial uprising in 1215, as a result of which he was forced to issue a comprehensive charter guaranteeing customary feudal and political rights. Magna Carta is concerned primarily with the rectification of past abuses of feudal privileges, but it also discloses the significant overlap of lord-vassal relationships with the emerging constitutional doctrine of limited monarchy and government under the law. John repudiated Magna Carta shortly after issuing it and died in 1216 in the midst of another baronial rebellion. Magna Carta was reissued repeatedly, with certain variations, during the generations that followed.

From *English Historical Documents*, vol, 3, *1189-1327*, ed. and tr. Harry Rothwell; London, Eyre & Spottiswoode, 1975, pp. 316-324. Reprinted by permission.

John, by the grace of God, king of England, lord of Ireland, duke of Normandy and Aquitaine, and count of Anjou, to the archbishops, bishops, abbots, earls, barons, justiciars, foresters, sheriffs, stewards, servants, and to all his bailiffs and faithful subjects, greetings. Know that we, out of reverence for God and for the salvation of our soul and those of all our ancestors and heirs, for the honour of God and the exaltation of holy church, and for the reform of our realm, on the advice of our venerable fathers, Stephen, archbishop of Canterbury, primate of all England and cardinal of the holy Roman church, [and other bishops and magnates]:

[1] In the first place have granted to God, and by this our present charter confirmed for us and our heirs for ever that the English church shall be free, and shall have its rights undiminished and its liberties unimpaired; and it is our will that it be thus observed; which is evident from the fact that, before the quarrel between us and our barons began, we willingly and spontaneously granted and by our charter confirmed the freedom of elections which is reckoned most important and very essential to the English church, and obtained confirmation of it from the lord pope Innocent III; the which we will observe and we wish our heirs to observe it in good faith for ever. We have also granted to all free men of our kingdom, for ourselves and our heirs for ever, all the liberties written below, to be had and held by them and their heirs of us and our heirs.

[2] If any of our earls or barons or others holding of us in chief by knight service dies, and at his death his heir be of full age and owe relief he shall have his inheritance on payment of the old relief, namely the heir or heirs of an earl £100 for a whole earl's barony, the heir or heirs of a baron £100 for a whole barony, the heir or heirs of a knight 100s, at most, for a whole knight's fee; and he who owes less shall give less according to the ancient usage of fiefs.

[6] Heirs shall be married without disparagement, yet so that before the marriage is contracted those nearest in blood to the heir shall have notice.

[7] A widow shall have her marriage portion and inheritance forthwith and without difficulty after the death of her husband; nor shall she pay anything to have her dower or her marriage portion or the inheritance which she and her husband held on the day of her husband's death; and she may remain in her husband's house for forty days after his death, within which time her dower shall be assigned to her.

[8] No widow shall be forced to marry so long as she wishes to live without a husband, provided that she gives security not to marry without our consent if she holds of us, or without the consent of her lord of whom she holds, if she holds of another.

[10] If anyone who has borrowed from the Jews any sum, great or small, dies before it is repaid, the debt shall not bear interest as long as the heir is under age, of whomsoever he holds; and if the debt falls into our hands, we will not take anything except the principal mentioned in the bond.

[12] No scutage or aid shall be imposed in our kingdom unless by common counsel of our kingdom, except for ransoming our person, for making our eldest son a knight, and for once marrying our eldest daughter; and for these only a

reasonable aid shall be levied. Be it done in like manner concerning aids from the city of London.

[13] And the city of London shall have all its ancient liberties and free customs as well by land as by water. Furthermore, we will and grant that all other cities, boroughs, towns, and ports shall have all their liberties and free customs.

[20] A free man shall not be amerced for a trivial offence except in accordance with the degree of the offence, and for a grave offence he shall be amerced in accordance with its gravity, yet saving his way of living; and a merchant in the same way, saving his stock-in-trade; and a villein shall be amerced in the same way, saving his means of livelihood—if they have fallen into our mercy: and none of the aforesaid amercements shall be imposed except by the oath of good men of the neighbourhood.

[21] Earls and barons shall not be amerced except by their peers, and only in accordance with the degree of the offence. . . .

[27] If any free man dies without leaving a will, his chattels shall be distributed by his nearest kinsfolk and friends under the supervision of the church, saving to every one the debts which the deceased owed him.

[30] No sheriff, or bailiff of ours, or anyone else shall take the horses or carts of any free man for transport work save with the agreement of that freeman.

[31] Neither we nor our bailiffs will take, for castles or other works of ours, timber which is not ours, except with the agreement of him whose timber it is.

[38] No bailiff shall in future put anyone to trial upon his own bare word, without reliable witnesses produced for this purpose.

[39] No free man shall be arrested or imprisoned or disseised or outlawed or exiled or in any way victimized, neither will we attack him or send anyone to attack him, except by the lawful judgment of his peers or by the law of the land.

[40] To no one will we sell, to no one will we refuse or delay right or justice.

[41] All merchants shall be able to go out of and come into England safely and securely and stay and travel throughout England, as well by land as by water, for buying and selling by the ancient and right customs free from all evil tolls, except in time of war and if they are of the land that is at war with us. And if such are found in our land at the beginning of a war, they shall be attached, without injury to their persons or goods, until we, or our chief justiciar, know how merchants of our land are treated who were found in the land at war with us when war broke out; and if ours are safe there, the others shall be safe in our land.

[45] We will not make justices, constables, sheriffs or bailiffs save of such as know the law of the kingdom and mean to observe it well.

[46] All barons who have founded abbeys for which they have charters of the kings of England or ancient tenure shall have the custody of them during vacancies, as they ought to have.

[48] All evil customs connected with forests and warrens, foresters and warreners, sheriffs and their officials, river-banks and their wardens shall immediately be inquired into in each county by twelve sworn knights of the same county who are

to be chosen by good men of the same county, and within forty days of the completion of the inquiry shall be utterly abolished by them so as never to be restored, provided that we, or our justiciar if we are not in England, know of it first.

[52] If anyone has been disseised of or kept out of his lands, castles, franchises or his right by us without the legal judgment of his peers, we will immediately restore them to him: and if a dispute arises over this, then let it be decided by the judgment of the twenty-five barons who are mentioned below in the clause for securing the peace: for all things, however, which anyone has been disseised or kept out of without the lawful judgment of his peers by King Henry, our father, or by King Richard, our brother, which we have in our hand or are held by others, to whom we are bound to warrant them, we will have the usual period of respite of crusaders, excepting those things about which a plea was started or an inquest made by our command before we took the cross; when however we return from our pilgrimage, or if by any chance we do not go on it, we will at once do full justice therein. . . .

[54] No one shall be arrested or imprisoned upon the appeal of a woman for the death of anyone except her husband.

[61] Since, moreover, for God and the betterment of our kingdom and for the better allaying of the discord that has arisen between us and our barons we have granted all these things aforesaid, wishing them to enjoy the use of them unimpaired and unshaken for ever, we give and grant them the under-written security, namely, that the barons shall choose any twenty-five barons of the kingdom they wish, who must with all their might observe, hold and cause to be observed, the peace and liberties which we have granted and confirmed to them by this present charter of ours, so that if we, or our justiciar, or our bailiffs or any one of our servants offend in any way against anyone or transgress any of the articles of the peace or the security and the offence be notified to four of the aforesaid twenty-five barons, those four barons shall come to us, or to our justiciar if we are out of the kingdom, and, laying the transgression before us, shall petition us to have that transgression corrected without delay. And if we do not correct the transgression, or if we are out of the kingdom, if our justiciar does not correct it, within forty days, reckoning from the time it was brought to our notice or to that of our justiciar if we were out of the kingdom, the aforesaid four barons shall refer that case to the rest of the twenty-five barons and those twenty-five barons together with the community of the whole land shall distrain and distress us in every way they can, namely, by seizing castles, lands, possessions, and in such other ways as they can, saving our person and the persons of our queen and our children, until, in their opinion, amends have been made; and when amends have been made, they shall obey us as they did before. And let anyone in the land who wishes take an oath to obey the orders of the said twenty-five barons for the execution of all the aforesaid matters, and with them to distress us as much as he can, and we publicly and freely give anyone leave to take the oath who wishes to take it and we will never prohibit anyone from taking it. Indeed, all those in the land who are unwilling of

themselves and of their own accord to take an oath to the twenty-five barons to help them to distrain and distress us, we will make them take the oath as aforesaid at our command. And if any of the twenty-five barons dies or leaves the country or is in any other way prevented from carrying out the things aforesaid, the rest of the aforesaid twenty-five barons shall choose as they think fit another one in his place, and he shall take the oath like the rest. In all matters the execution of which is committed to these twenty-five barons, if it should happen that these twenty-five are present yet disagree among themselves about anything, or if some of those summoned will not or cannot be present, that shall be held as fixed and established which the majority of those present ordained or commanded, exactly as if all the twenty-five had consented to it; and the said twenty-five shall swear that they will faithfully observe all the things aforesaid and will do all they can to get them observed. And we will procure nothing from anyone, either personally or through anyone else, whereby any of these concessions and liberties might be revoked or diminished; and if any such thing is procured, let it be void and null, and we will never use it either personally or through another.

[63] Wherefore we wish and firmly enjoin that the English church shall be free, and that the men in our kingdom shall have and hold all the aforesaid liberties, rights and concessions well and peacefully, freely and quietly, fully and completely, for themselves and their heirs from us and our heirs, in all matters and in all places for ever, as is aforesaid. An oath, moreover, has been taken, as well on our part as on the part of the barons, that all these things aforesaid shall be observed in good faith and without evil disposition. Witness the above-mentioned and many others. Given by our hand in the meadow which is called Runnymede between Windsor and Staines on the fifteenth day of June, in the seventeenth year of our reign.

READING 4

Statutes of Edward I

These documents from the reign of Edward I (1277-1307) illustrate the effort of the royal government to control baronial lands by establishing inquiries to investigate the grounds for baronial rights to jurisdiction over such lands (*Quo Warranto*: "By what warrant?"), and by restricting the process of endless links of

Documents A and C from *Sources of English Constitutional History*, ed. and tr. Carl Stephenson and Frederick G. Marcham; New York, Harper & Row, 1972, pp. 169, 174. Document B is from *The Chronicle of Walter of Guisborough*, ed. Harry Rothwell; (Camden Society, vol. 89, 3rd series), London, 1957, p. 216. Tr. by David S. Spear.

subinfeudation (*Quia Emptores*). Predictably, the inquiries *Quo Warranto* led to conflicts between the king and some magnates who had held rights for time out of mind, but who lacked formal proof. This episode recounts one incident in the proceedings, and its importance lies in John of Warenne's response to Edward's justices, which reveals an alternate theory of government for the kingdom.

A.   *QUO WARRANTO* (STATUTE OF GLOUCESTER OF 1278)

In the year of grace 1278, the sixth of the reign of King Edward, son of King Henry, at Gloucester in the month of August, the same king, having summoned the more discreet men of his kingdom, both greater and lesser, has made provision for the betterment of his kingdom and the fuller administration of justice, as is demanded by the kingly office. . . .

The sheriffs shall have it commonly proclaimed throughout their bailiwicks—that is to say, in cities, boroughs, trading towns, and elsewhere—that all those who claim to have any franchises by charters of the king's predecessors, kings of England, or by other title, shall come before the king or before the itinerant justices on a certain day and at a certain place to show what sort of franchises they claim to have, and by what warrant[1] [they hold them]. . . . And if those who claim to have such franchises, do not come on the day aforesaid, those franchises shall then be taken into the king's hand by the local sheriff in the name of distress; so that they shall not enjoy such franchises until they come to receive justice. . . .

B.   BARONIAL RESPONSE TO THE STATUTE OF GLOUCESTER

Not long afterwards the king (Edward I) upset some of the magnates of the land by sending out his justiciars to find out by what right (*quo warranto*) they held their lands. If they had no good claim, their lands were seized at once. Among those magnates called to appear before the king's justiciars was (John) Earl of Warenne. When asked by what warrant he held his lands, he produced in their presence an ancient and rusty sword, saying, "Here, my lords, here is my warrant. My ancestors rode beside William the Bastard and conquered their lands by this sword. And by this sword I will defend my lands against anyone who wishes to seize them. For it was not the king himself who conquered and subdued these lands, but our ancestors who were with him as comrades and partners." And the magnates agreed with the Earl of Warenne and with his response, and full of turmoil and dissent they withdrew.

---

[1]The Latin phrase here is *quo warranto*.

C.   STATUTE OF *QUIA EMPTORES* (1290)

Whereas the buyers of lands and tenements belonging to the fiefs of magnates and other men have in times past frequently entered upon their fiefs to the prejudice of the same [lords], because the free-holders of the said magnates and other men have sold their lands and tenements to such purchasers to be held in fee by themselves and their heirs of the feoffors and not of the principal lords of the fiefs, whereby those same principal lords have often lost the escheats, marriages, and wardships of lands and tenements belonging to their fiefs; and whereas this has seemed very hard and burdensome to those magnates and other lords, being in such cases manifest disinheritance: [therefore] the lord king in his parliament at Westminister [held] after Easter in the eighteenth year of his reign. . . , at the suggestion of the magnates of his realm, has granted, provided, and established that henceforth every freeman shall be permitted to sell his land or tenement, or a part of it, at pleasure; yet so that the feoffee shall hold that land or tenement of the same principal lord [of whom the feoffor held] and by the same services and customs by which the feoffor earlier held. . . .

READING 5

Louis VI Subdues a Recalcitrant Baron

Suger (1081-1151), abbot of the French royal monastery of St-Denis, was a great admirer of Louis VI (1108-1137), who was himself the strongest king since the Carolingian era, and whom Suger depicts as the ideal Christian peacekeeping monarch. Thomas of Marle, whom Suger clearly dislikes, seems, in fact (on the basis of independent evidence) to have been every bit as unpleasant as he is depicted in this passage.

defender of other peoples

A king is obliged by virtue of his office to crush with his strong right hand the impudence of tyrants. For such men freely provoke wars, take pleasure in plunder, oppress the poor, destroy the churches, and give themselves free reign to do whatsoever they wish. And if left to their own devices, such men are further inflamed, for the forces of evil seek always to crush those who are slipping out of their grip while happily stoking the passions of those whom they hope to hold fast for all eternity.

From Suger, *Vie de Louis VI Le Gros*, ed. Henri Waquet; Paris, Société d'Edition "Les Belles Lettres," 1964, pp. 172-79. Tr. by David S. Spear.

One such wicked man was Thomas of Marle. For while King Louis was busy fighting in the wars which we mentioned earlier, Thomas ravaged the regions around Laon, Reims, and Amiens. Indeed, the devil encouraged him in these things, for the devil as we know is accustomed to leading fools to their damnation. Thomas devastated the region with the fury of a wolf. No fear of ecclesiastical penalty persuaded him to spare the clergy; no feeling of humility convinced him to spare the people. Everyone was slaughtered, everything destroyed. He snatched two prize estates from the nuns of Saint-John of Laon. And treating the two castles of Crécy-sur-Serre and Nouvion-Catillon as his own, Thomas equipped them with new ramparts and tall towers. In a word, he transformed them into a dragon's lair and a den of thieves, exposing the nearby inhabitants to the miseries of fire and plunder.

Fed up with the intolerable afflictions of this man, the churchmen of France met together (on December 6, 1114) at a great general council at Beauvais. There they passed a sentence of condemnation against the enemies of Jesus Christ. The venerable papal legate Cuno, bishop of Praeneste, was particularly moved by the numerous pleas of the church and the cries of the orphans and the poor. He drew the sword of Saint Peter against Thomas of Marle, and with the unanimous assent of the council, declared him excommunicated, ripped from him *in absentia* the titles and honors of knighthood, branded him a criminal, and declared him unworthy of being called a Christian.

Heeding the wishes of so great a council, King Louis moved quickly against Thomas. Accompanied by his army and the clergy (to whom the king was ever devoted), he turned at once against the heavily defended castle of Crécy. There, thanks to his men at arms, or should we say on account of divine aid, Louis achieved swift victory. He seized the new towers as if they were no more than the huts of peasants; he drove out the criminals; he piously slaughtered the impious; and as for those who had showed no pity, he in turn showed no pity towards them. Anyone seeing the castle engulfed in flames would have understood that, "His whole world shall join Him in the fight against His frenzied foes." (Wisdom of Solomon 5:21).

Flushed by the success of his decisive victory, the king moved quickly against the other illegally held castle, Nouvion. There he was approached by a man who reported the following: "Please know, your majesty, that this wicked castle is harboring a group of men so despicable that hell alone is worthy of housing them. These are the very men who, when you ordered the commune of Laon to be suppressed, set fire not only to the city but also to the cathedral and several other churches. They martyred all of the nobles in the city who dared to come to the aid of their bishop. Worse, these men brutally murdered Bishop Gaudry himself[1], defender of the church and anointed of Christ, leaving his naked body exposed to the beasts and birds of prey, and cutting off the very finger which held his episcopal

---

[1] This is the same unfortunate Gaudry bishop of Laon who appears in chapter 5, p. 119.

ring. Now these horrible men, advised by the evil Thomas of Marle himself, have seized the castle keep[2]."

Driven now by a double anger, King Louis attacked the illegal castle. He burst the walls asunder, like the gates of hell, freeing the innocent, punishing the guilty most severely, and avenging the injuries of the many. Thirsting for justice, Louis decreed that all those murderers he came across would hang from the gibbet, their bodies left for the kites, the crows, and the vultures to feed upon. They richly deserved this punishment since they had not feared to harm the Lord's anointed.

Having levelled the illegitimate castles, and having restored to the nuns of Saint-John their lost estates, the king turned to deal with the city of Amiens. There a certain tyrant named Adam had fortified himself in the city's keep and had laid waste to the city's churches and neighborhoods. Louis besieged the tower for nearly two years, finally taking it from the defenders. Having taken the tower, he completely destroyed it, bringing peace to the region at last, and thereby carrying out his duties as king, for "it is not for nothing that (rulers) hold the power of the sword." (Romans 13:4) And Louis deprived the evil Thomas and his heirs of the lordship of the city of Amiens forever.

READING 6

Philip Augustus on the Governance of the Realm, 1190

Philip II "Augustus" (1180-1223) was a contemporary of four successive kings of England: Henry II, Richard I, John, and Henry III. This ordinance, establishing a regency government during Philip's absence on the Third Crusade, contrasts sharply with John's Magna Carta. It projects the image of a king whose duties to his subjects are governed by conscience rather than by baronial pressures.

In the name of the holy and indivisible Trinity. Amen. Philip, by the grace of God King of the French.

It is the duty of a King to look after the interests of his subjects by all possible means and to place the public welfare before his own private advantage. Since we are most eagerly and with all our strength fulfilling our vow to make a journey to

From *Sources for the History of Medieval Europe*, ed. and tr. Brian Pullan; Oxford, Basil Blackwell, 1966, pp. 254-257. Reprinted by permission.

[2] The keep was the central tower of a medieval castle.

aid the Holy Land, on the advice of the Most High we have determined to ordain how to deal with the business of the kingdom that must be transacted and how to dispose of our last mortal possessions if we should die upon the journey.

First, therefore, we ordain that our bailiffs shall in each provostship on our estates appoint four wise and law-abiding men who will bear honest witness, and the business of the village shall be transacted only with their advice or with that of at least two of them. At Paris, however, we appoint six honest and law-abiding men whose names are T[hibaud le Riche], A[thon de la Grève], E[brouin le Changeur], R[obert of Chartres], B[audouin Bruneau?] and N[icolas Boisseau?].

In lands of ours which have been specified by name, we have appointed our bailiffs, who shall each month fix one day called the assize, on which all who make a complaint shall receive justice and their rights without delay through the bailiffs, and we shall likewise receive justice and our rights; and a record shall be kept there of all fines which are due to us.

Further, it is our will and command that our dearest mother Queen Adèle, with our dearest uncle and vassal William, Archbishop of Reims, shall every four months fix one day on which they shall hear at Paris the complaints of the men of our Kingdom, and there deal with them to the honour of God and the profit of the realm.

We further ordain that on that day representatives of each of our villages and also our bailiffs who hold assizes shall appear before them to describe in their presence the affairs of our land.

If any of our bailiffs has committed a crime, other than murder, robbery, homicide or treason, and if the Archbishop, the Queen and others who attend to hear of the offences committed by our bailiffs are agreed upon this, we order them to inform us, three times in every year, by letters written on the aforesaid days, which bailiff has offended, and what he has done, and from whom he has received money, gifts or services for causing us or our vassals to lose their rights.

Our bailiffs shall in a similar fashion send us information about our provosts.

The Queen and Archbishop shall not be empowered to remove our bailiffs from their bailiwicks save for murder, robbery, homicide or treason; nor shall bailiffs have the power to remove provosts, save for one of these crimes. We, on God's advice, once these persons have informed us of the facts of the case, will inflict a punishment which will serve as a fitting deterrent to others.

Likewise, the Queen and Archbishop shall report to us three times a year concerning the state of our realm and its affairs.

If it happens that an episcopal see[1] or the headship of a royal abbey falls vacant, we wish the canons of the church or the monks of the monastery which is vacant to come before the Queen and Archbishop, as they would come before us, and ask them for freedom to elect; and we wish the Queen and Archbishop to grant this to them without opposition. We advise the canons and monks to elect a pastor who

---

[1] An episcopal see is a bishopric.

will be pleasing to God and useful to the realm. The Queen and Archbishop shall keep the *regalia* in their hands until the chosen candidate has been consecrated and blessed, and then the *regalia* shall be handed to him without opposition.

We further ordain that if a prebend or ecclesiastical benefice falls vacant, when the *regalia* come into our hands, the Queen and Archbishop shall confer them in the best and most honourable fashion possible upon honourable and learned men, taking the advice of Brother Bernard. Our donations, which we have made by letters patent, shall be excepted from this.

We forbid all prelates of churches and vassals of ours to pay *taille*[2] or other taxes whilst we are on God's service. If the Lord God's will be done and death befalls us, we strictly forbid all men of our land, both clergy and laity, to pay *taille* until our son—may God keep him safe and sound for his service—reaches the age at which, by the grace of the Holy Spirit, he can rule the Kingdom.

Should anyone wish to make war upon our son, and the revenues that he has be not sufficient, then all our vassals must assist him with their persons and their property, and the churches shall extend to him the aid which they are accustomed to render to us.

We forbid our provosts and bailiffs to arrest any man or seize his property, whilst he is willing to give good guarantors that he will appear for trial in our court, except in cases of homicide, murder, robbery or treason.

We further ordain that all our revenues, dues and emoluments shall be brought to Paris at three dates: firstly on the Feast of St. Remigius, secondly at the Purification of the Blessed Virgin and thirdly on Ascension Day; and they shall be handed over to our aforesaid burghers, and to Pierre le Maréchal. Should any of these happen to die, Guy de Garlande shall appoint another in his place.

When our revenues are received, Adam, our clerk, shall be present and record the receipts; and each of the burghers shall have a key to each of the coffers in the Temple in which our treasure is stored, and the Temple itself shall have one. We will give instructions in our letters as to how much of this treasure shall be sent to us.

We ordain that, should we happen to die on the journey we are making, the Queen and Archbishop and the Bishop of Paris, and the Abbots of St. Victor and St. Denis, and Brother Bernard shall divide our treasure into two parts. They shall distribute one-half as they choose in order to repair churches which have been destroyed as a result of our wars, so that the worship of God can take place within them. They shall give some of the same half to those who have been ruined by our taxes; and the rest of the same half to those whom they choose and whom they believe to be most in need, for the salvation of our soul and that of our father King Louis and those of our ancestors. We order the guardians of our treasure and all the men of Paris to keep the other half of the treasure for the needs of our son until he reaches an age at which he can rule the Kingdom with the advice of God and by his own intellect.

---

[2] A specific type of direct tax.

If death should befall both us and our son, we order the aforesaid seven men to distribute our treasure as they choose for the sake of our soul and his. As soon as the news of our death arrives, we wish our treasure, wherever it is, to be taken to the house of the Bishop of Paris, and there kept under guard, and afterwards it shall be disposed of as we have ordained.

We instruct the Queen and Archbishop to keep in their own hands as many as they decently can of the honours, such as abbeys, deaneries and certain other offices, which are in our gift when they fall vacant until we return from serving God; and those that they cannot retain, they shall give and assign in a godly fashion on the advice of Brother Bernard and they shall do this to the honour of God and the profit of the realm. But should we die on the journey, we wish them to give the honours and offices in the churches to those whom they perceive to be most worthy of them.

That this may be firmly established, we order this charter to be authenticated by our seal and by the addition of the royal signature below.

Done at Paris, in the year of the Incarnate Word 1190, in the eleventh year of our reign, with those whose names and signatures are appended below present in our palace. The signature of Count Thibaut, our Seneschal. The signature of Guy the Butler. The signature of Matthew the Chamberlain. The signature of Ralph the Constable. Given at a time when the Chancery was vacant.

READING 7

Louis IX Receives Certain Relics

Matthew Paris, a monk of St. Albans Abbey, was born around 1200 and died in or shortly after 1259. He was an Englishman who, despite his name, was probably neither born nor educated in Paris. He was thus a contemporary but not a countryman of St. Louis. Nevertheless, he was in a position to be well informed about the affairs of Western Christendom: St. Albans was a much visited abbey, a day's journey from London on the main road to the north. Matthew was personally acquainted with Henry III, his queen Eleanor of Provence, and important barons, bishops, and royal officials.

The passage below illustrates the importance of relics and religious ceremonial in intensifying the sense of holiness associated with the French monarchy. The relics described here were

From Matthew Paris, *History of the English*, tr. J.A. Giles; vol 1, London, Henry G. Bohn, 1852.

among the most significant in Christendom. Whether the cross in
question was actually the "True Cross" remains a matter of debate,
but it did have a verifiable pedigree running back to the fourth
century. St. Louis took relics very seriously and was not easily
fooled. His "beautiful chapel at Paris" described toward the end
of the passage is known as La Sainte-Chapelle and remains to this
day one of the architectural marvels of Europe.

In this year, [1241] the holy cross of our Lord, which, after the time of Saladin,
had remained at Damietta until the unfortunate battle, in which that city had been
first gained and afterwards lost, when it fell into the hands of the Saracens, was
brought into the kingdom of France, by the agency of the French king and his
mother, Blanche, and by the grace of Christ seconding their pious wishes: they
gave a large sum of money in order to obtain possession of the same. When this
cross was first sold, it was bought by the Venetians for twenty thousand pounds,
and they obtained it from the two sons of J., king of Jerusalem, who wanted money
to make war on the Greeks; and afterwards Baldwin pawned it for a still larger sum
of money, and lastly sold it to Louis, the French king.

On the Friday next preceding Easter-day, on which day our Lord Jesus Christ
was nailed to the life-giving-cross for the redemption of the world, this said cross
was carried to Paris from the church of St. Antoine, where it had been placed on a
vehicle of some kind, on which the king mounted with the two queens, namely,
Blanche of Castile, his mother, and Margaret of Provence, his wife, and his
brothers, and in the presence of the archbishops, bishops, abbots, and other
religious men, as well as the French nobles, and surrounded by a countless host of
people, who were awaiting this glorious sight with great joy of heart, raised the
cross above his head with tears, whilst the prelates who were present cried with a
loud voice, "Behold the cross of our Lord." After all had worshipped it with due
reverence and devotion, the king himself, barefooted, ungirt, and with his head
bare, and after a fast of three days, following the example of the noble and august
Heraclius,[1] carried it in wool to the cathedral church of Notre Dame at Paris; the
brothers of the king, too, after having purified themselves by similar acts of
devotion, by confessions, fasting, and prayers, followed him on foot with the two
queens.

They also carried the crown of thorns (which divine mercy had, as has been
before stated, given to the kingdom of France the year before), and raising it on
high on a similar vehicle to the other, presented it to the gaze of the people. Some
of the nobles supported the arms of the king and his brothers, whilst carrying this
pious burden, lest they should become fatigued by holding their hands constantly
raised, and give way beneath this priceless treasure. This was done circumspectly

---

[1]The East Roman Emperor (610-641) who liberated the "true cross" from the Persians.

at the wish of the prelates, that so holy a thing might be handled reverently by those whose prudent conduct had gained so much glory, after the example of Heraclius, whom we have before mentioned. When they arrived at the cathedral church, all the bells in the city were set ringing, and after special prayers had been solemnly read, the king returned to his great palace, which is in the middle of the city, carrying his cross, his brothers carrying the crown, and the priests following in a regular procession (a sight more solemn or more joyful than which the kingdom of France had never seen), and each and all then, with clasped hands, glorified God, who thus showed his especial love for the French kingdom above all others, and for affording to it his consolation and protection.

Thus, therefore, our Lord Jesus Christ, the King of kings, the Lord of lords, whose judgments are a great deep, in whose hands are the hearts of kings, giving health to whomsoever he wills, in a short space of time endowed and enriched the kingdom of France with these three precious gifts, namely, the aforesaid crown and cross of our Lord, of which we have now made mention, and the body of the blessed Edmund of Canterbury, the archbishop and confessor, which was now manifestly shining forth with unusual miracles. The French king therefore ordered a chapel of handsome structure, suitable for the reception of his said treasure, to be built near his palace, and in it he afterwards placed the said relics with due honour. Besides these the French king had, in his beautiful chapel at Paris, the garment belonging to Christ, the lance, that is to say, the iron head of the lance, and the sponge, and other relics besides; on which account the pope granted an indulgence of forty days to all who went to them in the chapel at Paris for the sake of paying their devotions.

READING 8

Philip the Fair *vs.* Boniface VIII

This emphatic statement of the papal monarchy doctrine is by no means the assertion of papal self-confidence that it might seem. It was issued in November 1302 by Pope Boniface VIII (1294-1303) as he was nearing the end of his stormy pontificate. King Edward I of England and Philip IV (1285-1314) of France had been advancing the doctrine of royal authority against the claims of the international church. Boniface responded to Philip of France with *Unam Sanctam*—somewhat less than the assertion of papal self-confidence

From *The Crisis of Church and State, 1050-1300*, ed. Brian Tierney; Prentice-Hall, Englewood Cliffs, N.J., 1964, pp. 188-189, 191.

that it may appear, given the threat. Less than a year after its issue, Philip sent a band of French and Italian troops to confront Boniface at his residence at Anagni. Boniface died three weeks later, in a state of shock and humiliation.

A. *UNAM SANCTAM*, 1302

That there is one holy, Catholic and apostolic Church we are bound to believe and to hold, our faith urging us, and this we do firmly believe and simply confess; and that outside this Church there is no salvation or remission of sins, as her spouse proclaims in the Canticles, "One is my dove, my perfect one. She is the only one of her mother, the chosen of her that bore her" (Canticles 6:8); which represents one mystical body whose head is Christ, while the head of Christ is God. In this Church there is one Lord, one faith, one baptism. At the time of the Flood there was one ark, symbolizing the one Church. It was finished in one cubit and had one helmsman and captain, namely Noah, and we read that all things on earth outside of it were destroyed. This Church we venerate and this alone, the Lord saying through his prophet, "Deliver, O God, my soul from the sword, my only one from the power of the dog" (Psalm 21:21). He prayed for the soul, that is himself, the head, and at the same time for the body, which he called the one Church on account of the promised unity of faith, sacraments and charity of the Church. This is that seamless garment of the Lord which was not cut but fell by lot. Therefore there is one body and one head of this one and only Church, not two heads as though it were a monster, namely Christ and Christ's vicar, Peter and Peter's successor, for the Lord said to this Peter, "Feed my sheep" (John 21:17). He said "My sheep" in general, not these or those, whence he is understood to have committed them all to Peter. Hence, if the Greeks or any others say that they were not committed to Peter and his successors, they necessarily admit that they are not of Christ's flock, for the Lord says in John that there is one sheepfold and one shepherd.

We are taught by the words of the Gospel that in this Church and in her power there are two swords, a spiritual one and a temporal one. For when the apostles said "Here are two swords" (Luke 22:38), meaning in the Church since it was the apostles who spoke, the Lord did not reply that it was too many but enough. Certainly anyone who denies that the temporal sword is in the power of Peter has not paid heed to the words of the Lord when he said, "Put up thy sword into its sheath" (Matthew 26:52). Both then are in the power of the Church, the material sword and the spiritual. But the one is exercised for the Church, the other by the Church, the one by the hand of the priest, the other by the hand of kings and soldiers, though at the will and sufferance of the priest. One sword ought to be under the other and the temporal authority subject to the spiritual power. For, while the apostle says, "There is no power but from God and those that are ordained of God" (Romans 13: 1), they would not be ordained unless one sword was under the other and, being inferior, was led by the other to the highest things. For, according to the blessed Dionysius, it is the law of divinity for the lowest to be led to the highest through intermediaries. In the order of the universe all things are not kept in order in the same fashion and immediately but the lowest are ordered by the intermediate and inferiors by superiors. But that the spiritual power excels any earthly one in dignity and nobility we ought the more openly to confess in proportion as spiritual things excel temporal ones. Moreover we clearly perceive this from the giving of tithes, from benediction and sanctification, from the acceptance of this power and from the very government of things. For, the truth bearing witness, the spiritual power has to institute the earthly power and to judge it if it has not been good. So is verified the prophecy of Jeremiah [1: 10] concerning the Church and the power of the Church, "Lo, I have set thee this day over the nations and over kingdoms" etc.

Therefore, if the earthly power errs, it shall be judged by the spiritual power, if a lesser spiritual power errs it shall be judged by its superior, but if the supreme spiritual power errs it can be judged only by God not by man, as the apostle witnesses, "The spiritual man judgeth all things and he himself is judged of no man" (1 Corinthians 2:15). Although this authority was given to a man and is exercised by a man it is not human but rather divine, being given to Peter at God's mouth, and confirmed to him and to his successors in him, the rock whom the Lord acknowledged when he said to Peter himself "Whatsoever thou shalt bind" etc. (Matthew 16:19). Whoever therefore resists this power so ordained by God resists the ordinance of God unless, like the Manicheans, he imagines that there are two beginnings, which we judge to be false and heretical, as Moses witnesses, for not "in the beginnings" but "in the beginning" God created heaven and earth (Genesis 1:1). Therefore we declare, state, define and pronounce that it is altogether necessary to salvation for every human creature to be subject to the Roman Pontiff.

B.   THE INCIDENT AT ANAGNI, 1303

Behold, Reverend Father, at dawn of the vigil of the Nativity of the Blessed Mary just past, suddenly and unexpectedly there came upon Anagni a great force of armed men of the party of the King of France and of the two deposed Colonna cardinals. Arriving at the gates of Anagni and finding them open, they entered the town and at once made an assault upon the palace of the Pope and upon that of the Marquis, the Pope's nephew. . . .

After a time, however, the Marquis, nephew of the Pope, realizing that defense was no longer possible, surrendered to Sciarra and the captain, so that they spared his own life and those of his sons and companions. In this fashion were the Marquis and one of his sons taken and thrown into prison, while another son escaped by means of a hidden passage. When the Pope heard this reported, he himself wept bitterly, yet not even the Pope was in a position to hold out longer. Sciarra and his forces broke through the doors and windows of the papal palace at a number of points, and set fire to them at others, till at last the angered soldiery forced their way to the Pope. Many of them heaped insults upon his head and threatened him violently, but to them all the Pope answered not so much as a word. And when they pressed him as to whether he would resign the Papacy, firmly did he refuse—indeed he preferred to lose his head—as he said in his vernacular: "*E le col, e le cape!*" which means: "Here is my neck and here my head." Therewith he proclaimed in the presence of them all that as long as life was in him, he would not give up the Papacy. Sciarra, indeed, was quite ready to kill him, but he was held back by the others so that no bodily injury was done the Pope. Cardinal Peter of Spain was with the Pope all through the struggle, though the rest of his retinue had slipped away. Sciarra and the captain appointed guards to keep the Pope in custody after some of the papal doormen had fled and others had been slain. Thus [were] the Pope and his nephew taken in Anagni on the said vigil of the Blessed Mary at about the hour of vespers and it is believed that the Lord Pope put in a bad night.

The soldiers, on first breaking in, had pillaged the Pope, his chamber and his treasury of utensils and clothing, fixtures, gold and silver and everything found therein so that the Pope had been made as poor as Job upon receiving word of his misfortune. Moreover, the Pope witnessed all and saw how the wretches divided his garments and carted away his furniture, both large items and small, deciding who would take this and who that, and yet he said no more than: "The Lord gave and the Lord taketh away, etc." And anyone who was in a position to seize or to lay hold upon something, took and seized it and carried it off . . . .

PART THREE

THE LATE MIDDLE AGES

The late Middle Ages (*c*. 1300-1500) are difficult to characterize. The era was one of plague, depression, and strife, but it also witnessed the Italian Renaissance, the invention of printing, and the early voyages of discovery.

The Hundred Years War (1337-1453) brought death, starvation, and intermittent anarchy to the French countryside while driving the English monarchy to the brink of bankruptcy and forcing it to make significant concessions to Parliament. England suffered widespread disorder, a bloodcurdling peasants' revolt, the deposition and murder of two kings, and a drawn-out civil war between rival aristocratic factions—the so-called "Wars of the Roses" (1455-1485). Spain, too, was afflicted by civil strife, as were Italy and central Europe. Yet by the close of the period strong monarchies had reemerged in France, England, and Spain, and the Italian Renaissance had reached its height.

The late-medieval Church was similarly troubled. The popes moved from faction-ridden Rome to Avignon in 1309 and remained there for more than a century. Between 1378 and 1415 the Church was torn by schism as two popes, and later three, contended for the spiritual supremacy of Christendom. The period ended with the papacy reunited and planted firmly back in Rome, but drained of much of its former prestige and international authority. The Protestant Reformation was just beyond the horizon.

The civil and economic unrest of the late Middle Ages was aggravated enormously by the onset of bubonic plague. Descending on Europe in 1348, the Black Death carried off perhaps a third of its population in the ensuing two years and returned periodically during the next three centuries. As a consequence of plague, warfare, and famine, Europe's population was lower in 1500 than in 1300, and most of its major cities had diminished accordingly. But in the last half of the fifteenth century the population reversed its long downward trend and commerce began to revive. By 1500 there were clear signs that Europe had surmounted its late-medieval crisis. Western Civilization was moving into an era of renewed prosperity and global expansion.

CHAPTER **10**

CONSTITUTIONAL EUROPE

The Hundred Years War widened the gulf between the French and English systems of royal governance, propelling France toward the absolutism of early-modern times while advancing the authority of Parliament in England. The war was far too expensive for either government to support with ordinary revenues, but whereas the French monarchy, under King Charles V, succeeded in establishing the right to tax its subjects relatively freely on the grounds of the military emergency, the English monarchy had to obtain Parliament's permission for extraordinary taxes, and therefore Parliament—more specifically the House of Commons—enjoyed considerable leverage. It insisted more and more that the monarchy grant its petitions in return for its own permission to levy new taxes, and, on rare occasions, it even exercised the right to impeach royal ministers (document 1). The next document describes a "constitutional" movement amidst the horrors of the Hundred Years War in fourteenth-century France—a movement led by the Paris merchant Étienne Marcel, who was subsequently assassinated. The recovery of French military fortunes in the next century is illustrated by the next two documents (3 and 4)—on Joan of Arc and the military juggernaut of King Charles VII.

Sir John Fortescue, writing in the fifteenth century, distinguishes sharply and perhaps unfairly between the English and French regimes (document 5); his views should be compared with those of the French historian Philippe Commynes, on monarchical authority in France (document 6).

The German monarchy (or Holy Roman Empire), battered by generations of struggle with the papacy and German princes, emerged from the Middle Ages in crippled condition (document 7). The Roman papacy was similarly weakened by its long exile in Avignon, its lapse into schism, its conflicts with Church councils, and its declining moral reputation (documents 8-11).

READING 1

Documents Relating to
Crown and Parliament in England

These documents illustrated the changing relationship between crown and parliament during the period of the Hundred Years War, and the split within parliament between lords and commons. It was the commons (smallholding shire knights and representatives from towns) who wrung the most important privileges from the financially strapped monarchy. Step by step, the crown was surrendering its initiative as parliament established control over direct taxation and used that power to compel the king to grant its petitions. On the principle of "redress before supply," parliament was insisting that the king enact its petitions into law without alteration. Behind the mask of courtly and respectful language, one can discern some sharp-eyed negotiating over difficult constitutional issues.

A. THE PARLIAMENT OF 1348

The knights of the shires and the others of the commons were told that they should withdraw together and take good counsel as to how our lord the king could be aided to his greatest advantage and to the least burdening of his people and at last gave their response:

Thus the said poor commons, to their own excessive hurt, grant to our lord the king three fifteenths[1] to be levied during three years, on condition that this aid shall be assigned and kept solely for the war of our lord the king and shall not be assigned to pay old debts; and also, no imposition, tax, nor loan be levied by the privy council without their grant and assent.

And afterwards the said commons were told that all individual persons who wished to present petitions in this parliament should do so, and the commons presented their petitions in the manner following:

Item. The commons pray the petitions presented in the last parliament shall be observed; and that by no bill presented in this parliament shall the responses already granted be changed: for the commons acknowledge no such bill as may be presented by any one to effect the contrary.

From *English Historical Documents, vol. iv,* ed. A.R. Myers; New York, Oxford University Press, 1969, pp. 443, 446-447, 455, 460-462.

[1] A "fifteenth" was a tax of one-fifteenth of the value of all of a person's property apart from real estate. Unlike modern taxes, which are levied on real estate or income, these assessments applied to the worth of an individual's movable goods.

Response: At an earlier time the king, by the advice of the prelates and lords of the land, made answer to the petitions of the commons regarding the law of the land, to the effect that neither the laws held in times past nor the process of the same law could be changed without making a new statute.

And there were two causes which specifically affected our lord the king: first, concerning the war which our lord the king had undertaken against his adversary of France, the question was what shall be done when the truce has ended? The other cause, concerning the peace of England, and how and in what manner it could best be kept. And the knights of the shire and the commons were told that they must treat together and what they felt they must show to the king and his council. These knights and commons discussed together on these matters for four days, and at last they answered:

Very dread lord, as for your war and the array of it, we are so ignorant and simple that we do not know, nor are we able, to counsel on these matters. Wherefore we pray your gracious lordship to have us excused from your order, and may it please you, by the advice of the great and wise men of your council to ordain on this point what shall seem best to you.

B. THE "GOOD" PARLIAMENT OF 1376

Richard Lyons, merchant of London, was impeached and accused by the commons for many deceptions, extortions, and other crimes committed by him against our lord the king and against his people, both when he was in attendance on the household of the king and when he was collector of the king's customs, because he has put and caused to be put certain new imposition on wools and on merchandise without the assent of parliament; and he has levied and collected those impositions largely for his own use and the use of those who attend the king.

Thereupon the said Richard was ordered to prison during the king's pleasure, to be put to fine and ransom, according to the amount and heinousness of his offense, and that he lose his liberty [citizenship] in the city of London, and that he never hold office from the king, nor enter the council or the palace of the king.

C. THE PARLIAMENT OF 1401

The commons showed to our lord the king that in several parliaments before this time their common petitions have not been answered before they made their grant of some aid or subsidy to our lord the king. And therefore they prayed our lord the king that for the great ease and comfort of the commons, our lord the king might be pleased to grant to the commons that they might have knowledge of the answers to their petitions before any such grant had thus been made.

D. THE PARLIAMENT OF 1407

The king our sovereign lord sitting in the council chamber, the lords spiritual and temporal summoned to this present parliament being with him, they discussed amongst themselves the estate of the realm, and the means necessary for its defense against its enemies, and they agreed that it would not be possible to resist their malice, unless our sovereign lord the king should be granted in this present parliament some notable aid and subsidy. And on this the lords were then asked the question, "What aid would suffice and be necessary in this case?" To which demand and question the lords answered severally that considering the needs of the king on the one hand, and the poverty of the people on the other, the least aid that would suffice would be to have one and a half tenths from the cities and boroughs and one and a half fifteenths from the other lay people, etc. On which, by the king's command, the commons were bidden to send before our lord the king and the lords a certain number of persons of their company to hear and report to their companions what our lord the king should have commanded them. When this was reported to the commons, they were much disturbed, saying and affirming that it was a great prejudice and derogation of their liberties. And when our lord the king heard that, he granted and declared with the advice and assent of the same lords in the following manner. That is to say, that in this present parliament and those to be held in the future, the lords may well discuss together with regard to the state and remedies—always provided that the lords for their part and the commons on their part shall not make any report to our lord the king about any grant made by the commons and assented to by the lords, until the lords and commons are of one assent and agreement in this matter; and then it shall be reported in manner and form as is customary, that is, by the mouth of the speaker of the commons for the time being, so that the lords and commons may have the thanks of our lord the king. Moreover our lord the king wishes, with the assent of the lords, that the proceedings in this present parliament set forth above shall not be turned to the prejudice or derogation of the liberty of the commons, but he wishes that he and all the other estates shall be as free as they were before.

E. THE PARLIAMENT OF 1414

Our sovereign lord, your humble and true lieges beseech unto your very righteousness that from this time forward, no law ever be made and engrossed as a law or statute, which should change the wording and the intention asked by the speaker[2] without the assent of the commons.

---

[2] Speaker of the House of Commons.

READING 2

Jean Froissart, *The Rise and Fall of Étienne Marcel*

In 1356 the French suffered their second great military disaster of the Hundred Years War: they were routed at Poitiers by an English army led by King Edward III's eldest son, Edward the Black Prince, who captured the French king, John "the Good," and held him for ransom. John's son and heir, Charles duke of Normandy (the future King Charles V), tried to uphold the royal cause but could not rule as king while his father still lived. He was confronted by a bloody and brutal peasants' uprising known as the Jacquerie revolt (omitted here for the sake of readers of delicate sensibilities) and by a uniquely assertive Estates General led by a Parisian cloth merchant named Étienne Marcel, identified in this passage as the Provost of Merchants, whose effort at government through legislature cost him his life. The revolt of Marcel tainted constitutional government in France for more than a century.

If the English and their allies were jubilant at the capture of King John [the Good] at Poitiers, the kingdom of France was deeply disturbed. There was cause enough, for it brought loss and suffering to people of all condition, and the wiser heads predicted that greater evils were to come. Their sovereign was a prisoner and all the best of their knights were also in prison or dead.

In addition, those knights and squires who had returned from the battle were so blamed and detested by the commons that they were reluctant to go into the big towns.

So all the prelates of the church, bishops and abbots, all the nobility, lords and knights, the Provost of the merchants of Paris [Étienne Marcel] and the burgesses, and the councilors of the French towns, met together in Paris to consider how the realm should be governed until their king should be set free. They also wanted to find out what had happened to the vast sums which had been raised in the past through tithes, levies on capital, forced loans, coinings of new money, and all the other extortionate measures by which the population had been tormented and oppressed while the soldiers remained underpaid and the county inadequately protected. But of these matters no one was able to give an account.

It was therefore agreed that the prelates should elect twelve good men from among them, with powers, as representatives of the clergy, to devise suitable means of dealing with the situation described. The barons and knights also elected

From *Chronicles*, tr. Geoffrey Brereton; Penguin Books, Baltimore, 1968, pp. 146-150, 155-161.

twelve of the wisest and shrewdest of their number to attend to the same matters, and the burgesses twelve in the same way. It was then decided by common consent that these thirty-six persons should meet frequently in Paris to discuss the affairs of the realm and put them in order. Questions of all kinds were to be referred to the Three Estates. Their acts and ordinances were to be binding on all the other prelates, nobles, and common people of the cities and towns. Nevertheless, even at the beginning, several of those elected were viewed unfavorably by the Duke of Normandy and his council.[1]

As a first measure, the Three Estates stopped the coining of the money then being minted and took possession of the dies. Secondly, they required the Duke to arrest his father's Chancellor and the other financial officers and former councilors of the king, in order that they should render a true account of all the funds which had been levied and collected on their advice. When these high officials heard of this, they completely disappeared and were wise to do so.

Next, they appointed on their own authority officials with the duty of raising and collecting all the levies, taxes, tithes, loans, and other duties payable to the crown, and they had new coinage of fine gold minted.

At that time a knight called Sir Regnault de Cervoles, commonly known as the Archpriest, took command of a large company of men-at-arms assembled from many countries. These found that their pay had ceased with the capture of King John and could see no way of making a living in France. They therefore went towards Provence, where they took a number of fortified towns and castles by assault and plundered the whole country as far as Avignon. Pope Innocent VI and his cardinals who were at Avignon were in such fear of them that they hardly knew where to turn, and they kept their household servants armed day and night. After the Archpriest and his men had pillaged the whole region, the Pope and his college opened negotiations with him. He entered Avignon with most of his followers by friendly agreement, was received with as much respect as if he had been the king of France's son, and dined several times at the palace with the Pope and the cardinals. All his sins were remitted him and when he left he was given forty thousand crowns to distribute among his companions.

At that time also there arose another company of men-at-arms and irregulars from various countries, who subdued and plundered the whole region between the Seine and the Loire. As a result, no one dared to travel between Paris and Vendôme, or Paris and Orléans, or Paris and Montargis, and no one dared to remain there. These companies often carried their raids almost to Paris, or at other times towards Orléans or Chartres. They ranged the country in troops of twenty, thirty, or forty and they met no one capable of putting up a resistance to them.

These activities of what were known as the Free Companies [mercenaries] who attacked all travellers carrying valuables, began under the administration of the

---

[1] The Duke of Normandy was the dauphin Charles, son and heir of the captured King John the Good; on John's death he was crowned King Charles V (1364-1380).

Three Estates. The nobles and prelates began to grow tired of the institution of the Estates and left the Provost of the Merchants and some of the burgesses of Paris to go their own way, finding that these were interfering more than they liked with the conduct of affairs.

It happened one day that the Provost of the Merchants assembled a great crowd of the common people of Paris who supported him, all wearing similar caps by which they could recognize each other. He went to the palace surrounded by his men and entered the Duke of Normandy's room, where he asked him very sharply to shoulder responsibility for the affairs of the realm and give some thought to them, so that the kingdom—which would eventually be his—should be protected from the depredations of the Free Companies. The Duke replied that he would be quite ready to do so if he had the means at his disposal, but that it should be done by whoever collected the revenue and taxes belonging to the realm.

I do not know exactly how it happened, but such an angry argument arose that there, in the presence of the Duke of Normandy, three of the chief members of his council were killed, so close to him that his robe was splashed with blood and he himself was in great danger. But he was given one of the people's caps to put on his head, and was forced to pardon the murder of his three knights.

The Provost of the Merchants and his faction, knowing that they had incurred the resentment and hatred of their sovereign lord the Duke of Normandy, began to feel uneasy. Now it happened that inside Paris itself there had remained a large number of English and Navarrese mercenaries who had been retained by the Provost and the commons to help defend them against the Duke of Normandy. A disturbance arose between them and the Parisians, in which more than sixty of the soldiers were killed. The Provost of the Merchants was highly incensed by this and blamed the Parisians bitterly; but nevertheless, to appease the people, he took some hundred and fifty of the soldiers and imprisoned them in the Louvre, telling the citizens that he would punish them according to their crimes. This quieted the Parisians and after nightfall the Provost, who wished to propitiate the English mercenaries, released them from prison and sent them on their way.

When the English all assembled at Saint-Denis, they decided to avenge their comrades and the treatment inflicted on themselves. They sent a declaration of war to the Parisians and began to rove about outside the city killing and hacking to pieces any of the inhabitants who were bold enough to venture outside. The people of Paris fell into such distress and confusion that they no longer knew whom to trust. They began to murmur and be suspicious of everyone. The Duke of Normandy, for his part would not intervene as long as the Parisians were still ruled by the Provost of the Merchants. He sent them a public notification in writing that he would not make peace with them unless twelve of the citizens, to be chosen by himself, were surrendered to him at discretion. It is easy to understand why the Provost and others who knew they were inculpated were filled with alarm. They saw clearly enough, on considering the situation, that things could not continue as they were for long, for the people of Paris were beginning to cool in their enthusiasm for them and their party. They entered into secret negotiations with the English soldiers who were harrying Paris. A pact was made between the two parties, according to which the Provost and his supporters were to seize possession of the Porte Saint-Honoré and the Porte Saint-Antoine and to open those two gates at midnight to a combined force of English and Navarrese, who would come ready armed to ravage and destroy Paris.

On the very night when this was to happen, an inspiration from God awoke some of the citizens who had an understanding with the Duke of Normandy. These learnt that Paris was to be plundered and destroyed. They immediately armed themselves and all their friends and caused the news to be whispered about secretly, so as to gain more supporters.

Well-armed and numerous, they raised the banner of France to the cry of "Up with the king and the duke!" and were followed by the people. They went to the Porte Saint-Antoine where they found the Provost of the Merchants with the keys of the gate in his hands. Bitter accusations were hurled at the Provost and he was attacked and forced back. The people were in a tumult, clamoring and hooting. They shouted: "Death to the Provost and his friends! They have betrayed us! Kill them!"

In the midst of the commotion the Provost would gladly have escaped had he been able to, but was so close-pressed that he could not. Sir Jean de Charny hit him on the head with an axe and stretched him on the ground. Then he was struck by others who did not leave off until he was dead, together with six others of his faction. A search was made through the streets and the city was put in a state of defense and strong guards posted over it for the remainder of the night.

As soon as the Provost and his supporters had been killed or caught, which took place of the evening of Tuesday, 31 July 1358, messengers were sent in haste with the news to the Duke of Normandy, who was at Meaux. He was naturally delighted and prepared to come to Paris. But before his arrival, the King of Navarre's Treasurer, Josseran de Mâcon, and Charles Toussac, an alderman of Paris, were executed as traitors In the Place de Greve. The bodies of the Provost and the others killed with him were dragged to the courtyard of St. Catherine's Church, in the Val des Ecoliers. Gashed and naked as they were, they were laid in front of the cross in the courtyard and left there for a long time, so that any who wished to see them could do so. Afterwards they were thrown into the Seine.

READING 3

Waurin on Joan of Arc

This passage on Joan of Arc (*c.* 1412-1431), from the French
historian Jean de Waurin's contemporary chronicle, is less adula-
tory than most other accounts, and all the more interesting for that
reason.

While Orléans was besieged, there came to King Charles of France, at Chinon
where he was then staying, a young girl who described herself as a maid of twenty
years of age or thereabout, named Joan, who was clothed and habited in the guise
of a man. This Joan had remained a long time at an inn and she was very bold in
riding horses and leading them to drink and also in performing other feats and
exercises which young girls are not accustomed to do; and she was sent to the king
of France by a knight named Sir Robert de Baudricourt, captain of the palace of
Vaucoulleurs appointed on behalf of King Charles. This Sir Robert gave her horses
and five or six companions, and likewise instructed her, and taught her what she
ought to say and do, and the way in which she could conduct herself, since she
asserted that she was a maid inspired by divine providence, and sent to King
Charles to restore him and bring him back into the possession of all his kingdom
generally, from which he was, as she said, wrongfully driven away and put out.
And the maid was, at her coming, in very poor estate; and she was about two
months in the house of the king, whom she many times admonished by her
speeches, as she had been instructed, to give her troops and aid, and she would repel
and drive away his enemies, and exalt his name, enlarging his lordships, certifying
that she had had a sufficient revelation concerning this. And she was then
considered at court only as one deranged and deluded, because she boasted herself
as able to achieve so great an enterprise, which seemed to the great princes a thing
impossible, considering that all they together could not effect it. Nevertheless,
after the maid had remained a good space at the king's court, she was brought
forward and aided, and she raised a standard whereon she had painted the figure
and representation of Our Lord Jesus Christ; indeed, all her words were full of the
name of God. And she was many times examined by famous clerks and men of
great authority in order to inquire and know more fully her intention, but she
always held to her purpose, saying that if the king would believe her she would
restore him to his dominion. Maintaining this purpose she accomplished some
operations successfully, whereby she acquired great renown, fame, and exaltation.

This maid went with the Duke of Alençon from Chinon to Poitiers, where he
ordered that the marshal should take provisions and artillery and other necessary

From *English Historical Documents*, vol. IV, ed. A.R. Myers; Oxford University Press, New
York, 1969, pp. 242-243.

things to Orléans in force, whither the maid Joan wished to go; and she made request that they would give her a suit of armor to arm herself, which was delivered to her. Then, with her standard raised, she went to Blois where the muster was being made, and then to Orléans with the others; and she was always armed, in complete armor, and on this same journey many men-at-arms placed themselves under her.

When the maid had come into the city of Orléans, they gave her a good reception, and some were greatly rejoiced at seeing her in their company. And when the French troops who had brought the provisions into Orléans returned to the king, the maid remained there. And she was urged to go out to skirmish with the others by La Hire and some captains, but she made answer that she would not go unless the men-at-arms who had brought her were also with her: these were recalled from Blois and from the other places whither they had now withdrawn. And they returned to Orleans, where they were joyfully received by the maid. So she went out to them to welcome them, saying that she had well seen and considered the governance of the English, and that if they would believe in her she would make them all rich.

So she began that day to sally out of the town, and went with great alacrity to attack one of the English towers, which she took by force; and going on from that time she did some very marvelous things.

READING 4

Chartier, *Chronique du Roi Charles VII*

The Dauphin Charles, the future Charles VII (1422-61), 1450, owed much to Joan of Arc for saving his Valois dynasty at the nadir of its fortunes and for urging his coronation at Reims Cathedral in 1422. But as the contemporary chronicler Jean Chartier makes clear, when Joan fell into the hands of the English, Charles made little effort to rescue her. Nevertheless, from Joan of Arc's time on, the tide turned decisively in favor of the French who, well before Charles VII's death in 1461, had driven the English from all of France except the port of Calais on the English Channel. Charles, in short, was the king who won the Hundred Years War, and this passage explains one part of how he did it.

From *English Historical Documents*, vol. iv, ed. A.R. Myers; New York, Oxford University Press, 1969, pp. 262-263.

Whoever might wish to make mention of all the valiant men and of their deeds which have been done during the recovery of Normandy would find it too long for recital or writing. But nevertheless one must make some mention and record of the matter for those who in time to come may wish to read or hear the method and means of the miraculous recovery of this duchy. First of all, the king of France imposed good order on the conduct of his men-at-arms. He caused all those men to be equipped with good and sure arms and weapons; and each had two mounted archers. And these men were paid every month, so that they did not dare nor venture during this war and conquest of Normandy to take any of the people prisoner for ransom, whether they were in obedience of the English or of their own side; nor did they seize any food without paying, except from the English or their adherents, in which case they could take it lawfully.

Just as important was the provision that the king had made in his artillery for warfare, and he had a number of bombards, great cannons, culverins, so that never in the memory of man did a Christian king have such numerous artillery, or so well furnished with powder, shot, and all things necessary to approach and take towns and castles, nor had more carriages to drag them nor gunners more experienced to handle them, which gunners were paid from day to day.

And it was a marvelous thing to see the bulwarks, ditches, moats, and mines before all the towns and castles that were besieged during the war; for there was not a town taken by composition [i.e., through engineering] which could not have been taken by assault, but the king, through his kindness, always wished to take them by composition, to avoid the shedding of human blood and the destruction of his own country.

READING 5

John Fortescue on the English and French Monarchies

Sir John Fortescue (*c.* 1394-*c.* 1476) was a distinguished English jurist who served as chief justice of the King's Bench. Shifting political configurations resulting from the Wars of the Roses drove him for a time into exile in France but did not diminish his admiration for the English system of government. In the following passage from *The Governance of England* (*c.* 1470), Fortescue contrasts French "royal lordship" with English "political and royal lordship." His bias toward the English system will be evident.

From Sir John Fortescue, *The Governance of England,* ed. and tr. Charles Plummer; Oxford, The Clarendon Press, 1885, pp. 109-115. Revised by Joe W. Leedom.

There are two types of kingdoms, one of which is called a royal lordship, and the other is called a political and royal lordship.[1] They differ in that the first king may rule his people by such laws as he makes himself, and therefore he may set taxes and other impositions on them as he himself wishes, without their assent. The second king may not rule his people by laws other than those they assent to, and therefore he may set no impositions upon them without their own assent.

It may perhaps be marvelled at by some men why one realm is a royal lordship alone and the prince rules it by his law, called the royal law, and why another kingdom is a royal and political lordship and the prince rules it by a law called the royal and political law, since these two princes are of equal stature. This doubt may be answered in this manner: that the first constitution of these two realms upon the incorporation of them is the cause of this diversity. Now it seems to me it is shown openly enough why one king rules royally alone and the other politically and royally: for one kingdom began of and by the might of the prince, and the other began by the desire and institution of the people of the prince.

Now the French king reigns upon his people royally; yet neither St. Louis, once king there, nor any of his progenitors ever set taxes or other impositions upon the people of that land without the assent of the Three Estates, which, when they are assembled, are like the parliament in England.[2] And many of his successors kept this order until recently, when Englishmen made such war in France that the Three Estates dared not come together. And so because of that, and because of the great necessity which the French king had of good for the defence of that land, he took it upon himself to set taxes and other impositions upon the commons without the assent of the Three Estates; yet he would not and has not set such charges upon the nobles for fear of rebellion. And because the commons there, though they have complained, have not rebelled and are not ready to rebel, the French kings have every year since set such charges upon them, and augmented such charges, so that the commons are so impoverished and destroyed that they may hardly live. Truly they live in the most extreme poverty and misery, though they dwell in the most fertile land in the world. And because of this the French king does not have men of his own realm able to defend it, except for the nobles who bear no such impositions; rather, the king is forced to make his armies and retinues for the defence of his land up of foreigners, Scots, Spaniards, men of Germany, and of other nations, or else all his enemies might overrun him, for he has no defences of his own, except his castles and fortresses. Lo, this is the fruit of his royal law.

If the realm of England, which is an island, were ruled under such a law and such a prince, it would then be a prey to all other nations, and they would conquer, rob, or devour it, as was proved in the time of the Britons. But this land is ruled under a better law, and therefore the people of it are not in such penury, but rather they are

---

[1] The Latin for these two types of government, a *dominium regale* and a *dominium politicum et regale,* was widely used in later discussions of the English government.

[2] The first Estates General, as the French parliament came to be known, did not actually meet until 1303.

wealthy and have all things necessary to the sustenance of nature. And so they are mighty, and able to resist the adversaries of this realm, and to beat other realms that do, or would do them wrong. Lo, this is the fruit of the royal and political law under which we live.

READING 6

Philippe de Commynes on the French Monarchy

One of the most gifted French historians of the late Middle Ages, Philippe de Commynes (d. 1509) dealt astutely with the reigns of Louis XI (1461-1483) and Charles VIII (1483-1498). Compare the opinions of Commynes and Fortescue on the taxation power of the French crown.

Of all the kings in this world ours has least reason to say: "I have the privilege of levying on my subjects what I please." And those who ascribe these words to him to make him appear greater do him no honor; on the contrary, they cause him to be hated and feared by his neighbors, who would not want to live under his domination for anything in the world. But if our king, or those who want to exalt him or promote his reputation, were to say: "I have subjects who are so good and loyal that they never refuse me anything I request of them, and I am more feared and better obeyed by my subjects than any other prince in the world; my subjects endure all misfortunes and afflictions with more patience than any others, and bear less resentment for past sufferings," it seems to me that this would be very much to his credit, and I am sure that this is so. He should not say: "I take whatever I want and it is my prerogative, which I intend to keep." King Charles V [of France] never used such terms. As a matter of fact I have never heard any king say this, but I have heard it from their servants, who thought that they were doing their master a good turn. But, in my opinion, they misunderstood the interests of their lord, and they spoke this way in order to show humility before him and because they did not know what they were saying.

As an example of the goodness of the French, the first instance which comes to mind from our time is the convocation of the Three Estates in Tours [in 1484], after the decease of our good master, King Louis, may he rest in peace, which took place

From *The Memoirs of Philippe de Commynes,* ed. Samuel Kinser, tr. Isabelle Cazeaux; Columbia, S.C., 1969, pp. 359-361. Copyright University of South Carolina Press, 1969. Reprinted by permission.

in 1483. It might have been thought at the time that such an assembly would be dangerous, and some persons of low estate and little virtue said then, and many times since, that it was a crime of lese majesty to consider having a meeting of the estates, and that it would only serve to diminish the authority of the king. But these are the very persons who commit a crime against God, the king, and the people. These words serve only those who are in positions of authority and esteem without having deserved it in any way, who are not qualified for their office, and who have never done anything except whisper in ears and talk about things of little value; these people are opposed to these great assemblies for fear that they may be recognized for what they are and that their practices may be condemned.

At the time everyone, whether of high, middle, or low rank, considered the kingdom to be very costly to maintain, for the people had endured and suffered for twenty years and more great and horrible taxes, and which amounted to some three million francs a year more than ever before. For Charles VII never levied more than 1,800,000 francs a year, and King Louis, his son, in the year of his death, raised 4,700,000 francs, not including funds for artillery and other supplies. And it was indeed pitiful to see and hear of the poverty of the people. But one good thing about our good master was that he did not hoard anything in the treasury; he collected everything and spent everything. He built large edifices to fortify and defend the towns and other places of the kingdom, and he did this to a much larger extent than all the kings who preceded him. He was very generous to the churches. In certain respects it would have been better if he had been less liberal, because he robbed the poor to give to those who had no need of it. In short, no one is perfect in this world.

And in this kingdom, which was so oppressed in many ways after the death of our king, was there any division against the king who now reigns? Did princes and their subjects rise up in arms against their young king? Did they wish to replace him with another? Did they wish to deprive him of his authority? Did they want to restrain him so that he would be unable to perform his role as a king and issue commands? Certainly not. Still, there were some people vainglorious enough to say that such things would have happened, had they not prevented it. People did the opposite of everything I said in my questions: for all of them came to him, whether they were princes, lords, or ordinary townsmen; all of them acknowledged him as their king and swore allegiance to him. The princes and the lords made their requests humbly, on their knees, handing in their demands in the form of petitions, and they established a council to which twelve of them were named. And then the king, who was only thirteen years old, gave orders, according to the advice of this council.

At the above-mentioned assembly of the Three Estates, certain requests and remonstrances were made with great humility for the good of the kingdom always remitting everything to the king's good pleasure and that of his council, and granting him whatever was asked of them, and whatever was shown by written documents to be necessary for the king's expenses, without saying anything. And the sum requested was 2,500,000 francs, which was enough, and all that heart could desire, and, if anything, it was too much rather than too little, unless something else should come up. And the estates begged that at the end of two years they should meet again, and in case the king did not have enough money, they would grant him as much as he pleased; and if he were engaged in war or if anyone were to offend him, they would put at his disposal their persons and their possessions without refusing him anything that he might need.

Is it with such subjects, who give so liberally to him, that the king should allege a privilege of being able to take at his pleasure? Would it not be fairer to God and to the world to raise money in this manner than with unordered will? For no prince can levy taxes otherwise than by authorization, as I said, unless he does it by tyranny and is excommunicated. But many are so stupid that they do not know what they can do or not in this respect.

READING 7

The Golden Bull of Emperor Charles IV, 1356

The Golden Bull of 1356 is important less as an agent of constitutional change than as a recognition and regularization of political arrangements that had long been developing. The document must be read very carefully. Some of its phrases are empty verbiage, whereas its utter silence on the traditional papal role in disputed elections is most eloquent. The pope's exclusion from German politics should be understood in the light of Charles IV's prior concession to the papacy that he would exercise no authority in Italy without papal permission. In short, Germany and Italy were becoming disentangled at last.

Charles IV pretends that the Golden Bull is a product of imperial initiative, but its provisions were actually hammered out in an assembly of German princes. The Bull describes the emperor in grandiose terms as "ruler of the world," yet it is designed, point by point, to enhance the authority of the seven electoral princes and to assure the autonomy and indivisibility of their dominions at imperial expense. Charles was himself both emperor and, as hereditary king of Bohemia, an electoral prince. A careful

From *Select Historical Documents of the Middle Ages*, ed. E.F. Henderson, London, 1892, pp. 220-221; and O.J. Thatcher and E.N. MacNeal, *A Source Book for Mediaeval History*, New York, 1905, pp. 284-300.

reading will disclose the identities of the other six electors.

In the name of the holy and indivisible Trinity, amen. Charles the Fourth, by the favor of divine mercy emperor of the Romans, always augustus, and king of Bohemia, as a perpetual memorial does this. Every kingdom divided against itself shall be desolated, for its princes have become the companions of thieves. Tell us, pride, how would you have reigned over Lucifer had you not had discord to aid you? Tell us, hateful Satan, how would you have cast Adam out of paradise if you had not divided him from his obedience? You have often spread discord among the seven electors of the holy empire, through whom the holy empire ought to be illuminated.

We, through the office by which we possess the imperial dignity, are doubly bound—both as emperor and by the electoral right that we enjoy—to put an end to future danger of discord among the electors themselves, to whose number we, as king of Bohemia, are known to belong. And so we have promulgated, decreed, and recommended for ratification these laws for the purpose of cherishing unity among the electors, and of bringing about a unanimous election, and of closing all avenues to that detestable discord and to the dangers that arise from it.

We decree and determine that, whenever the electoral princes are summoned, each one of them shall be bound to furnish on demand an escort and safe-conduct to his fellow electors or their representatives, within his own lands and as much farther as he can, for the journey to and from the city where the election is held. Any electoral prince who refuses to furnish escort and safe-conduct shall be liable to the penalties for perjury and to the loss of his electoral vote for that occasion. If there should arise any enmity or hostility between two electoral princes, it shall not be allowed to interfere with the safe-conduct which each is bound to furnish to the other.

It shall be the duty of the archbishop of Mainz to send notice of the approaching election to each of the electoral princes by his messenger, containing the following: first, the date on which the letter should reach the prince to whom it is directed; then the command to the electoral prince to come or to send his representatives to Frankfürt-am-Main, three months from that date. The form of the letter of notification and of the credentials of the representatives are appended to this document.

When news of the death of the king of the Romans has been received at Mainz, within one month from the date of receiving it the archbishop of Mainz shall send notice to all the electoral princes. But if the archbishop neglects or refuses to send such notices, the electoral princes are commanded to assemble on their own motion and without summons within three months from the death of the emperor, for the purpose of electing a king of the Romans and future emperor.

Mass shall be celebrated on the day after the arrival of the electors. The archbishop of Mainz administers this oath, which the other electors repeat:

"I, archbishop of Mainz, archchancellor of the empire for Germany, electoral prince, swear on the holy gospels here before me, and by the faith which I owe to God and to the holy Roman empire, that with the aid of God, and according to my best knowledge and judgment, I will cast my vote for a person fitted to rule the Christian people. I will give my vote freely, uninfluenced by any agreement, price, bribe, promise, or anything of the sort, by whatever means it may be called. So help me God and all the saints."

After the electors have taken this oath, they shall proceed to the election, and shall not depart from Frankfürt until the majority have elected a king of the Romans and future emperor, to be ruler of the world and of the Christian people. If they have not come to a decision within thirty days from the day on which they took the above oath, after that they shall live on bread and water and shall not leave the city until the election has been decided.

Such an election shall be as valid as if all the princes had agreed unanimously and without difference upon a candidate. If any one of the princes has been hindered or delayed for a time, but arrives before the election is over, he shall be admitted and shall take part in the election at the stage that had been reached at the time of his arrival. According to the ancient and approved custom, the king of the Romans elect, immediately after his election and before he takes up any other business of the empire, shall confirm and approve by sealed letters for each and all of the electoral princes, ecclesiastical and secular, the privileges, charters, rights, liberties, concessions, ancient customs, and dignities, and whatever else the princes held and possessed from the empire at the time of the election; and he shall renew the confirmation and approval when he becomes emperor. The original confirmation shall be made by him as king, and the renewal as emperor. It is his duty to do this graciously and in good faith, and not to hinder the princes in the exercise of their rights.

In the case where three of the electors vote for a fourth electoral prince, his vote shall have the same value as that of the others to make a majority and decide the election.

It is known and recognized throughout the world that the king of Bohemia, the count palatine of the Rhine, the duke of Saxony, and the margrave of Brandenburg, by virtue of the principalities that they possess, have the right to vote in the election of the king of the Romans along with their co-electors, the ecclesiastical princes, and that they with the ecclesiastical princes are the true and legal electoral princes of the holy empire. In order to prevent disputes arising among the sons of these secular electoral princes, we have fixed the succession by the present law which shall be valid forever. On the death of one of the secular electoral princes his right, voice, and vote in the election shall descend to his first-born son who is a layman; if the son has died before this, to the son's first-born son who is a layman. If the first-born lay son of the elector has died before this, without legitimate lay sons, by virtue of the present law the succession shall go to the elector's next oldest lay son and then to his heirs, and so on according to the law of primogeniture. In case the heir is under age the paternal uncle of the heir shall act as guardian and administrator until the heir comes of age, which shall be at eighteen years.

When any electorate falls vacant for lack of heirs, the emperor or king of the Romans shall have the power to dispose of it, as if it reverted to the empire, saving the rights, privileges, and customs of the kingdom of Bohemia, according to which the inhabitants of that kingdom have the right to elect their king in case of a vacancy.

We also decree that no count, baron, noble, vassal, burgrave, knight, client, citizen, burgher, or other subject of the churches of Cologne, Mainz, or Trier, of whatever status, condition, or rank shall be cited, hailed, or summoned to any authority before any tribunal outside of the territories of these churches and their dependences, or before any judge, except the archbishops and their judges. We refuse to hear appeals based on the authority of others over the subjects of these princes.

We extend this right by the present law to the secular electoral princes, the count palatine of the Rhine, the duke of Saxony, and the margrave of Brandenburg, and to their heirs, successors, and subjects forever.

It is known that the right of voting for the king of the Romans and future emperor inheres in certain principalities, the possessors of which have also the other offices, rights, and dignities belonging to these principalities. We decree, therefore, by the present law that the electoral vote and other offices shall always be so united and conjoined that the possessor of one of these principalities shall possess and enjoy the electoral vote and all the offices, dignities, and appurtenances belonging to it, that he shall be regarded as an electoral prince, that he and no other shall be accepted by the other electoral princes and admitted to participation in the election and all other acts which regard the honor and advantage of the holy empire, and that no one of these rights shall ever be taken from him.

READING 8
Petrarch's Description of the Papal Court at Avignon, *c.* 1340-1353

This somber portrait of the Avignon papacy, by the Italian humanist Petrarch (1304-1374), illustrates at once the papacy's diminishing reputation and Petrarch's addiction to rhetorical exaggeration. He was by no means the first critic to contrast papal wealth with apostolic poverty, nor were the Roman popes of the High Middle Ages immune from such criticism. But Petrarch's blade is particularly sharp and well-polished, and his identification of fourteenth-century Avignon with ancient, hedonistic Babylon gained wide circulation.

From *Readings in European History*, vol. 1, ed. James H. Robinson; Boston, Ginn & Company, 1904, pp. 502-503.

. . . Now I am living in France, in the Babylon of the West. The sun in its travels sees nothing more hideous than this place on the shores of the wild Rhone, which suggests the hellish streams of Cocytus and Acheron. Here reign the successors of the poor fishermen of Galilee; they have strangely forgotten their origin. I am astounded, as I recall their predecessors, to see these men loaded with gold and clad in purple, boasting of the spoils of princes and nations; to see luxurious palaces and heights crowned with fortifications, instead of a boat turned downwards for shelter.

Instead of holy solitude we find a criminal host and crowds of the most infamous satellites; instead of soberness, licentious banquets; instead of pious pilgrimages, unnatural and foul sloth; instead of the bare feet of the apostles, the snowy coursers of brigands fly past us, the horses decked in gold and fed on gold, soon to be shod with gold, if the Lord does not check this slavish luxury. In short, we seem to be among the kings of the Persians or Parthians, before whom we must fall down and worship, and who cannot be approached except presents be offered. O ye unkempt and emaciated old men, is it for this you labored? Is it for this that you have sown the field of the Lord and watered it with your holy blood? But let us leave the subject.

READING 9

William of Ockham on Imperial and Papal Power

The distinguished philosopher William of Ockham (c. 1290-1349), whom we have encountered before, was no friend of the Avignon papacy. In this passage he contrasts the papacy as it should be with what, in his opinion, it had become.

We may summarize what is involved in the sublimity of the pope's principate, because this consists of three things. First, that it is a principate in respect of spiritual things only, which are of greater dignity than secular things. Second, that it is a principate over free men, not over slaves, because no one is by divine law a slave of the pope. Third, that the pope can by divine law regularly or casually do all things that are necessary to the organization and government of the faithful, although his ordinary and regular power is limited by definite boundaries, which he is not regularly permitted to transgress. And what those boundaries are is clear from our argument, though it is not clear in which cases those things that are not regularly granted to him may be permitted him. Perhaps it is impossible to give a fixed general rule for these special cases; but in such cases the greatest caution

From Ewart Lewis, *Medieval Political Ideas,* vol. 2; A.A. Knopf, New York, 1954, pp. 613-615.

must be used, according to the discretion and counsel of the wisest men, most sincerely zealous for justice, without any exception of persons, whether subjects or rulers, whether poor or rich, if they can be found. If, however, such men are not available, no action should be taken, lest the pope, because of the ignorance under which in fact he often labors, should dangerously transgress the ancient boundaries and make decisions which may be null and void by divine law itself.

We shall show how the church of Avignon, doing heavy and enormous injuries to all the faithful of Christ, is attempting to rule all Christians tyrannically, and how in order to do this more freely and without fear, but not without the mark of tyranny, it persecutes those who are so bold as to dispute about its power and about its good intention, so that in universities and other schools no doctor or lector dare to propose or accept for discussion and determination in any way any question that concerns the power of the pope, although to dispute about the power of the pope ought to be welcome and acceptable both to the pope and to all his subjects, that they may be subject only so far as is expedient, and no further. This knowledge is necessary to the pope also, lest he transgress the ancient boundaries set by his fathers. And therefore, if the pope strikes fear into those who dispute about his power, he deservedly opens himself to the suspicion that he does not intend to be restricted by the legitimate boundaries of his proper power but intends to rule his subjects tyrannically.

Moreover, it is not only right for learned men to inquire discreetly and with good intention what power the pope has, but it is also expedient and necessary for them to judge his deeds, if those deeds cannot possibly proceed from a good intention: that is, to decide that they are bad and reprehensible and at the proper place and time to assert this and intimate it to others; because everyone is permitted to judge concerning manifest things. Therefore, although when papal deeds could have been the result of good intentions they should have the benefit of the doubt, yet when they are such as could not have been done with good intentions, anyone is permitted to judge them; for such deeds of a pope are bound to be regarded as blameworthy.

READING 10
The Declaration of the Cardinals, 1378

Under strong international pressure, the Avignon pope Gregory XI moved the papal court back to Rome. Like many of his predecessors, he found the city difficult to govern, and he decided to return to Avignon. But Gregory died in 1378 before he could carry out

From *A Source Book for Mediaeval History*, ed. and Tr. O.J. Thatcher and E.N. McNeal; New York, Charles Scribner's Sons, 1905, pp. 325-326.

his plan, and the resulting events, related here by the cardinals, gave rise to the great schism. Having declared their election of the Italian Urban VI null and void, they elected another pope and returned with him to Avignon. Urban VI stayed on in Rome and appointed new cardinals.

The Declaration of the Cardinals thus pinpoints the origin of the schism, but it is not so much an objective account of events as a self-serving interpretation of them. Other sources make it clear that the cardinals elected Urban VI willingly, *before* being pressured by a mob of Romans who were unaware of the election. As archbishop of Bari, Urban had been an efficient but colorless ecclesiastical administrator. As pope he surprised everyone by launching a campaign against clerical wealth and taking steps to reduce the cardinals' revenues. It was at that point that they repudiated Urban, fled Rome, and manufactured their cover story.

. . . After the apostolic seat was made vacant by the death of our lord, pope Gregory XI, who died in March, we assembled in conclave for the election of a pope, as is the law and custom, in the papal palace, in which Gregory had died. . . . Officials of the city with a great multitude of the people, for the most part armed and called together for this purpose by the ringing of bells, surrounded the palace in a threatening manner and even entered it and almost filled it. To the terror caused by their presence they added threats that unless we should at once elect a Roman or an Italian they would kill us. They gave us no time to deliberate but compelled us unwillingly, through violence and fear, to elect an Italian without delay. In order to escape the danger which threatened us from such a mob, we elected Bartholomew, archbishop of Bari, thinking that he would have enough conscience not to accept the election, since everyone knew that it was made under such wicked threats. But he was unmindful of his own salvation and burning with ambition, and so, to the great scandal of the clergy and of the Christian people, and contrary to the laws of the church, he accepted this election which was offered him, although not all the cardinals were present at the election, and it was extorted from us by the threats and demands of the officials and people of the city. And although such an election is null and void, and the danger from the people still threatened us, he was enthroned and crowned, and called himself pope and apostolic. But according to the holy fathers and to the law of the church, he should be called apostate, anathema, Antichrist, and the mocker and destroyer of Christianity.

READING 11

Decrees of the Conciliar Movement

The great schism stimulated a movement by reform-minded churchmen to reorganize ecclesiastical governance on more or less the parliamentary model, with the papacy sharing its authority with Church councils. The following documents illustrate the rise and fall of the conciliar movement.

The Council of Pisa (documents A and B) elected a "conciliar" pope but failed in its attempt to dethrone the popes of Rome and Avignon, both of whom asserted the traditional claim that the pope could be judged by no one. Against this claim, the churchmen at Pisa, and later at Constance (documents C, D, and E), affirmed the power of councils over popes and demanded that councils be convened on a regular basis. But the Council of Constance's success in healing the schism diminished the need of conciliar governance. Councils continued to meet regularly until the mid-fifteenth century, when the conciliar movement disintegrated under the pressure of papal opposition (document F).

A. THE COUNCIL OF PISA CLAIMS JURISDICTION, 1409

This holy and general council, representing the universal church, decrees and declares that the united college of cardinals was empowered to call the council, and that the power to call such a council belongs of right to the aforesaid holy college of cardinals, especially now when there is a detestable schism. The council further declared that this holy council, representing the universal church, caused both claimants of the papal throne to be cited in the gates and doors of the churches of Pisa to come and hear the final decision [in the matter of the schism] pronounced, or to give a good and sufficient reason why such sentence should not be rendered.

B. THE OATH OF REFORM
FROM THE COUNCIL OF PISA, 1409

We, each and all, bishops, priests, and deacons of the holy Roman Church, congregated in the city of Pisa for the purpose of ending the schism and of restoring the unity of the Church, on our word of honor promise God, the holy Roman Church, and this holy council now collected here for the aforesaid purpose, that, if any one of us is elected pope, he shall continue the present council and not dissolve

From *A Source Book for Mediaeval History*, ed. and Tr. O.J. Thatcher and E.N. McNeal; New York, Charles Scribner's Sons, 1905, pp. 327-332.

it, nor, so far as is in his power, permit it to be dissolved until, through it and with its advice, a proper, reasonable, and sufficient reformation of the universal church in its head and in its members shall have been accomplished.

C. *HAEC SANCTA*[1] FROM THE COUNCIL OF CONSTANCE, 1415

This holy synod of Constance, being a general council, and legally assembled in the Holy Spirit for the praise of God and for ending the present schism, and for the union and reformation of the church of God in its head and in its members, in order more easily, more securely, more completely, and more fully to bring about the union and reformation of the church of God, ordains, declares, and decrees as follows: And first it declares that this synod, legally assembled, is a general council, and represents the catholic church militant and has its authority directly from Christ; and everybody, of whatever rank or dignity, including also the pope, is bound to obey this council in those things which pertain to the faith, to the ending of this schism, and to a general reformation of the church in its head and members. Likewise it declares that if anyone, of whatever rank, condition, or dignity, including also the pope, shall refuse to obey the commands, statutes, ordinances, or orders of this holy council, or of any other holy council properly assembled, in regard to the ending of the schism and to the reformation of the church, he shall be subject to the proper punishment; and unless he repents, he shall be duly punished; and if necessary, recourse shall be had to other aids of justice.

D. THE REFORM PROGRAM OF THE COUNCIL OF CONSTANCE, 1417

The holy council at Constance determined and decreed that before this holy council shall be dissolved, the future pope, by the grace of God soon to be elected, with the aid of this holy council, or of men appointed by each nation, shall reform the church in its head and in the Roman curia, in conformity to the right standard and good government of the church. And reforms shall be made in the following matters: 1. In the number, character, and nationality of the cardinals. 2. In papal reservations. 3. In annates, and in common services and little services. 4. In the granting of benefices and expectancies. 5. In determining what cases may be tried in the papal court. 6. In appeals to the papal court. 7. In the offices of the *cancellaria,* and of the penitentiary. 8. In the exemptions and incorporations made during the schism. 9. In the matter of commends. 10. In the confirmation of elections. 11. In the disposition of the income of churches, monasteries, and benefices during the time when they are vacant.[2] 12. That no ecclesiastical property be alienated. 13. It

---

[1]"This Council"; the titles of conciliar decrees are taken from their opening words. Had we followed that custom, the present sourcebook would have been titled "Many Students."

[2]Annates, expectancies, and similar financial measures were payments made to the papacy by appointees to ecclesiastical offices.

shall be determined for what causes and how a pope may be disciplined and deposed. 14. A plan shall be devised for putting an end to simony. 15. In the matter of dispensations. 16. In the provision for the pope and cardinals. 17. In indulgences. 18. In assessing tithes.

E. *FREQUENS* FROM THE COUNCIL OF CONSTANCE, 1417

A good way to till the field of the Lord is to hold general councils frequently, because by them the briers, thorns, and thistles of heresies, errors, and schisms are rooted out, abuses reformed, and the way of the Lord made more fruitful. But if general councils are not held, all these evils spread and flourish. We therefore decree by this perpetual edict that general councils shall be held as follows: The first one shall be held five years after the close of this council, the second one seven years after the close of the first, and forever thereafter one shall be held every ten years. One month before the close of each council the pope, with the approval and consent of the council, shall fix the place for holding the next council. If the pope fails to name the place the council must do so.

F. *EXECRABILIS*: PIUS II DENOUNCES CONCILIARISM, 1460

The execrable and hitherto unknown abuse has grown up in our day, that certain persons, imbued with the spirit of rebellion, and not from a desire to secure a better judgment, but to escape the punishment of some offence which they have committed, presume to appeal from the pope to a future council, in spite of the fact that the pope is the vicar of Jesus Christ and to him, in the person of St. Peter, the following was said: "Feed my sheep" [John 21:16] and "Whatsoever thou shalt bind on earth shall be bound in heaven" [Matt. 16:18]. Wishing therefore to expel this pestiferous poison from the church of Christ and to care for the salvation of the flock entrusted to us, and to remove every cause of offence from the fold of our Saviour, with the advice and consent of our brothers, the cardinals of the holy Roman church, and of all the prelates, and of those who have been trained in the canon and civil law, who are at our court, and with our own sure knowledge, we condemn all such appeals and prohibit them as erroneous and detestable.

CHAPTER 11

ECHOES OF THE FUTURE

The documents that follow provide an appropriately confused picture of the fourteenth and fifteenth centuries as an era of death, disorder, and renaissance. The Black Death (document 1) produced enormous suffering, grief, and economic upheaval. The elimination of perhaps one third of the population resulted in a violent shift from land shortage to labor shortage, prompting property owners in both northern and southern Europe to seek legislation to freeze wages (documents 2 and 3). These measures angered peasants and laborers and sometimes drove them into rebellion. Yet throughout the horrors of the late Middle Ages European culture continued to flourish.

Indeed, the fifteenth century marks the apex of the Italian Renaissance. A glance at Renaissance writings, no less than at Renaissance art, discloses a characteristic blend of classicism, secularism, and Christianity. Renaissance humanists such as Coluccio Salutati could write about Christian virtue and salvation (document 4) while popes such as Nicholas V were collecting classical books and showering patronage on classical scholars (document 5). Conversely, Florence, the nexus of Renaissance culture could, in the midst of the High Renaissance (1490s), fall under the spell of a fire-and-brimstone Dominican preacher, Savonarola, who believed he was receiving messages directly from God (document 6)—and the Florentine people could afterwards condone his being burned at the stake (document 7).

A similar brew of Christian and worldly motives underlay the earlier voyages of exploration (document 8), which also profited from major advances in geographical understanding (document 9). Documents 10 and 11 illustrate the contributions of the late Middle Ages to the emergence of modern science; documents 12 and 13, conversely, point to the heightening of religious conflict on the eve of the Protestant Reformation.

We conclude with a celebration of the study and writing of history by the fifteenth-century English writer William Caxton, which ends with the wise words; History "enhaunceth noble men and depresseth wicked men and fooles." If you hate reading Middle English you are welcome to skip this passage, but it will be your loss.

READING 1

Boccaccio's *Decameron* on the Black Death in Florence, 1348

This eyewitness account is provided by the Florentine humanist,Giovanni Boccaccio (1313-1375), one of the best minds and keenest observers of his time. Except for a touch of civic pride, Boccaccio writes with remarkable objectivity.

In the year of our Lord 1348, there happened at Florence, the finest city in all Italy, a most terrible plague; which, whether owing to the influence of the planets, or that it was sent from God as a just punishment for our sins, had broken out some years before in the Levant, and after passing from place to place and making incredible havoc all the way, had now reached the west. There, in spite of all the means that art and human foresight could suggest, such as keeping the city clear from filth, the exclusion of all suspected persons, and the publication of copious instructions for the preservation of health, and notwithstanding manifold humble supplications offered to God in processions and otherwise, it began to show itself in the spring of the aforesaid year, in a sad and wonderful manner. Unlike what had been seen in the east, where bleeding from the nose is the fatal prognostic, here there appeared certain tumors in the groin or under the arm-pits, some as big as a small apple, others as an egg; and afterwards purple spots in most parts of the body; in some cases large and but few in number, in others smaller and more numerous— both sorts the usual messengers of death. To the cure of this malady neither medical knowledge nor the power of drugs was of any effect; whether because the disease was in its own nature mortal, or that the physicians (the number of whom, taking quacks and women pretenders into the account, was grown very great) could form no just idea of the cause, nor consequently devise a true method of cure; whichever was the reason, few escaped; but nearly all died the third day from the first appearance of the symptoms, some sooner, some later, without any fever or other accessory symptoms. What gave the more virulence to this plague, was that, by being communicated from the sick to the hale, it spread daily, like fire when it comes in contact with large masses of combustibles. Nor was it caught only by conversing with or coming near the sick, but even by touching their clothes, or anything that they had before touched. It is wonderful, what I am going to mention; and had I not seen it with my own eyes, and were there not many witnesses to attest it besides myself, I should never venture to relate it, however worthy it were of belief. Such, I say, was the quality of the pestilential matter, as to pass not only

From *The First Century of Italian Humanism,* ed. Ferdinand Schevill; New York, F.S. Crofts & Co., 1928, pp. 32-34.

from man to man, but, what is more strange, it has been often known, that anything belonging to the infected, if touched by any other creature, would certainly infect and even kill that creature in a short space of time. One instance of this kind I took particular notice of: the rags of a poor man just dead had been thrown into the street. Two hogs came up, and after rooting amongst the rags and shaking them about in their mouths, in less than an hour they both turned round and died on the spot.

These facts, and others of the like sort, occasioned various fears and devices amongst those who survived, all tending to the same uncharitable and cruel end; which was, to avoid the sick and every thing that had been near them, expecting by that means to save themselves. And some, holding it best to live temperately and to avoid excesses of all kinds, made parties and shut themselves up from the rest of the world; eating and drinking moderately of the best, and diverting themselves with music and such other entertainments as they might have within doors; never listening to anything from without to make them uneasy. Others maintained free living to be a better preservative, and would balk no passion or appetite they wished to gratify, drinking and revelling incessantly from tavern to tavern, or in private houses (which were frequently found deserted by the owners and therefore common to every one), yet strenuously avoiding, with all this brutal indulgence, to come near the infected.

And such, at that time, was the public distress that the laws, human and divine, were no more regarded; for the officers, to put them in force, being either dead, sick, or in want of persons to assist them, every one did just as he pleased. A third sort of people chose a method between these two: not confining themselves to rules of diet like the former, and yet avoiding the intemperance of the latter; but eating and drinking what their appetites required, they walked everywhere with perfumes and nosegays to smell to, as holding it best to corroborate the brain: for the whole atmosphere seemed to them tainted with the stench of dead bodies, arising partly from the distemper itself, and partly from the fermenting of the medicines within them. Others with less humanity, but perchance, as they supposed, with more security from danger, decided that the only remedy for the pestilence was to avoid it. Persuaded, therefore, of this and taking care for themselves only, men and women in great numbers left the city, their houses, relations, and effects, and fled into the country, as if the wrath of God had been constrained to visit those only within the walls of the city, or else concluding that none ought to stay in a place thus doomed to destruction.

READING 2

The Corn Statute of Florence, 1348

Wage control legislation occurred throughout Europe, as this
Florentine statue shows.

The peasants and tillers of the soil, all those who by indigence work and
cultivate the land for a wage and by the day, may not ask, demand, or have a salary
or wage higher than below mentioned: From the calends[1] of November to the
calends of February each year, three sous and six deniers of small florins per day,
or per task, providing themselves with all their expenses. From the calends of
February to the calends of June, four sous of small florins per day or per task,
providing themselves with all their expenses. From the calends of June to the
calends of November they may not demand more than three sous of small florins
per day or per task, under pain of one hundred sous each time for the contravener.
And if the contravener cannot pay the fine he shall remain one month in the prison
of the commune of Florence, and the punishment shall be executed thus. In this
matter the oath of him who would have wished the work performed or he who
would have paid the price shall be held.

READING 3

The Ordinance of Laborers, 1349

Edward III of England (1327-1377) sent copies of this ordinance to
all his sheriffs. Its purpose is self-explanatory.

The king to the sheriff of Kent, greeting. Because a great part of the people, and
especially of workmen and servants, have lately died in the pestilence, many seeing
the necessities of masters and great scarcity of servants, will not serve unless they
may receive excessive wages, and others preferring to beg in idleness rather than
by labor to get their living; we, considering the grievous incommodities which of

From Georges Duby, *Rural Economy and Country Life in the Medieval West*, tr. Cynthia
Postan; Columbia University of South Carolina Press, 1968, pp. 525.

From *Translations and Reprints from the Original Sources of European History*, vol. 2;
Philadelphia, University of Pennsylvania Press, 1902, pp . 3-5.

[1]The calends was the first day of the month.

the lack especially of plowmen and such laborers may hereafter come, have upon deliberation and treaty with the prelates and the nobles and learned men assisting us, with their unanimous counsel ordained:

That every man and woman of our realm of England, of what condition he be, free or bond, able in body, and within the age of sixty years, not living in merchandize, nor exercising any craft, nor having of his own whereof he may live, nor land of his own about whose tillage he may occupy himself, and not serving any other; if he be required to serve in suitable service, his estate considered, he shall be bound to serve him which shall so require him; and take only the wages, livery, meed, or salary which were accustomed to be given in the places where he oweth to serve, the twentieth year of our reign of England, or five or six other common years next before.[1] Provided always, that the lords be preferred before others in their bondmen or their land tenants, so in their service to be retained; so that, nevertheless, the said lords shall retain no more than be necessary for them. And if any such man or woman being so required to serve will not do the same, and that be proved by two true men before the sheriff, bailiff, lord, or constable of the town where the same shall happen to be done, he shall immediately be taken by them or any of them, and committed to the next gaol, there to remain under strait keeping, till he find surety to serve in the form aforesaid.

If any reaper, mower, other workman or servant, of what estate or condition he be, retained in any man's service, do depart from the said service without reasonable cause or license, before the term agreed, he shall have pain of imprisonment; and no one, under the same penalty, shall presume to receive or retain such a one in his service.

No one, moreover, shall pay or promise to pay to anyone more wages, liveries, meed, or salary than was accustomed, as is before said; nor shall anyone in any other manner demand or receive them, upon pain of doubling of that which shall have been so paid, promised, required or received, to him who thereof shall feel himself aggrieved; and if none such will sue, then the same shall be applied to any of the people that will sue; and such suit shall be in the court of the lord of the place where such case shall happen.

And if lords of towns or manors presume in any point to come against this present ordinance, either by them or by their servants, then suit shall be made against them in the form aforesaid, in the counties, wapentakes, and trithings, or such other courts of ours, for the penalty of treble that so paid or promised by them or their servants. And if any before this present ordinance hath covenanted with any so to serve for more wages, he shall not be bound, by reason of the said covenant, to pay more than at another time was wont to be paid to such a person; nor, under the same penalty, shall presume to pay more.

And because many strong beggars, as long as they may live by begging, do refuse to labor, giving themselves to idleness and vice, and sometimes to theft and other abominations; no one upon the said pain of imprisonment, shall, under the

---

[1] That is, wages were to be fixed at pre-plague levels paid in 1347 or before.

color of pity or alms, give anything to such, who are able to labor, or presume to favor them in their idleness, so that thereby they may be compelled to labor for their necessary living.

READING 4
Coluccio Salutati on the Active Life

Coluccio Salutati (1331-1406) was a major Florentine humanist and civic official who in 1375 became chancellor of Florence. His writings stress the connection between humanistic scholarship and service to the city-state. In his letter to Pellegrino, Salutati praises the active life over the contemplative life in the context of Christian piety and salvation. In another of his letters, however, he praises the monastic life, thus reflecting the medieval rhetorical tradition of celebrating the virtues of both action and contemplation.

In some respects Salutati is simply echoing St. Francis (see pages 156 to 160) while in others he is expressing the new civic humanism of the Renaissance. Can you separate the old ideas from the new?

Do not believe, my Pellegrino, that to flee from turmoil, to avoid the view of pleasant things, to enclose oneself in a cloister, or to isolate oneself in a hermitage, constitute the way of perfection. Within yourself is that which imprints upon your work the title of perfection, which receives those things which do not touch you, rather cannot touch you, if your mind and your spirit withdraws within itself, if it does not search outside of itself. If the spirit will not receive within itself these exterior objects—the square, the forum, the court, the most crowded place of the city they will be for you a very remote retreat and a perfect solitude. If instead, either in the recollection of distant things or in the fascination of present ones, our spirit turns outwardly, I do not know what it profits to live a solitary life. For it is a characteristic of the spirit to think always of something, whether this be a thing comprehended by the senses, represented by the memory, constructed by the power of the intellect, or created by the feeling of desire. And tell me, Pellegrino, who do you believe was more beloved by God: Paul,[1] the inactive hermit, or the

From *Renaissance Italy: Was It the Birthplace of Modern Europe?* ed. Gene A. Brucker; New York, Holt, Rinehart, and Winston, Inc., 1958, pp. 35-36. Reprinted by permission of Gene A. Brucker and the publisher.

[1] St. Paul the Hermit (d. *c.* 347), not Paul the Apostle.

busy Abraham? Among the superior ones, there are more who dedicate themselves to the active life than occupy themselves solely with spiritual things, just as there are many more who save themselves in the active life than are chosen from the contemplative life.

You should not be pleased with your prayers; you should not believe that you have approached more closely to heaven; you should not condemn me for remaining in the secular world. Without doubt you, fleeing from the world, can fall from heaven to earth, while I, remaining in the world, can raise my heart to heaven. And if you provide for, serve, and think of your family, children, relatives, friends, you cannot fail to raise your heart to the heavens and please God. Perhaps, occupied in mundane things, you will please Him more, since you will not aspire for yourself alone to be in communion with God, but in conjunction with Him, who holds dear the things necessary for the family, pleasing to friends, salutary for the state, you will labor, to the extent that He gives you the opportunity.

And thus to conclude, while contemplation is better, more divine, and more sublime, still it must be united with action. Nor is it always necessary to remain fixed in that summit of speculation. And tell me, I pray you, what is examined in the Last Judgment, if not the works of mercy, even though neglected or incomplete? Whoever will have clothed the nude, fed the hungry, given drink to the thirsty, buried the dead, released the imprisoned, he will hear that most sweet appeal: "Come, blessed by My Father, enjoy the Kingdom prepared for you from the beginning of the world."

READING 5

Vespasiano on the Founding of the Papal Library by Nicholas V

Vespasiano (1421-1498) was a writer and bookseller who, it is said, was put out of business by the influx of inexpensive printed books. In this selection from his *Lives of the Artists,* Vespasiano praises Pope Nicholas V (1447-1455) for founding the Vatican Library and supporting humanist scholars. In both these activities, Nicholas was playing the role of an enlightened Renaissance despot.

Owing to the jubilee of 1450 a great quantity of money came in by this means to

From *Readings in European History,* vol. 1, ed. James Harvey Robinson; Boston, Ginn & Company, 1904, pp. 529-530.

the apostolic see, and with this the pope commenced building in many places, and sent for Greek and Latin books, wherever he was able to find them, without regard to price. He gathered together a large band of writers, the best that he could find, and kept them in constant employment. He also summoned a number of learned men, both for the purpose of composing new works and of translating such existing works as were not already translated, giving them most abundant provision for their needs meanwhile; and when the works were translated and brought to him, he gave them large sums of money, in order that they should do more willingly that which they undertook to do.

He made great provision for the needs of learned men. He gathered together great numbers of books upon every subject, both Greek and Latin, to the number of five thousand volumes. So at his death it was found by inventory that never since the time of Ptolemy had half that number of books of every kind been brought together. All books he caused to be copied, without regard to what it cost him, and there were few places where his Holiness had not copiers at work. When he could not procure a book for himself in any way, he had it copied.

After he had assembled at Rome, as I said above, many learned men at large salaries, he wrote to Florence to Messer Giannozzo Manetti, that he should come to Rome to translate and compose for him. And when Manetti left Florence and came to Rome, the pope, as was his custom, received him with honor, and assigned to him, in addition to his income as secretary, six hundred ducats, urging him to attempt the translation of the books of the Bible and of Aristotle, and to complete the book already commenced by him, *Contra Judaeos et gentes;* a wonderful work, if it had been completed, but he carried it only to the tenth book. Moreover he translated the New Testament, and the Psalter, . . . with five apologetical books in defense of this Psalter, showing that in the Holy Scriptures there is not one syllable that does not contain the greatest of mysteries.

It was Pope Nicholas' intention to found a library in St. Peter's, for the general use of the whole Roman curia, which would have been an admirable thing indeed, if he had been able to carry it out, but death prevented his bringing it to completion. He illumined the Holy Scriptures through innumerable books, which he caused to be translated; and in the same way with the works of the pagans, including certain works on grammar, of use in learning Latin—the *Orthography* of Messer Giovanni Tortelle, who was of his Holiness' household and worked upon the library, a worthy book and useful to grammarians; the *Iliad* of Homer; Strabo's *De situ orbis* he caused to be translated by Guerrino, and gave him five hundred florins for each part—that is to say, Asia, Africa, and Europe; that was in all fifteen hundred florins. Herodotus and Thucydides he had translated by Lorenzo Valla, and rewarded him liberally for his trouble; Xenophon and Diodorus, by Messer Poggio; Polybius, by Nicolo Perotto, whom, when he handed it to him, he gave five hundred brand-new papal ducats in a purse, and said to him that it was not what he deserved, but that in time he would take care to satisfy him.

READING 6

Savonarola in Florence

Girolamo Savonarola (1452-1498), a spellbinding Dominican preacher, settled in Florence in 1490 at a time when Florence was the center of the Renaissance at its height—the time of Leonardo da Vinci. Savonarola became prior of the Dominican house of San Marco in Florence in 1491, and in subsequent years his preaching captivated the Florentine populace. He won further acclaim by persuading an invading French army to spare Florence, and in 1496 he persuaded the Florentine people to engage in "the burning of the Vanities", in which they cast into a bonfire their cosmetics, fake hair, and pornographic books. But he fell afoul of the corrupt Borgia pope, Alexander VI (whom he insulted publicly, frequently, and deservedly); and Alexander, referring to Savonarola as a "meddlesome friar," arranged to have him tried for heresy. The Florentines, frightened by the papal action—and perhaps growing tired of Savonarola—raised no serious objections to his being burned at the stake. Both Savonarola's successes and failures shed light on the scope and meaning of the Renaissance.

A. FROM SAVONAROLA'S *COMPENDIUM REVELATIONUM*, 1497

Almighty God, seeing that the sins of Italy continue to multiply, especially those of her princes, both ecclesiastical and secular, and unable to bear them any longer, decided to cleanse his church with a mighty scourge. He wanted this scourge to be foretold in Italy for the welfare of his chosen people, so that, forewarned, they might prepare. Since Florence lies in the center of Italy as the heart of a man, God deigned to choose her for the task of making the proclamation. And so, choosing me, useless and unworthy among all his servants, he arranged for me to come to Florence on the orders of my superiors in the year of our lord 1489. And in the same year I began publicly to expound the *Book of the Apocalypse* in our church of San Marco. I continually set forth three things: first, that the renovation of the Church would come about in these times; second, that all of Italy would be mightily scourged before God brought about this renovation; third, that these two things would come about soon. I labored to prove these three conclusions by rational arguments, by figures from scriptures, and by other analogies and parables

From Donald Weinstein, *Savonarola and Florence*; Princeton, 1970, pp. 68-71.

that can only be derived from scriptures. Later I began to reveal that I knew these events by a different light than that of the understanding of scripture alone. At last I began to disclose the matter more openly, admitting that my words were divinely inspired. One of the things I repeated often was: "Thus says the Lord God, 'The sword of the Lord shall be over the earth swiftly and soon!'" And another was: "Let the just rejoice and exult, prepare your minds against temptation by reading, meditation and prayer, and free yourselves from a second death." These words were not from the holy scriptures, as some thought, but newly come forth from heaven at just that time.

Then, as the king of the French was approaching and a revolution in the Florentine state was imminent [in 1494], although God's sword had appeared to me, as well as the great spilling of blood in this city, nevertheless, I began fervently to hope that this prophecy was not without some conditions, that if the people were repentant the most indulgent God might abate at least a part of his judgment. Thus, on 1 November and on the two days following, I spared neither voice nor lungs and, as everyone knows, I cried out so loudly from the pulpit as almost to wear myself out, "O Italy, these adversities have come to you because of your sins; O Florence these adversities have come to you because of your sins; O clergy, this tempest has arisen on your account. O nobles, O wise men, O humble folk, the mighty hand of God is upon you; neither power nor wisdom nor light can withstand it. The Lord is awaiting you, that he might show his pity on you. Convert, therefore, to the Lord with all your heart, because he is kind and compassionate. If you do not, he will avert his eyes from you forever."

B. GUICCIARDINI ON SAVONAROLA AND FLORENCE, 1561

The pope had accused Savonarola of slanderously preaching against the comportment of the clergy and the papal court, of stirring up discord in Florence, and of disseminating doctrine that was not entirely orthodox. For these reasons, the Dominican had been several times summoned to Rome, but he had refused to appear, alleging various excuses. Finally, the pope separated him from the fellowship of the church.[1] As a result of this excommunication he abstained from preaching for several months, and had he abstained longer he would have obtained absolution without any difficulty. For the pope personally took little account of Savonarola, and was moved to proceed against him more as a result of the suggestions and persuasion of the monk's adversaries.

But it seemed to Savonarola that his reputation was declining as a result of his silence, or that, at any rate, the object of his endeavors was impeded by it, since his

From Francesco Guicciardini, *The History of Florence*, Tr. D. Weinstein; Princeton, 1972, pp. 356-58.

[1]Pope Alexander VI, in 1497.

purpose was mainly served by his vehemence in preaching. And so, scorning the pope's commandments, he publicly affirmed that the excommunication that had been promulgated against him was unjust and invalid, contrary to the will of God and harmful to the public weal.

His preaching stirred up great dissensions. For on the one hand his adversaries, whose authority among the people grew greater every day, detested such disobedience and reproved him because his foolhardiness might result in changing the pope's mind [about an alliance with Florence]. On the other hand, his partisans defended him, alleging that divine works should not be interfered with because of simple concern over human consequences, nor should popes be permitted under such justifications to commence meddling in the affairs of the republic. Finally this quarrel became so heated that one of the Dominican monks who was a disciple of Savonarola and one of the Franciscans agreed upon a trial by fire in the presence of the entire populace, so that the Dominican being either spared or burned would make it clear to everybody whether Savonarola was a prophet or a fraud. For he had earlier preached that as a sign of the truth of his predictions he would obtain, when there was need for it, the grace from God to pass through the fire without harm. But now he was angry that the decision to carry on the experiment had been made without his knowledge, so he cleverly tried to prevent it; but since the matter had already gone so far on its own momentum it was necessary finally to proceed further. So on the chosen day, the two friars, accompanied by all the brothers of their order, came to the piazza which is in front of the public palace; but there the Franciscan learned that Savonarola had ordered his friar to bear the Host in hand when he entered into the flames. At this the Franciscans began to protest, alleging that their opponents were seeking to place the authority of the Christian faith in danger, since if the Host should be burned, the faith of the ignorant would decline considerably. And since Savonarola, who was present, insisted on this order, it was impossible for the experiment to proceed. Savonarola lost so much prestige by this that on the next day his adversaries seized arms and stormed the monastery of San Marco where he was living and led him, with two of his friars, to the public prison.

Savonarola was then examined under torture (although not very dolorous) and later the deposition of these examinations was published. According to this trial record (which cleared him of all the calumnies imputed to him, such as covetousness or having held secret dealings with princes) the things which he had prophesied were declared to have been predicted, not on the basis of divine revelation, but as his own opinion based on deep study of the scriptures; nor had he been moved by any malign intention or cupidity to acquire ecclesiastical eminence, but rather he had greatly desired that his work should result in the convocation of a council which would reform the corrupt manners of the clergy and bring back the Church of God to a state as similar as possible to what it had been at the time of the Apostles.

On the basis of this deposition, confirmed by Savonarola, but in such concise terms that his words could be given various interpretations, he and the two other friars were, by sentence of the General of the Dominican Order and by Bishop Romolino, stripped of their holy orders and left to the jurisdiction of the secular court, by whom they were hanged and burned. To this spectacle of degradation and torture there thronged no less a multitude of men than those who, on the day appointed for the experiment of entering into the fire, had rushed to the same place in expectation of the miracle which he had promised. Savonarola's death did not extinguish the diversity of judgments and emotions of the citizens, because many still reputed him to be an impostor, and many believed that the confession which had been published had been falsely fabricated or else that his delicate physical state had been much more influenced by the pain of the torture than by the truth.

READING 7
Azurara on the Motives of Prince Henry the Navigator

Gomes Eannes de Azurara (d. 1474) was advanced to the offices of chief archivist and royal chronicler of the kingdom of Portugal a year after he wrote this account. He is our best authority for the early Portuguese voyages down the west coast of Africa sponsored by Prince Henry the Navigator (1394-1460)—whom Azurara calls "the Lord Infant" or "the Prince." Prince Henry played a part in the Portuguese capture of the North African port of Ceuta in 1415. Afterward, from his court at Sagres in Portugal, he collected geographical and navigational data from the expeditions that he sent westward to the Atlantic islands and southward down the African coast. Azurara, writing as a court historian, is obviously providing an unflawed portrait.

We imagine that we know a matter when we are acquainted with the doer of it and the end for which he did it. And since in former chapters we have set forth the Lord Infant as the chief actor in these things, giving as clear an understanding of him as we could, it is meet that in this present chapter we should know his purpose in doing them. And you should note well that the noble spirit of this Prince, by a sort of natural constraint, was ever urging him both to begin and to carry out very great deeds. For which reason, after the taking of Ceuta he always kept ships well armed against the Infidel, both for war, and because he had also a wish to know the

From *The Chronicle of the Discovery and Conquest of Guinea*, vol. 1, tr. C.R. Beazley and E. Prestage; London, Hakluyt Society Publications, Inc., 1899, pp. 27-30.

land that lay beyond the isles of Canary and Cape Bojador [Morocco], since before his own time, neither by writings, nor by the memory of man, was known with any certainty the nature of the land beyond that Cape. Some said indeed that Saint Brandan had passed that way; and there was another tale of two galleys rounding the Cape, which never returned. But this doth not appear at all likely to be true, for it is not to be presumed that if the said galleys went there, some other ships would not have endeavored to learn what voyage they had made. And because the said Lord Infant wished to know the truth of this—since it seemed to him that if he or some other lord did not endeavor to gain that knowledge, no mariners or merchants would ever dare to attempt it—(for it is clear that none of them ever trouble themselves to sail to a place where there is not a sure and certain hope of profit)—and seeing also that no other prince took any pains in this matter, he sent out his own ships against those parts, to have manifest certainty of them all. And to this he was stirred up by his zeal for the service of God and of the King Edward his Lord and brother, who then reigned. And this was the first reason of his action.

The second reason was that if there chanced to be in those lands some population of Christians, or some havens, into which it would be possible to sail without peril, many kinds of merchandise might be brought to this realm, which would find a ready market, and reasonably so, because no other people of these parts traded with them, nor yet people of any other that were known; and also the products of this realm might be taken there, which traffic would bring great profit to our countrymen.

The third reason was that, as it was said that the power of the Moors in that land of Africa was very much greater than was commonly supposed, and that there were no Christians among them, nor any other race of men; and because every wise man is obliged by natural prudence to wish for a knowledge of the power of his enemy; therefore the said Lord Infant exerted himself to cause this to be fully discovered, and to make it known determinately how far the power of those infidels extended.

The fourth reason was because during the one and thirty years that he had warred against the Moors, he had never found a Christian king, nor a lord outside this land, who for the love of our Lord Jesus Christ would aid him in the said war. Therefore he sought to know if there were in those parts any Christian princes, in whom the charity and the love of Christ was so ingrained that they would aid him against those enemies of the faith.

The fifth reason was his great desire to make increase in the faith of our Lord Jesus Christ and to bring to Him all the souls that should be saved—understanding that all the mystery of the Incarnation, Death, and Passion of our Lord Jesus Christ was for this sole end—namely the salvation of lost souls—whom the said Lord Infant by his travail and spending would fain bring into the true path. For he perceived that no better offering could be made unto the Lord than this; for if God promised to return one hundred goods for one, we may justly believe that for such great benefits, that is to say for so many souls as were saved by the efforts of this Lord, he will have so many hundreds of guerdons in the kingdom of God, by which his spirit may be glorified after this life in the celestial realm. For I that wrote this history saw so many men and women of those parts turned to the holy faith, that even if the Infant had been a heathen, their prayers would have been enough to have obtained his salvation. And not only did I see the first captives, but their children and grandchildren as true Christians as if the Divine grace breathed in them and imparted to them a clear knowledge of itself.

But over and above these five reasons I have a sixth that would seem to be the root from which all the others proceeded: and this is the inclination of the heavenly wheels. For, as I wrote not many days ago in a letter I sent to the Lord King, that although it be written that the wise man shall be Lord of the stars, and that the courses of the planets (according to the true estimate of the holy doctors) cannot cause the good man to stumble; yet it is manifest that they are bodies ordained in the secret counsels of our Lord God and run by a fixed measure, appointed to different ends, which are revealed to men by his grace, through whose influence bodies of the lower order are inclined to certain passions. And if it be a fact, speaking as a Catholic, that the contrary predestinations of the wheels of heaven can be avoided by natural judgment with the aid of a certain divine grace, much more does it stand to reason that those who are predestined to good fortune, by the help of this same grace, will not only follow their course but even add a greater increase to themselves.

READING 8

Toscanelli on Sailing West to Go East

Paolo del Pozzo Toscanelli (1397-1482), a great geographer and mapmaker of the fifteenth century, makes it clear in this intriguing passage—written in 1474, some years before Columbus's first voyage—that Columbus was by no means the first European to believe that one might encounter Asiatic lands by sailing westward across the Atlantic. Toscanelli, prefiguring Columbus in other ways, shows how Italians were establishing contacts with Iberia in order to exploit seagoing explorations.

To Ferdinand Martins, Canon of Lisbon, Paolo the physician gives greeting.

It was pleasing to me to have intelligence concerning your health, and concerning your favour and familiar friendship with that most generous and magnificent

From *A Source Book in Geography*, ed. George Kish; Cambridge, Harvard University Press, 1978, pp. 306-307.

prince, your King. Whereas I have spoken with you elsewhere concerning a shorter way of going by sea to the lands of spices, than that which you are making by Guinea; the most serene King now wishes that I should give some explanation thereof, or rather that I should so set it before the eyes of all, that even those who are but moderately learned might perceive that way and understand it.

But though I know that this could be shown by the spherical form, which is that of the world; nevertheless I have determined to show it in the way in which charts of navigation show it, and this both that it may be more readily understood, and that the work may be easier.

Wherefore I send to His Majesty a chart[1], made by my hands, wherein your shores are shown, and the islands from which you may begin to make a voyage continually westwards, and the places whereunto you ought to come, and how much you ought to decline from the pole or from the equinoctal line, and through how much space, i.e., through how many miles, you ought to arrive at the places most fertile in all spices and gems. And do not wonder if I call those places where the spices are western, whereas they are commonly called east: because to those that sail by navigation those places are ever found in the west, though if we go by land they will always be found in the east.

It is said only merchants stay in these islands; for here there is so great an abundance of men sailing with merchandise, that in all the rest of the world they are not as they are in a most noble port called Zaiton, for they say that every year a hundred large ships of pepper are brought into that port, without counting other ships bearing other spices. That country is very populous, and very rich, with a multitude of provinces and kingdoms and cities without number, under one prince who is called the Great Kan [sic], which name in Latin means *rex regum* (king of kings), whose seat and residence are chiefly in the province of Katay.[2] His ancestors desired to have fellowship with the Christians. For it is now two hundred years since they sent to the Pope and asked for several men learned in the faith, in order that they might be enlightened. But those who were sent went back, being hindered on their journey. In the time of Eugenius,[3] also, one came to Eugenius and spoke of their great goodwill towards Christians. And I held speech with him for a long time on many things, on the greatness of the royal buildings, and on the greatness of the rivers of wondrous breadth and length, and on the multitude of cities on the banks of the rivers; and how on one river there are established about two hundred cities, and marble bridges of great breadth and length adorned with columns on every side. This country is worthy of being sought by the Latins, not only because from thence may be obtained vast grains of gold and silver and gems of every kind, and of spices that are never brought to us; but also because of the wise men, learned philosophers and astrologers, by whose genius and arts that

---

[1]Now lost.

[2]i.e., Cathay = China.

[3]Eugenius IV (1431-47).

mighty and magnificent province is governed and wars are also waged. These things I write to give some little satisfaction to your demand, in so far as the shortness of the time allowed, and my occupations suffered; being ready to satisfy your Royal Majesty in the future as much further as may be desired. Given at Florence, 25th June 1474.

READING 9

Roger Bacon on Experimental Science

The Oxford Franciscan Roger Bacon (d. 1292) explored such subjects as optics, alchemy, and languages. The excerpt below is a brief and rather clouded summary, from the last part of Bacon's *Opus Majus,* of the necessity for experimentation. Bacon's work, like that of many of his contemporaries, deals with the themes of reason and faith, tradition and innovation. It shows that the "experimental sciences" were still infused with theology and tinged with alchemy and magic. It also discloses the degree to which Bacon, and other scholars of his time, had absorbed the philosophical and scientific legacy of Classical Antiquity.

Having laid down fundamental principles of the wisdom of the Latins so far as they are found in language, mathematics, and optics, I now wish to unfold the principles of experimental science, since without experience nothing can be sufficiently known. For there are two modes of acquiring knowledge, namely, by reasoning and experience. Reasoning draws a conclusion and makes us grant the conclusion, but does not make the conclusion certain, nor does it remove doubt so that the mind may rest on the intuition of truth, unless the mind discovers it by the path of experience; since many have the arguments relating to what can be known, but because they lack experience they neglect the arguments, and neither avoid what is harmful nor follow what is good. For if a man who has never seen fire should prove by adequate reasoning that fire burns and injures things and destroys them, his mind would not be satisfied thereby, nor would he avoid fire, until he placed his hand or some combustible substance in the fire, so that he might prove by experience that which reasoning taught. But when he has had actual experience of combustion his mind is made certain and rests in the full light of truth. Therefore reasoning does not suffice, but experience does.

From *The Opus Majus of Roger Bacon,* tr. Robert Belle Burke; Philadelphia, University of Pennsylvania Press, 1928, pp. 583-585, 587. Reprinted by permission.

This is also evident in mathematics, where proof is most convincing. But the mind of one who has the most convincing proof in regard to the equilateral triangle will never cleave to the conclusion without experience, nor will he heed it, but will disregard it until the experience is offered him by the intersection of two circles, from either intersection of which two lines may be drawn to the extremities of the given line; but then the man accepts the conclusion without any question. Aristotle's statement, then, that proof is reasoning that causes us to know is to be understood with the proviso that the proof is accompanied by its appropriate experience, and is not to be understood of the bare proof. His statement also in the first book of the *Metaphysics* that those who understand the reason and the cause are wiser than those who have empiric knowledge of a fact, is spoken of such as know only the bare truth without the cause. But I am here speaking of the man who knows the reason and the cause through experience. These men are perfect in their wisdom, as Aristotle maintains in the sixth book of the *Ethics*, whose simple statements must be accepted as if they offered proof, as he states in the same place.

He therefore who wishes to rejoice without doubt in regard to the truths underlying phenomena must know how to devote himself to experiment. For authors write many statements, and people believe them through reasoning which they formulate without experience. Their reasoning is wholly false. For it is generally believed that the diamond cannot be broken except by goat's blood, and philosophers and theologians misuse this idea. But fracture by means of blood of this kind has never been verified, although the effort has been made; and without that blood it can be broken easily. For I have seen this with my own eyes, and this is necessary, because gems cannot be carved except by fragments of this stone.

But experience is of two kinds; one is gained through our external senses, and in this way we gain our experience of those things that are in the heavens by instruments made for this purpose, and of those things here below by means attested by our vision. Things that do not belong in our part of the world we know through other scientists who have had experience of them. As, for example, Aristotle on the authority of Alexander sent two thousand men through different parts of the world to gain experimental knowledge of all things that are on the surface of the earth, as Pliny bears witness in his *Natural History*. This experience is both human and philosophical, as far as man can act in accordance with the grace given him; but this experience does not suffice him, because it does not give full attestation in regard to things corporeal owing to its difficulty, and does not touch at all on things spiritual. It is necessary, therefore, that the intellect of man should be otherwise aided, and for this reason the holy patriarchs and prophets, who first gave sciences to the world, received illumination within and were not dependent on sense alone. The same is true of many believers since the time of Christ. For the grace of faith illuminates greatly, as also do divine inspirations, not only in things spiritual, but in things corporeal and in the sciences of philosophy; as Ptolemy states in the *Centilogium*, namely, that there are two roads by which we arrive at the knowledge of facts, one through the experience of philosophy, the other through divine inspiration, which is far the better way, as he says.

Since this Experimental Science is wholly unknown to the rank and file of students, I am therefore unable to convince people of its utility unless at the same time I disclose its excellence and its proper signification. This science alone, therefore, knows how to test perfectly what can be done by nature, what by the effort of art, what by trickery, what the incantations, conjurations, invocations, deprecations, sacrifices, that belong to magic, mean and dream of, and what is in them, so that all falsity may be removed and the truth alone of art and nature may be retained. This science alone teaches us how to view the mad acts of magicians, that they may be not ratified but shunned, just as logic considers sophistical reasoning.

READING 10

Nicole Oresme *On The Book of the Heavens and the World of Aristotle*

Nicole Oresme (1320-1382), bishop of Lisieux, a mathematician and scientist of fourteenth-century France, raises here the scientific possibility that the apparent daily rotation of the heavens might be explained in other ways. He deals with the apparent motion of the sun and moon by a principle of "relativity," which influenced Einstein's thinking on the motion of light. His conclusion is disappointing to modern audiences, but is perhaps to be expected of a bishop.

One could support well and give luster to the opinion that the earth, and not the heavens, is moved with a daily movement. First, I wish to state that one could not demonstrate the contrary by any experience. Secondly I will show that the contrary cannot be demonstrated by reasoning. And thirdly, I will put forth reasons in support of it.

One experience commonly cited in support of the daily motion of the heavens is the following: we see with our sense the sun and moon and many stars rise and set from day to day. This could not be except by the movement of the heavens. Another experience cited is this: if the earth is so moved, it makes a complete turn in a single natural day. Therefore, we and the trees and the houses are moved towards the east very swiftly, and so it should seem to us that the air and the wind blow continuously and very strongly from the east. But the contrary appears by

From Richard C. Dales, *The Scientific Achievement of the Middle Ages;* Philadelphia, University of Pennsylvania Press, 1973. pp. 131-133, 135-137.

experience. Similarly, if the earth is moved very swiftly in turning from west to east, and it has been posited that one throws a stone directly above, then it ought to fall, not on the place from which it left, but rather a good distance to the west. But in fact the contrary is apparent.

I make the supposition that local motion can be sensibly perceived only in so far as one may perceive one body to be differently disposed with respect to another. In support of this I give the following illustration: if a person is in one ship called *A* which is moved very carefully, i.e., without pitching or rolling, and this person sees nothing except another ship called *B*, which is moved in every respect in the same manner as *A* in which he is situated, I say that it will seem to this person that neither ship is moving. And if *A* is at rest and *B* is moved, it will appear and seem to him that *B* is moved. On the other hand, if *A* is moved and *B* is at rest, it will appear to him as before that *A* is at rest and that *B* is moved. The reason for this is because these two bodies, *A* and *B*, are continually changing their dispositions with respect to each other in the same manner throughout when *A* is moved and *B* is at rest as they were conversely when *B* is moved and *A* is at rest. I say then that if the upper of the two parts of the universe, i.e., the heavens, should today move with a diurnal movement, just as it is, and the lower part should not, and tomorrow the contrary should prevail, we could not perceive this change in any way, but everything would seem to be the same today and tomorrow. It would seem to us continually that the part where we are situated was at rest and that the other part was always moved, just as it seems to a person who is in a moving ship that the trees outside are moved.

To the second experience the response is this: not only is the earth so moved diurnally, but with it the water and the air, in such a way that the water and the lower air are moved differently than they are by wind and other causes. It is like this situation: if air were enclosed in a moving ship, it would seem to the person situated in this air that it was not moved.

To the third experience, which seems more effective, i.e., the experience concerning the arrow or stone projected upwards, one would say that the arrow is trajected upwards and simultaneously with this trajection it is moved eastward very swiftly with the air through which it passes. For this reason, the arrow returns to the place on the earth from which it left. Thus if a person were on a ship moving toward the east very swiftly without his being aware of the movement, and he drew his hand downward, describing a straight line against the mast of the ship, it would seem to him that his hand was moved with rectilinear movement only.

Where it is said that if the heavens would not make a rotation from day to day, all astronomy would be false, etc., I answer that this is not so, because all aspects, conjunctions, oppositions, constellations, figures, and influences of the heavens would be completely just as they are. The tables of the movements and all other books would be just as true as they are, except that in regard to the daily movement one would say that it is in the heavens "apparently" but in the earth "actually." There is no effect which follows from the one assumption more than from the others.

With the theory of the diurnal movement of the heavens it becomes necessary to posit an excessively great speed. This will become clear to one who considers thoughtfully the height or the distance of the heaven, its magnitude, and that of its circuit: for if such a circuit is completed in one day, one could not imagine or conceive of how the swiftness of the heaven is so marvelously and excessively great. It is so unthinkable and inestimable. Since all the effects which we see can be accomplished, and all the appearances saved, by substituting for this diurnal movement of the heavens a small operation, i.e., the diurnal movement of the earth, which is very small in comparison with the heavens, and since this can be done without making the number of necessary operations so diverse and outrageously great, it follows that if the heaven rather than the earth is moved, then God and nature would have made and ordained things for nought. But this is not fitting.

Yet, nevertheless, everyone holds, and I believe, that they—the heavens—and not the earth, are so moved, for "God created the orb of the earth, which will not be moved" (Psalms 92:1).

READING 11

Jan Hus, *Charges of Heresy at the Council of Constance*

Jan Hus (1374-1415), a reformer from Bohemia whose skepticism of the authority of the papacy and the Catholic clergy enraged them both, was invited to the Council of Constance (1415) on the promise of an imperial safe conduct and was then burned at the stake. His heretical views, which influenced later generations of reformers, including Martin Luther, are recorded here.

There is only one holy universal Church, which is the totality of the predestined. Priests living criminally in any manner whatever pollute the priestly power.

The papal dignity arose from Caesar and the papal preeminence and the institution emanated from the Caesar's power.

No one may reasonably assert without revelation about himself or another that he is the head of a particular holy church; nor the Roman pontiff that he is the head of the Roman church.

No one occupies the place of Christ or Peter unless he follows Him in morals; for in no other respect is it more appropriate to follow, nor has he otherwise

From Matthew Spinka, *John Hus at the Council of Constance*; New York, Columbia University Press, 1965, pp. 260-265.

received the procuratorial power from God; because for that vicarial office both the conformity of morals and of the instituting authority are required.

The pope is not the manifest or true successor of the prince of the apostles, Peter, if he lives in a manner contrary to Peter. And if he is avaricious, then he is the vicar of Judas Iscariot by living avariciously. For the same reason the cardinals are not the manifest and true successors of the college of Christ's other apostles unless they live after the manner of the apostles, observing the commands and counsels of the Lord Jesus Christ.

The priest of Christ living in accordance with His law, having knowledge of Scripture and a desire to edify the people, ought to preach, an alleged excommunication notwithstanding; and subsequently, that if the pope or another orders a priest so disposed not to preach, the inferior ought not to obey.

By ecclesiastical censures of excommunications, suspensions, interdicts, the clergy subject the lay people to themselves for their own exaltation and the increase of avarice, and by malice protect and prepare Antichrist's way.

If the pope is wicked then like the apostle Judas he is a devil, a thief, and son of perdition, and not the head of the holy Church militant; for he is not even its member, since the grace of predestination is the bond whereby the body of the Church and every member of it is linked indissolubly with the head.

The pope ought not to be called the most holy even according to office, for otherwise a king ought also to be called the most holy according to office, and executioners and public criers ought to be called saints; indeed, even the devil should be called holy as being an official of God.

If the pope lives in a manner contrary to Christ, even if he had ascended by a rightful and legitimate election according to the established human constitution, he has nevertheless ascended otherwise than through Christ. For Judas Iscariot was elected to the episcopacy rightfully and legitimately by Jesus Christ who is God; nevertheless, he entered by another way into the sheepfold of the sheep.

The condemnation of the forty-five articles of Wyclif decreed by the doctors is irrational and unjust, and the reason alleged for it is wrongly conceived.

There is not a spark of apparent evidence that there should be one head ruling the Church in spiritual matters that should always abide with the Church militant; that is evident, since it is known that the Church has been without a pope for a long time.

The apostles and the faithful priests of the Lord had firmly ruled the Church in things necessary to salvation before the papal office was instituted. They would do so if there were no pope—as is highly possible—until the Day of Judgment.

No one is secular lord, no one is prelate, no one is bishop while he is in mortal sin.

READING 12

Martin Luther, *Disputation Against Scholastic Theology*

This critique of high medieval (scholastic) theology by Martin Luther (1483-1576), the founder of the Protestant Reformation, makes clear the gulf between scholastics such as Thomas Aquinas in the thirteenth century and Luther in the sixteenth. Aquinas had emphasized human dignity and nobility—and the power of human reason to go so far as to prove the existence of God (Chapter six, Reading eight). Luther on the other hand, like many other Protestant reformers, emphasized human depravity and the limitations of human reason when compared to the infinite perfections of God.

Man, being a bad tree, can only will and do evil.

It is false to state that man's will is free to choose between either of two opposites. Indeed, the will is not free, but captive. It is false to state that the will can by nature conform to correct precept. As a matter of fact, without the grace of God the will produces an act that is perverse and evil. It does not, however, follow that the will is by nature evil, that is, evil in essence, as the Manichaeans maintain. It is nevertheless innately and inevitably evil and corrupt.

No act is done according to nature that is not an act of concupiscence against God. Every act of concupiscence against God is evil.

The best and infallible preparation for grace and the sole means of obtaining grace is the eternal election and predestination of God. On the part of man, however, nothing precedes grace except ill will and even rebellion against grace. In brief, man by nature has neither correct precept nor good will.

It is not true that an invincible ignorance[1] excuses one completely (all the scholastics notwithstanding); for ignorance of God and oneself and good works is by nature always invincible.

There is no moral virtue without either pride or sorrow, that is, without sin. We are never the lords of our actions, but servants. This is in opposition to the philosophers. We do not become righteous by doing righteous deeds but, having been made righteous, we do righteous deeds. This is in opposition to the philosophers.

From Brian Tierney, et al., *Great Issues in Western Civilization, vol i*; New York, Random House, 1976, pp. 500-503.

[1] Invincible ignorance was that doctrine that some people were simply incapable of understanding the Christian message. This was applied especially to the Jews, who seemed to show no inclination to convert.

Virtually the entire *Ethics* of Aristotle is the worst enemy of grace. This is in opposition to the scholastics. It is an error to say that no man can become a theologian without Aristotle. Indeed, no one can become a theologian unless he becomes one without Aristotle. To state that a theologian who is not a logician is a monstrous heretic—this is a monstrous statement.

In vain does one fashion a logic of faith, a substitution brought about without regard for limit and measure. This is in opposition to the new dialecticians. No syllogistic form[2] is valid when applied to divine terms. Nevertheless, it does not for that reason follow that the truth of the doctrine of the Trinity contradicts syllogistic forms. If a syllogistic form of reasoning holds in divine matters, then the doctrine of the Trinity is demonstrable and not the object of faith.

Briefly, the whole of Aristotle is to theology as darkness is to light.

READING 13

William Caxton *Proem* to the *Polychronicon*, 1482

We conclude with the eloquent prologue ("proem") by the fifteenth-century English writer William Caxton (1422-1491), writing in Middle English, to Ranulf Higden's fourteenth-century Latin history of the world (Britain in particular), the *Polychronicon*. Those who are befuddled by Middle English are permitted to close the book here. Caxton established the first printing press in England.

Grete thankynges, lawde and honoure we merytoryously be bounde to yelde and offre unto wryters of hystoryes, whiche gretely have prouffyted oure mortal lyf, that shewe unto the reders and herers by the ensamples of thynges passyd what thynge is to be desyred and what is to be eschewed. For those thynges whiche oure progenytours dyde by the taste of bytternes and experyment of grete jeopardyes have enseygned, admonested and enformed us, excluded from suche peryllys, to knowe what is prouffytable to oure lyf and acceptable and what is unprouffytable and to be refused. He is, and ever hath been, reputed the wysest whiche by the experyence of adverse fortune hath byholden and seen the noble cytees, maners and variaunt condycions of the people of many dyverse regyons, for in hym is

From N.F. Blake, *Caxton's Own Prose*; Andre Deutsch, London, 1973, pp. 128-130.

[2] A form of reasoning advanced by Aristotle in which a logical conclusion is drawn from two premises.

presupposed the lore of wysedom and polycye by the experyment of jeopardyes and peryllys, which have growen of folye in dyverse partyes and contrayes. Yet he is more fortunat, and may be reputed as wyse, yf he gyve attendaunce withoute tastynge of the stormes of adversyte, that may be the redyng of historyes conteynyng dyverse customes, condycyons, lawes and actes of sondry nacions come unto the knowleche of and understandynge of the same wysedome and polyce. In whiche hystoryes so wreton in large and adourned volumes, he syttynge in his chambre or studye maye rede, knowe and understande the polytyke and noble acts of alle the worlde, as of one cyte, and the conflyctes, errours, troubles and vexacions done in the sayd unyversal worlde in suche wyse as he had ben and seen them in the propre places where as they were done. For certayne it is a greete benefyte unto a man that he can be reformed by other and straunge mennes hurtes and scathes, and by the same to knowe what is requysyte and prouffytable for his lyf and eschewe suche errours and inconvenytys, by whiche other men have ben hurte and lost theyr felycyte. Therefore the counseylles of auncyent and whyte-heeryd men, in whome olde age had engendyrd wysedome, ben gretely preysed of yonger men; and yet hystoryes soo moche more excelle them as the dyurnyte or length of tyme includeth moo ensamples of thynges and laudable actes than th'age of one man may suffyse to see.

Hystoryes ought not only to be judged moost prouffytable to yonge men whiche by the lecture, redynge and understandyng make them semblable and equale to men of greter age and to olde men, to whome longe lyf hath mynystred experymentes of dyverse thynges, but also th'ystoryes able and make ryght pryvate men digne and worthy to have the governaunce of empyres and noble royammes. Historyes moeve and withdrawe emperours and kynges fro vycious tyrannye, fro vecordyous sleuthe unto tryumphe and vyctorye in puyssaynt batayles. Historyes also have moeved ryght noble knyghtes to deserve eternal laude, whiche foloweth them for their vyctoryous merytes, and cause them more valyantly to entre in jeopardyes of batayles for the defence and tuicion of their countrey and publyke wele. Hystorye also afrrayeth cruel tyrauntys for drede of infamye and shame infynyte bycause of the detestable actes of suche cruel persones ben oftymes plantyd and regyustred in cronykes unto theyr perpetuel obprobrye and dyvulgacion of theyr infamye, as th'actes of Nero and suche other. Truly, many of hye and couragyous men of grete empryse, desyryng theyr fame to be perpetuelly conservyd by lyteral monumentis whiche ben the permanente recordes of every vyrtuouse and noble acte, have buylded and edefyed ryall and noble cytees, and for the conservacion of the wele publycke have mynystred and establysshed dyscrete and prouffytable lawes. And thus the pryncipal laude and cause of delelectable and amyable thynges in which mannes felycyte stondeth and resteth ought and maye wel be attributed to hystoryes.

Whyche worde *historye* may be descryved thus. Historye is a perpetuel conservatryce of thoos thynges that have be doone before this presente tyme and

---

[1] Daily.

also a cotydyan[1] wytnesse of bienfayttes, of malefaytes, grete actes, and tryumphal vyctoryes of all maner peple. And also yf the terryble, feyned fables of poetes have moche styred and moeved men to pyte and conservynge of justyce, how moche more is to be supposed that historye, assertryce of veryte and as moder of alle philosphye moevynge our maners to vertue, reformeth and reconcyleth ner hande alle thoos men which thurgh the infyrmyte of oure mortal natyre hath ledde the mooste parte of theyr lyf in ocyosyte and myspended theyr tyme, passed ryght soone oute of remembraunce; of which lyf and deth is egal oblyvyon. The fruytes of vertue ben immortall, specyally whanne they ben wrapped in the benefyce of hystoryes.

Other monymentes distributed in dyverse chaunges enduren but for a short tyme or season, but the vertu of historye, dyffused and spredd by the unyversal worlde, hath tyme whiche consumeth all other thynges as conservatryce and kepar of her werke. Hystorye, representyge the thynges lyke unto the wordes, enbraceth al utylyte and prouffite. It sheweth honeste and maketh vyces detestable. It enhaunceth noble men and depresseth wicked men and fooles.

ACKNOWLEDGEMENTS

The following selections are protected by copyright and were reprinted in this book by permission of the copyright owners.

1:2 Stevenson, J. (ed.). "The Edict of Milan, 313," pp. 300-302 in *A New Eusebius: Documents Illustrative of the History of the Church to A.D. 337.* London: Society for Promoting Christian Knowledge, 1957. Reprinted by permission of the Society for Promoting Christian Knowledge.

1:4 and 1:7 Pharr, C. (trans.). "Selections from the Code of Theodosius II," pp. 450-451, 473; and "More Selections from the Theodosian Code," pp. 170, 172, 387, 544 in *The Theodosian Code and Novels and the Sirmondian Constitutions.* Copyright 1952 by Clyde Pharr, renewed 1980 in the name of Roy Pharr. Reprinted by permission of Princeton University Press.

1:9 Garmonsway, G.N. (trans.). *The Anglo-Saxon Chronicle*, 2nd ed., Vv. 446, 449, 455, 456, 476, 473, 495, 501, 508, 514, 519, 528, 597. London: Everyman's Library Ltd., 1955. Reprinted by permission of David Campbell Publishers, Ltd.

2:1 Dawes, E., and Baynes, N.H. (eds. and trans.). "The Life of St. Daniel the Stylite," pp. 7, 18-19, 29, 36, 43-44, 70-71 in *Three Byzantine Saints.* Crestwood, New York: St. Vladimir's Seminary Press, 1977. Reprinted by permission of St. Vladimir's Seminary Press.

2:3 Sewter, E.R.A. (trans.). "Michael Psellus Describes the Battle of Manzikert, 1071," pp. 353-356 in *Fourteen Byzantine Rulers*. London: Penguin Classics, 1966. Copyright © E.R.A. Sewter, 1966. Reprinted by permission of Penguin Books Ltd.

2:4 Geanakoplos, D.J. "Basil II on the Protection of Peasants' Lands, 996," pp. 245-247 in *Byzantium, Church Society and Civilization as Seen through Contemporary Eyes*. Chicago: University of Chicago Press, 1984. Reprinted by permission of The University of Chicago Press.

2:6 Tierney, B. (ed.). "Pope Gelasius I on Priestly and Royal Power," pp. 13-14 in *The Crisis of Church and State, 1050-1300*. Englewood Cliffs, New Jersey: Prentice Hall Inc., 1964. Reprinted by permission of Prentice Hall Inc., a division of Simon & Schuster.

2:9 Webb, J.F. (trans.). "A Description of the Synod of Whitby" from Eddius, "The Life of St. Wilfred of Hexham," pp. 141-143 in *Lives of the Saints*. London: Penguin Classics, 1965. Copyright © J.F. Webb, 1965. Reprinted by permission of Penguin Books Ltd.

2:10 Darwood, N.J. (trans.). "From 'The Cow' (Sura 2) from the Koran," pp. 326-356 in *The Koran*. London: Penguin Classics, Third revised edition, 1968. Copyright © N.J. Darwood, 1956, 1959, 1966, 1968. Reprinted by permission of Penguin Books Ltd.

2:11 Guillaume, A. (ed. and trans.). "The 'Constitution of Medina,' 622" from Ibn Ishaq's "Life of the Prophet," pp. 231-233 in *The Life of Mohammed, a Translation of Ibn Ishaq's Sirat Rasul Allah*. Karachi: Oxford University Press, 1955. Reprinted by permission of Oxford University Press, Karachi, Pakistan.

2:12 Lerner, R., and Mahdi, M. (eds.). "Alfarabi's *The Political Regime*," pp. 32, 34, 36-38 in *Medieval Political Philosophy: A Sourcebook*. Copyright © 1963 by The Free Press. Reprinted by permission of The Free Press, a division of Macmillan, Inc.

2:13 Watt, W.M. "Al-Ghazali's *Deliverance from Error*," pp. 19-26 in *The Faith and Practice of Al-Ghazali*. Chicago: Kazi Publications, 1982. Reprinted by permission of Kazi Publications.

3:1 Tierney, B. (ed.). "Pope Gregory's Letter to Emperor Leo II, 727," pp. 19-20 in *The Crisis of Church and State, 1050-1300*. Englewood Cliffs, New Jersey: Prentice Hall Inc., 1964. Reprinted by permission of Prentice Hall Inc., a division of Simon & Schuster.

3:2 Emerton, E. (trans.). "Letter of St. Boniface," nos. viii, xv, xix in *The Letters of St. Boniface.* © 1940 Columbia University Press. Reprinted by permission of Columbia University Press.

3:4 Cantor, N.F. (ed.). "The Donation of Constantine," pp. 132-139 in *The Medieval World, 300-1300,* 2nd ed. Copyright © 1968 by Macmillan Publishing Company. Reprinted by permission of Macmillan Publishing Company.

3:5 Grant, A.J. (ed. and trans.). "Einhard's Life of Charlemagne," part 1, chaps. 7, 8, 9, 11 in *Early Lives of Charlemagne, by Eginhard and the Monk of St. Gall.* London: Chatto and Windus, 1922. Reprinted by permission of Random House, Inc., New York.

3:6 Ehler, S., and Morral, J.B. "Charlemagne's Letter to Pope Leo II, 796," p. 12 in *Church and State through the Centuries.* New York: Biblo and Tannen, Inc., 1967.

3:7 Easton, S.C., and Wieruszowski, H. "Documents Relating to the Imperial Coronation of Charlemagne," pp. 126-127, 127-128, 128, 129 in *The Era of Charlemagne.* Princeton: Van Nostrand Inc., 1961.

3:8 Loyn, H.R., and Percival, J. (eds.). "The General Capitulary of the Missi, Spring, 802," pp. 74-79 in *The Reign of Charlemagne.* London: Edward Arnold Ltd., 1975. Reprinted by permission of Edward Arnold Ltd., Sevenoaks, Kent.

4:1 Schloz, B.W. (ed. and trans.). "Nithard's Account of the Year 840," pp. 141-145, 174 in *Carolingian Chronicles.* Ann Arbor: University of Michigan Press, 1970. Reprinted by permission of University of Michigan Press.

4:3 Duby, G. "Survey of the Manor of Neuillay, c. 860," pp. 204-205 in *Rural Economy and Country Life in the Medieval West,* trans. Cynthia Postan. Charleston: University of South Carolina Press, 1972. Reprinted by permission of the University of South Carolina Press.

4:5 Lopez, R.S. (ed.). "Foundation Charter of Cluny," pp. 14-15 in *The Tenth Century.* Copyright © 1959 by Robert Sabatino Lopez. Reprinted by permission of Holt, Rinehart & Winston.

4:6 Hill, B.H., Jr. (ed.). "Widukind of Corvey's Account of the Battle of Lechfeld, 955," pp. 15-18 in *The Rise of the First Reich.* New York: John Wiley & Sons, 1969. Reprinted by permission of Boyd H. Hill, Jr.

4:7 Wright, F.A. (trans.). "A Chronicle of Otto's Reign," pp. 215-218 in *The Works of Liudprand of Cremona*. London: Routledge & Kegan Paul, Ltd., 1930. Reprinted in Boyd H. Hill, Jr. (ed.). *The Rise of the First Reich*. New York: John Wiley & Sons, 1969. Reprinted by permission of Routledge & Kegan Paul, Ltd., and Boyd H. Hill, Jr.

4:8 Lopez, R.S. (ed.). "An Account of the Lombard Kingdom in the Late Tenth Century" from *Instituta regalia et ministeria camere regnum Longobardum*, pp. 15-17 in *The Tenth Century*. Copyright © 1959 by Robert Sabatino Lopez. Reprinted by permission of Holt, Rinehart & Winston, Inc.

4:9 Magnusson, M., and Palsson, H. (eds. and trans.). "'Greenland Saga' Concerning the Discovery of North America" from *Graenlendiga Saga*, pp. 54-58 in *The Vinland Sagas: The Norse Discovery of America*. Copyright Magnus Magnusson and Hermann Palsson, 1965. Reprinted by permission of Penguin Books, Ltd.

5:1 Douglas, D.C., and Greenaway, G.W. (ed.). "The Customs of Newcastle-upon-Tyne," pp. 970-971 in *English Historical Documents, Volume II, 1042-1189*. Oxford: Oxford University Press, 1953. Reprinted by permission of Octopus Publishing Group Library for Methuen London.

5:2 Benton, J.F. (ed. and trans.). "The Revolt of the Laon Commune," pp. 167, 174-76 in *Self and Society in Medieval France: The Memoirs of Abbott Guibert of Nogent (1064? - c. 1125)*, based on the translation of C.C. Swinton Bland. Copyright © 1970 by John F. Benton. Reprinted by permission of Harper-Collins Publishers.

5:3 Cave, R.C., and Coulson, H.H. (eds.). "Guild Regulations for the Shearers of Arras," pp. 250-52 in *A Source Book for Medieval Economic History*. New York: Biblo & Tannen, Inc., 1965.

5:4 Peters, E. (ed.). "The Crusaders Take Jerusalem" from *The Chronicle of Fulcher of Chartres*, trans. Martha E. McGinty, pp. 76-79 in *The First Crusade*. Philadelphia: University of Pennsylvania Press, 1971. Reprinted by permission of the University of Pennsylvania Press.

5:5 Erickson, C. (ed.). "Bernard of Clairvaux on the Knights Templars," pp. 184-186 in *The Records of Medieval Europe*. Copyright © 1971 by Carolly Erickson. Reprinted by permission of Doubleday, a division of Bantam Doubleday Dell Publishing Group, Inc.

6:1 Anderson, W.B. (trans.). "Two Letters of Sidonius Apollinaris," pp. 239, 241, 275 in *Sidonius Apollinaris, Poems and Letters*, Volume II. Cambridge, Massachusetts: Harvard University Press, 1936. Reprinted by permission of the publishers and the Loeb Classical Library.

6:2 Jones, G. (trans.). "Gunnlaug's Feud," pp. 211-214 in *Erik the Red and Other Icelandic Sagas*. Oxford: Oxford University Press, 1980. Reprinted by permission of Oxford University Press.

6:3 Luquiens, F.B. (trans.). "The Trial of Ganelon," pp. 92-100 in *The Song of Roland*. Copyright 1952, and renewed 1980, by Macmillan Publishing Company. Reprinted by permission of Macmillan Publishing Company.

6:4 Flores, A. (ed.). "Marie de France, 'The Nightingale,'" pp. 330-33 in *Medieval Age*, trans. Muriel Kittel. New York: Dell Publishing, 1963. Reprinted by permission of Angel Flores.

6:5 Ryan, G. and Ripperger, H. (trans.). "St. Theodora," pp. 539-543 in Jacob of Voraigne, *The Golden Legend*. Copyright © 1941 by Longmans, Green and Co., Inc. Reprinted by permission of Random House, Inc.

6:6 Olson, C.C., and Crow, M.M. (eds.). "La Tour-Landry: A Marriage Proposal," pp. 52-53 in *Chaucer's World*. New York: Columbia University Press, 1948. Reprinted by permission of Columbia University Press.

6:7 O'Faolain, J., and Martines, L. "Giovanni Morelli: *Memoir*," pp. 169-170 in *Not In God's Image: Women in History From the Greeks to the Victorians*. Copyright © 1973 by Julia O'Faolain and Lauro Martines. Reprinted by permission of HarperCollins Publishers.

6:8 Marcus, R.J. (ed.). "Papal Protection of the Jews: A Bull of Gregory X, 1272," pp. 152-154 in *The Jew in the Medieval World*. Cincinnati: Sinai Press, 1938. Copyright 1938 Union of American Hebrew Congregations.

7:3 Wakefield, W.L., and Evans, A.P. (eds.). "An Account of the Albigensian Heresy," pp. 231-235 in *Heresies of the High Middle Ages*. New York: Columbia University Press, 1969. Reprinted by permission of Columbia University Press.

7:4 Moore, R.I. (ed. and trans.). "An Account of the Waldensian Heresy," pp. 144-145 in *The Birth of Popular Heresy*, Documents of Medieval History Series. Sevenoaks, Kent: Edward Arnold Ltd., 1975.

7:5 Schroeder, H.J. (ed. and trans.). "A Canon from the Fourth Lateran Council, 1215," pp. 238-239, 242-244 in *Disciplinary Decrees of the General Councils.* St. Louis: B. Herder Book Co., 1937. Copyright 1937 by B. Herder Book Co.

7:7 Tierney, B. (ed.). "Peter Abelard: *Sic et Non*," pp. 172-175 in *Sources of Medieval History*, 4th edition. New York: McGraw-Hill Book Company, 1983. Reprinted by permission of McGraw-Hill Book Company.

7:8 Gilby, T., O.P. (ed.). "St. Thomas Aquinas on the Existence of God," pp. 64-70 in St. Thomas Aquinas *Summa Theologiae.* New York: Image Books, 1969. Reprinted by permission of Eyre & Spottiswoode Publishers, London.

7:9 Lerner, R., and Mahdi, M. (trans. and ed.). "Bishop Etienne Tempier's Condemnations of 1277," in *Medieval Political Philosophy: A Sourcebook.* Copyright © 1963 by The Free Press. Reprinted by permission of The Free Press, a division of Macmillan Inc., on pp. 542-549 in Hyman, A. and Walsh, J.J., *Philosophy in the Middle Ages* (Cambridge, Massachusetts: Hackett Publishing Company, 1973).

7:10 Fremantle, A. "William of Ockham on Universals," pp. 208-209 in *The Age of Belief.* Copyright © 1954 by Anne Fremantle. Reprinted by permission of Curtis Brown Ltd.

8:2 Mierow, C.C. (trans.). "The Incident at Besancon," pp. 181-184 in Otto of Friesing, *The Deeds of Frederic Barbarossa.* New York: W.W. Norton & Company, 1966. Reprinted by permission of Columbia University Press and Dorothy Mierow.

8:4 Ross, J.B., and McLaughlin, M.M. (eds.). "Salimbene on the Emperor Frederick II," pp. 362-366 in *The Portable Medieval Reader.* Copyright 1949 by Viking Penguin, Inc. Copyright renewed © 1977 by James Bruce Ross and Mary Martin McLaughlin. Reprinted by permission of Viking Penguin, a division of Penguin Books USA Inc.

8:5 Schneider, H.W. (trans.). "Dante's *De Monarchia*," pp. 42-45 in Dante Alighieri, *On World Government or De Monarchia.* Copyright 1949, 1950, 1957 The Liberal Arts Press, renewed 1985 Herbert Wallace Schneider. Reprinted by permission of Herbert Wallace Schneider.

9:3 Rothwell, H. (ed. and trans.). "From Magna Carta, 1215," pp. 316-324 in *English Historical Documents, Vol. 3. 1189-1327.* London: Octopus Ltd., 1975. Reprinted by permission of Methuen London.

9:4 Stephenson, C., and Marcham, F.G. (ed. and trans.). "Quo Warranto (Statute of Gloucester of 1278)" and "Statute of Quia Emptores (1290)," pp. 169, 174 in *Sources of English Constitutional History*. Copyright © 1937 by Harper & Row, Publishers, renewed 1964 by Frederick George Marcham, James Stephenson, and Richard Stephenson. Reprinted by permission of HarperCollins Publishers.

9:6 Pullan, B. (ed. and trans.). "Philip Augustus on the Governance of the Realm, 1190," pp. 254-257 in *Sources for the History of Medieval Europe*. Oxford: Basil Blackwell Ltd., 1966. Reprinted by permission of Basil Blackwell Ltd.

9:8 Tierney, B. (ed.). "Unam Sanctam, 1302," "The Incident of Anagni," "Philip the Fair vs. Boniface VIII," pp. 188-189, 191 in *The Crisis of Church and State, 1050-1300*. Englewood Cliffs, New Jersey: Prentice Hall Inc., 1964. Reprinted by permission of Prentice Hall Inc., a division of Simon & Schuster.

10:1 Myers, A.R. (ed.). "The Parliament of 1348," "The Parliament of 1376," "The Parliament of 1401," "The Parliament of 1407," "The Parliament of 1414," pp. 443, 446-447, 455, 460-462 in *English Historical Documents, Vol. IV*. New York: Oxford University Press, 1969. Reprinted by permission of Octopus Publishing Group Library for Methuen London.

10:2 Brereton, G. "Jean Froissart, The Rise and Fall of Etienne Marcel," pp. 146-150, 155-161 in Jean Froissart, *Chronicles*. London: Penguin Classics, 1968. Copyright © Geoffrey Brereton, 1968. Reprinted by permission of Penguin Books Ltd.

10:3 and 10:4 Myers, A.R. (ed.). "Waurin on Joan of Arc," pp. 242-243; and "Chartier, Chronique du Roi Charles VII, 1450,) pp. 262-263 in *English Historical Documents, Vol. IV*. New York: Oxford University Press, 1969. Reprinted by permission of Octopus Publishing Group Library for Methuen London.

10:6 Kinser, S. (ed.) "Philippe de Commynes on the French Monarchy," pp. 359-361 of *The Memoirs of Philippe de Commynes*, trans. Isabella Cazeaux. Copyright University of South Carolina Press, 1969. Reprinted by permission of the University of South Carolina Press.

10:9 Lewis, E. "William of Ockham on Imperial and Papal Power," pp. 613-615 in *Medieval Political Ideas, Vol. II*. New York: Alfred A. Knopf, Inc., 1954. Reprinted by permission of Alfred A. Knopf, Inc.

11:1 Schevill, F. (ed.). "Boccaccio's Decameron on the Black Death in Florence, 1348," pp. 32-34 in *The First Century of Italian Humanism.* Copyright © 1928 by F.S. Crofts & Co.

11:3 Duby, G. "The Corn Statue of Florence, 1348," p. 525 in *Rural Economy and Country Life in the Medieval West,* trans. Cynthia Postan. Columbia, South Carolina: University of South Carolina Press, 1968. Reprinted by permission of the University of South Carolina Press.

11:4 Brucker, G.A. (ed.). "Coluccio Salutati on the Active Life," pp. 35-36 in *Renaissance Italy: Was It the Birthplace of Modern Europe?.* New York: Holt, Rinehart & Winston, 1958. Reprinted by permission of Gene A. Brucker and the publisher.

11:6 Weinstein, D. (ed.). "From Savonarola's *Compendium Revelationum,* 1497," pp. 68-71 in *Savonarola and Florence.* Copyright © 1970 by Princeton University Press. Reprinted by permission of Princeton University Press.

11:6B Alexander, Sidney (trans.). "Guicciardini on Savonarola and Florence, 1561," pp. 356-358 in Francesco Guicciardini, *The History of Italy.* New York and Toronto: Macmillan Publishing Company. Copyright © 1969 by Sidney Alexander. All rights reserved.

11:8 Kish, G. (ed.). "Toscanelli on Sailing West to Go East," pp. 306-307 in *A Source Book in Geography.* Copyright © 1978 by the President and Fellows of Harvard College. Reprinted by permission of Harvard University Press.

11:9 Burke, R.B. (trans.). "Roger Bacon on Experimental Science," pp. 583-585, 587 in *The Opus Majus of Roger Bacon.* Philadelphia: University of Pennsylvania Press, 1928. Reprinted by permission of the University of Pennsylvania Press.

11:10 Dales, R.C. "Nicole Oresme, On the Book of the Heavens and the World of Aristotle," pp. 131-133, 135-137 in *The Scientific Achievement of the Middle Ages.* Philadelphia: University of Pennsylvania Press, 1973. Reprinted by permission of the University of Pennsylvania Press.

11:11 Spinka, M. "Jan Hus, Charges of Heresy at the Council of Constance, 1415," pp. 260 ff. in *John Hus at the Council of Constance.* New York: Columbia University Press, 1965. Reprinted by permission of Columbia University Press.

11:12 Grimm, H.J. (ed.). "Martin Luther: Disputation Against Scholastic Theology," p. 572 in *Luther's Works, Vol. 31.* Copyright 1957 by Fortress Press. Reprinted by permission of Augsburg Fortress on pp. 500-503 in Tierney, B., et al., *Great Issues in Western Civilization, Vol. I* (New York: McGraw-Hill Book Company, 1976, 1992).

11:13 Blake, N.F. "William Caxton, Proem to the Polychronicon, 1482," pp. 128-130 in *Caxton's Own Prose.* London: Andre Deutsch, Ltd., 1973. Reprinted by permission of Andre Deutsch Ltd.